PLATO'S *THEAETETUS*

PLATO'S
THEAETETUS

DAVID BOSTOCK

CLARENDON PRESS · OXFORD
1988

Oxford University Press, Walton Street, Oxford OX2 6DP
Oxford New York Toronto
Delhi Bombay Calcutta Madras Karachi
Petaling Jaya Singapore Hong Kong Tokyo
Nairobi Dar es Salaam Cape Town
Melbourne Auckland
and associated companies in
Berlin Ibadan

Oxford is a trade mark of Oxford University Press

Published in the United States
by Oxford University Press, New York

British Library Cataloguing in Publication Data
Bostock, David
Plato's "Theaetetus".
1. Epistemology. Plato. Theaetetus.
Critical Studies
I. Title
121
ISBN 0–19–824489–4

Library of Congress Cataloging in Publication Data
Bostock, David.
Plato's Theaetetus/David Bostock.
Bibliography: p.
Includes index.
1. Plato. Theaetetus. I. Title.
B386.Z7B67 1988   121—dc19   88—10151
ISBN 0–19–824489–4

Set by Wyvern Typesetting Limited
Printed in Great Britain by
Biddles Ltd., Guildford and King's Lynn

PREFACE

Plato's *Theaetetus* is one of the most fascinating of all his dialogues. It has the charming style of his early writings, but the matter of the dialogue is deep, and the arguments reach a level of sophistication that is new. It is a mature Plato who is speaking to us, and yet at the same time a Plato who is once more probing, questioning, and exploring. The dialogue shows him wrestling with a new problem, one to which he had earlier given a somewhat facile answer, but which he now realizes requires very much more careful consideration. Even for the philosopher with wholly contemporary interests, it repays study. There are things that Plato has to say on his question 'What is knowledge?' that are of the greatest interest and importance. But for the student of Plato's thought it holds a place of special interest. Like the contemporary *Parmenides*, it shows us a Plato in transition, between the confident pronouncements of the middle dialogues, and the equally confident, but quite different, views of the later dialogues. This is a Plato who again is not sure of his way. He presents us with a *problem*. He has much to tell us about it, but he cannot tell us how it is to be resolved, for he no longer thinks that he knows the answer. That is the special attraction that the *Theaetetus* has for me.

This book is not intended for those who have no previous acquaintance with philosophy, but I hope it will be useful to undergraduates in their second or third years, who have at least begun upon the subject. I have tried to explain in reasonable detail any topic that goes beyond what they might be expected to be familiar with. I have referred from time to time to well-known views of Locke, Berkeley, and Hume, for the benefit of those who are already familiar with those authors, and similarly to views of Frege and Russell, and to work by Quine, Strawson, Kripke, and others. But I do not rely on a pre-existing knowledge of these authors, and what I say should be able to stand perfectly well on its own, with the references deleted. I have not presupposed any knowledge of Greek. For the benefit of those who do know the language, I have quite often shown (in brackets) the Greek word or phrase that my

English is translating. But those who do not may simply ignore these glosses, and should lose nothing thereby.

For the sake of those who will be reading the dialogue in translation, I have chosen one translation to quote from throughout, namely the one by John McDowell (*Plato: Theaetetus*, in the Clarendon Plato Series, Oxford, 1973). This should be readily available, and I imagine that anyone who is doing serious work on the *Theaetetus* will anyway wish to consult McDowell's extensive notes. But it should be possible to use this book in conjunction with any other translation instead, provided that it gives in the margin the standard way of referring to Plato's text (which hails from the edition of Stephanus in 1578). My line references are to the edition of the Greek text by Burnet, in the series of Oxford Classical Texts (Oxford, 1900). They may not exactly fit the lines of any English translation.

Like all authors, I have many many debts to countless others from whom I have learned over the years. But I should like to acknowledge one debt in particular, and that is to the inspiring teaching of the late G. E. L. Owen. He first guided me through the *Theaetetus*, a long time ago now, and the dialogue has been a delight to me ever since.

David Bostock

Merton College, Oxford
July 1987

CONTENTS

I

INTRODUCTION

1. CHRONOLOGY

(i) *General*

Plato wrote a large number of dialogues, and it is fairly certain that they have all survived. When studying any one of these dialogues it is natural to consider it in relation to others, in the hope that the obscurities of the one dialogue will be cleared up in another, or that its lacunae may be filled, or generally to see its doctrines in a larger perspective. For this comparison to be of any assistance it is obviously important to know the approximate *order* in which the dialogues were written, for of course it cannot be assumed—indeed it is obviously false—that Plato's views on all questions remained unchanged from his first dialogue to his last. But unfortunately the dating of the dialogues is a rather conjectural matter.[1]

What may now be called the 'orthodox' chronology is clearly and briefly given in ch. I of Ross, *Plato's Theory of Ideas*. It is this:

Early Dialogues	Middle Dialogues	Late Dialogues
including:	*Symposium*	*Parmenides*
Euthyphro	*Phaedo*	*Theaetetus*
Protagoras	*Republic*	*Sophist*
Euthydemus	*Phaedrus*	*Statesman*
Meno		*Philebus*
Gorgias		*Timaeus*
Cratylus		*Laws*
and others		

No one is at all confident of the order of the early dialogues, but we may reasonably ignore this problem, since it does not affect the

---

[1] Those familiar with Owen's important article of 1953, 'The Place of the *Timaeus* in Plato's Dialogues', will recognize that my discussion is heavily indebted to it.

interpretation of the *Theaetetus*. The middle and late dialogues are supposed to have been written in the order here specified, except that the order of the *Phaedo* and the *Symposium* is disputed, though on all accounts they are close in date, and the order of the *Philebus* and *Timaeus* is differently assigned by different writers. (Some prefer to count the *Parmenides* and the *Theaetetus* as the last of the middle dialogues, rather than the first of the late dialogues.) There are two main types of consideration used in establishing this order. One is the evidence provided by changes of literary style from one dialogue to another, and the other is the evidence provided by cross-references amongst the dialogues themselves and some very obvious continuities and discontinuities of theme. In fact, the latter type of evidence will take us *most* of the way towards the orthodox dating, as I now indicate.

(i) It is uncontroversial that the *Meno*, *Phaedo*, and *Republic* were written in that order. (*a*) The *Meno* introduces the idea that knowledge is really recollection, and attempts to establish this by an 'experiment', but remains somewhat tentative about the theory. The *Phaedo*, however, refers to this theory as one that is already familiar, and clearly alludes to the argument for it that is given in the *Meno*, before going on to present a new argument, which it evidently regards as decisive. (*b*) The *Meno* introduces the idea that it is often valuable to argue from a hypothesis, and provides an example of such an argument, but without paying much attention to the general theory involved. The *Phaedo* takes up this topic in more detail, and suggests that it is the right way for a philosopher to investigate any problem. The *Republic* is even more emphatic about this, and gives much further elaboration of the right way to treat hypotheses; but there is no other dialogue that recommends this method, save possibly the *Parmenides*.[2] (*c*) The *Phaedo* operates with a rather simple conception of the soul as a unitary entity, which is replaced in the *Republic* by a more sophisticated analysis of the soul as tripartite. The tripartite view is found also in the *Phaedrus* and the *Timaeus*.

(ii) It is uncontroversial that the *Theaetetus*, *Sophist*, and *States-*

---

[2] The *Parmenides* does ostensibly recommend the method of hypotheses, but the recommendation would appear to be ironical. At any rate, it is followed by an example of the method which seems very clearly to show that it cannot be trusted to yield sound results.

man were written in that order. The primary evidence here is that the *Sophist* opens with a reference back to the *Theaetetus* (as a discussion that occurred 'yesterday'), and a reference forward to the *Statesman*. The *Statesman* also opens with a reference back to the *Sophist* as having preceded. (And, incidentally, both the *Sophist* and the *Statesman* refer forward to a dialogue the *Philosopher*, which presumably Plato never wrote.) As well as these explicit cross-references, there are also suitable continuities of theme between the *Theaetetus* and the *Sophist*, and between the *Sophist* and the *Statesman*. The *Theaetetus* contrasts the followers of Heraclitus, those devotees of universal flux, with the adherents of Parmenides, who believed in a changeless unity. It proceeds to criticize Heraclitus, but declines the criticism of Parmenides, whereas this is a major theme in the *Sophist*. Again, the *Theaetetus* contains a long and inconclusive discussion of the problem of false belief, and this problem is once more discussed and finally resolved in the *Sophist*. One might also notice the interest in such 'topic-neutral' notions as being, sameness, and difference, which play a crucial part in the argument of the *Theaetetus* at 185–6, and are amongst the 'greatest kinds' discussed at some length in the *Sophist*. As for continuities between the *Sophist* and the *Statesman*, the most obvious point to mention here is the use of the method of 'collection and division' (which apparently supersedes the earlier method of 'hypotheses' as the true method to be practised by the philosopher). Both dialogues recommend and employ this method, the *Sophist* laying greater stress on its importance for philosophy, and the *Statesman* being more explicit on its limitations.

(iii) It is not *very* controversial to hold that the *Parmenides* links the two series we have mentioned: it comes after the *Republic* and before the *Theaetetus*. No one will dispute that the *Parmenides* comes after the *Republic*, for the *Parmenides* contains, in its first part, a forceful criticism of the theory of forms that is first clearly articulated in the *Phaedo*, and taken further in the *Republic*. (What is controversial is the question of how Plato reacted to this criticism which he himself had set out.) The main reason for supposing that the *Parmenides* comes before the *Theaetetus* is that at *Theaetetus* 183e Socrates refers to an occasion on which he 'met' Parmenides, and found him very impressive. It does not seem at all likely that the historical Socrates ever did meet with the historical Parmenides, or that—if he did—Plato should know anything about that meeting. (It would have occurred long before he was born.) Even if there was such a meeting, it is not clear why Plato should think it relevant to mention the point here, when he is very clearly discussing views which are a long way removed from the preoccupations of the historical Socrates. So it is much more likely that the reference is to be understood as a reference to the fictitious meeting portrayed in the dialogue *Parmenides*. This provides good ground for saying that the *Parmenides* was written before the *Theaetetus*, though it is also possible to explain the allusion by supposing that the *Parmenides* had been begun, but not finished, when the *Theaetetus* was written, or even that the *Parmenides* was at least planned at that stage. A second connection between the *Theaetetus* and the *Parmenides* is this. The *Theaetetus* is unique amongst Plato's dialogues in being a dialogue that is reported to us, but reported in direct speech and not in indirect speech. It even goes out of its way to explain that this was done on purpose to avoid the tedium of having to repeat 'then I said' and 'then he said' all the way through (143b–c). Now in earlier dialogues Plato has shown no reluctance to keeping up the reported speech all through the dialogue, but the *Parmenides* is clearly the last of his dialogues to be given in reported speech, and even there the reported speech only lasts for the first part of the dialogue; the second part lapses into direct speech. (In view of the nature of the argument in the second part, this is not altogether surprising.) It is therefore tempting to infer that at least the first part of the *Parmenides* was written before Plato decided that reported speech was tedious, and the opening of the *Theaetetus* then records this decision, which Plato adhered to in all the rest of his writings. But it must be admitted that this is rather a slim point to rely on, and it may perhaps have a different explanation.[3]

I am inclined to think that the two points mentioned, when taken together, do give us enough reason to say that the *Theaetetus* follows the *Parmenides*, or at least that it follows the first part of the *Parmenides*. But it is difficult to be sure of this, as there is very little overlap between the topics of which they treat, and there is certainly one point where an argument in the *Theaetetus* appears to be undermined by considerations raised in the second part of the

---

[3] The preface to the *Theaetetus*, which contains this apology for using direct speech, may perhaps have been added after the rest of the dialogue had been written (cf. pp. 10–11 below).

Parmenides.[4] At any rate, I think it is fair to say that there is very general agreement that the *Parmenides* and the *Theaetetus* are close to one another in date, even if their precise relationship is not altogether clear. So far, then, all is in accordance with what I called the 'orthodox' dating. I think we may add:

(iv) The *Phaedrus*, *Sophist*, *Statesman*, and *Philebus* were written in that order. These four dialogues all recommend or practise the method of 'collection and division', and it is quite clearly the *Phaedrus* that introduces that method for the first time. So the *Phaedrus* must precede the *Sophist* and the *Statesman*. It seems very probable[5] that the *Philebus* follows them, for its version of the method introduces some quite new (and very puzzling) considerations about 'the indefinite'. (It is tempting to connect these with what we are told of Plato's so-called 'unwritten doctrines', which clearly belong to his later years.) As for the beginning of this quartet of dialogues, all that one can say with any confidence is that the *Phaedrus* comes after the *Republic*, since the great speech that occupies most of its first half takes over without argument the tripartite view of the nature of the soul that had been argued in *Republic* iv, and it contains a new proof of the immortality of the soul, which clearly supersedes that of *Republic* x. (The new definition of the soul, on which this proof is based, reappears in *Laws* x, 895d–896a.) In other respects this first half of the *Phaedrus* returns to still earlier themes, notably the theory of recollection, from the *Meno* and the *Phaedo*, and of course the topic of love from the *Symposium*. On this ground one might suppose that the *Phaedrus* is close in date to the *Republic*. On the other hand its second half seems to suggest that the great speech should be treated with some reservation (e.g. 265b, 277d), and is very much more forward-looking. It introduces 'collection and division', as we have noted; it apparently recommends a more detailed investigation of the soul than the simple division into three parts; and its chief message is that there is after all room for a serious science of rhetoric. This evidently contradicts the *Gorgias*, and it is somewhat at odds with the attitude to rhetoric that is shared by the *Republic* and by the *Theaetetus* (172c–177b). It is possible, then, that while the first half of the *Phaedrus* was composed shortly after the *Republic*, the second half was not added until rather later.

---

[4] See pp. 214–15 below.
[5] The point has been disputed. See further p. 149, n. 4.

Let us pull these results together. By looking simply to the content of the dialogues, and not yet invoking any considerations about their literary style, we can confirm a great deal of the 'orthodox' chronology (see figure). This accounts for nearly all the dialogues

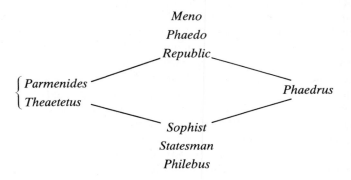

Meno
Phaedo
Republic
{ *Parmenides*
{ *Theaetetus*
Phaedrus
Sophist
Statesman
Philebus

that are at all relevant to the interpretation of the *Theaetetus*, but with two exceptions, namely the *Cratylus* and the *Timaeus*.

(v) The *Cratylus* was certainly written before the *Theaetetus*, but there also seem to be indications that it is not an early dialogue, but should be placed shortly after the *Republic*. It is clear that the *Cratylus* comes before the *Theaetetus* because of the way in which it introduces several themes that the *Theaetetus* then treats at much greater length, for example Protagoras' doctrine that man is the measure of all things (*Crat.* 386a–e), the paradox of falsehood (*Crat.* 429d–433b),[6] and the flux doctrine of Heraclitus (*Crat.* 439c–440c, and earlier). But the very fact that the *Cratylus* is interested in these topics, as well as its central concern with the nature of language, can be taken as a ground for dating it comparatively near to the *Theaetetus*. In addition, it is worth noting that the *Cratylus* takes the theory of forms for granted, and several of the things that it says about forms are very similar to things said in the discussion of imitation in *Republic* x, which is in this and other ways at variance with the doctrine of the main bulk of the *Republic*.[7] I therefore record it as my opinion that the *Cratylus* was written very shortly

---

[6] This paradox has also occurred earlier, at *Euthydemus* 283e–284c.
[7] For some parallels between the *Cratylus* and *Republic* x, see pp. 21–2.

after the last book of the *Republic*. This point, however, is not of very great significance for the understanding of the *Theaetetus*. What is much more important is the next issue.

(vi) The *Timaeus* certainly comes after the *Republic*, since its (somewhat peculiar[8]) introduction contains a recapitulation of the main themes of *Republic* ii–v, and a little later (at 29c3) it contains a clear reminiscence of the simile of the Divided Line at the end of *Republic* vi. But if we are looking simply to the content of the dialogue, and its allusions to other dialogues, I see no reason to say that it comes after any of the dialogues which are reckoned as late dialogues in the orthodox chronology. Its main topic is the nature of the physical world, which no other dialogue treats in comparable detail, but this is set against the background of a theory of forms which (with minor modifications) is essentially the theory of the middle period. Yet the late dialogues open with a trenchant critique of this theory, in the first part of the *Parmenides*, and although opinions differ on how Plato himself reacted to this critique it seems to me that the later dialogues (other than the *Timaeus*) do not clearly reaffirm the more extravagant claims of the middle period. In the *Theaetetus* the theory of forms (though present) is not much emphasized, and at first sight it does not appear to be very important to the main argument;[9] in the *Sophist* the theory is subjected to a further unfriendly criticism (248a–249d); the *Statesman* is, I would say, rather neutral on the topic; and the *Philebus* is evidently interested in a quite different metaphysic concerned with 'the definite' versus 'the indefinite'. Of course I do not mean to suggest that Plato gave up thinking in terms of forms altogether— that extreme view would be easy to refute—but that the confident pronouncements of the middle period, in particular concerning the 'separation' of forms from the physical world, do not recur in any dialogue after the *Parmenides*, save possibly the *Timaeus*. On this basis, then, it would be reasonable to infer that the *Timaeus* precedes the *Parmenides*, and my own suggested ordering would be: *Republic, Cratylus, Timaeus, Parmenides* (part I), *Theaetetus*. This is evidently a notable departure from the orthodox dating.

In fact the orthodox dating for the *Timaeus* rests on evidence I have so far been ignoring, namely the evidence of literary style (e.g.

---

[8] Ryle (1966), pp. 230–2, conjectures that this introduction was originally designed for the *Critias* and not the *Timaeus*. I find this conjecture attractive.

[9] But I shall suggest, as the book proceeds, that this first appearance is deceptive.

choice of this word or construction rather than that, sentence-rhythms, hiatus, and so on). Stylometric investigations have always been based upon the assumption that the *Laws* is Plato's last work, on the ground that it is unfinished and that we are told that it was 'on the wax', i.e. in manuscript, at Plato's death.[10] The procedure is then to compare the styles of different dialogues with that of the *Laws*, and to arrange them in order of greater or lesser resemblance to this terminus. Different stylometrists, working with rather different criteria, have reached rather different results about the general ordering of the dialogues, and certainly one cannot claim that the method gives a unanimous verdict. But the general opinion is that *nearly all* the tests so far conducted make the style of the *Timaeus* resemble that of the *Laws* more closely than does the style of the *Parmenides* and the *Theaetetus*, and that *many* of the tests make the *Timaeus* closer even than the *Sophist* and *Statesman*. (Most tests leave a noticeable break between *Parmenides* and *Theaetetus* on the one hand, and *Sophist* and *Statesman* on the other, while *Timaeus* and *Philebus* are usually closely associated. Different tests give widely different results for the *Cratylus*.) This explains the divergence between the 'orthodox' chronology and the one I have just sketched.

One may reasonably be somewhat sceptical about the presuppositions of stylistic studies of this sort. The obvious objection is that Plato was quite capable of deliberately varying his style from one occasion to another. For instance, the most prominent change of style is that hiatus is consciously avoided in *Timaeus*, *Sophist*, *Statesman*, *Philebus*, and *Laws*, but not in any other dialogue.[11] But this is obviously a *conscious* stylistic device, which Plato may well have decided to be suitable for some of his writings but not for others.[12] Again, the use of 'poetic' forms of speech is obviously the sort of thing that a skilled writer can put on and take off again. Besides, there is a further objection to the way Platonic stylometry is usually pursued, namely its assumption that the *Laws* can be treated as Plato's last work. As Owen (1953) has very fairly complained: 'Who would argue that the works which Descartes or Leibniz left in manuscript must have been their last?', and yet this is really all the evidence we have to support the assumption. Indeed,

---

[10] Diogenes Laertius iii. 37.
[11] I ignore the *Critias*, which is an unfinished fragment attached to the *Timaeus*.
[12] Cf. Ryle (1966), p. 297.

when one looks closely at the *Laws*, which is very long (345 pages), it becomes a plausible hypothesis that its internal inconsistencies are to be explained by its different parts being composed at different dates. There is nothing to overrule the suggestion that a fair part of it was composed very shortly after the *Republic*, though there is reason to suppose that Plato later revised it.[13] But if this is so then we do not know what chronological significance there may be in the stylistic resemblances between the *Timaeus* and the *Laws*. For all these reasons it seems to me very dangerous to rely purely on stylistic criteria for the dating of the dialogues, but I shall not attempt to go into the matter in any detail, merely expressing a general scepticism about the method.[14]

The stylometric evidence on the *Timaeus* was first challenged by Owen's article of 1953, to which Cherniss gave an influential reply in 1957, and the debate is by no means settled today. The question is important for understanding the development of Plato's views on the forms, for if the *Timaeus* does indeed come after the *Parmenides*, as the orthodox dating has it, then we can be sure that Plato was not led to modify his theory of forms in any important way as a result of the difficulties that the *Parmenides* sets out. But it is also important for the interpretation of the *Theaetetus*, and for much the same reason, as my next section will show. I record here my view that the *Timaeus* is a middle dialogue, written before the *Theaetetus* (and the *Parmenides*), but I shall not argue for it now. It will be more straightforward to look first at what the *Theaetetus* has to say, and I shall return to its relationship to the *Timaeus* at a later stage (Chapter IV, section 1).[15] But the next section will make it clear that the problem cannot be ignored.

[13] In the second book of his *Politics*, which is generally held to be an early work and written well before Plato's death, Aristotle comments extensively on *Laws* iii–vii. But the text that he is commenting on does not seem to be quite the same as the text that we have. Aristotle refers to the speaker as 'Socrates', whereas in our text the main speaker is an unnamed visitor from Athens, and he several times complains that the text omits topics which our text does not omit. (For details, see Morrow (1960).)

[14] The most influential stylometric study was that of Lutoslawski (1905). His methods are criticized in detail by Sayre (1983), Appendix B, who argues that, when they are purged of various distorting factors, they in fact yield the result that the *Timaeus* was composed before the *Parmenides*. (But Sayre's methods yield results as odd as Lutoslawski's, e.g. that the whole of the *Parmenides* was written later than either of its two parts.)

[15] I shall not, however, discuss the vexed question of the relationship between the *Timaeus* and the *Parmenides*.

Meanwhile, I add a short note on the chronological relation between the *Theaetetus* and its sequel the *Sophist*.

(ii) *The* Theaetetus *and the* Sophist

The usual view is that the *Theaetetus* and the *Sophist* are separated by some considerable lapse of time, during which Plato came to adopt the view that dialogues were more beautifully written in hiatus-avoiding Greek, even though that would hardly be the natural language of conversation. But it has been argued by Ryle (1966), pp. 27–32, that the *Theaetetus*, *Sophist*, and *Statesman* were originally written in close proximity, and designed to be delivered to the public as a connected trilogy.[16] I shall not be concerned to discuss all the varied speculations that Ryle brings in support of this claim, but there is one fact that is rather difficult to explain on the usual view, namely that the *Theaetetus* apparently ends by looking forward to the *Sophist*. The last words of the *Theaetetus* are 'Let's meet here again, Theodorus, tomorrow morning', and the first words of the *Sophist* are 'Here we are, Socrates, keeping the agreement we made yesterday'. This seems to show that when Plato finished the *Theaetetus* he was already looking forward to the *Sophist*.

One awkwardness for Ryle's view is the discrepancy between the dramatic settings of the two dialogues. The audience of the *Sophist* (and the *Statesman*) are listening in on a conversation between Socrates and others (mainly the others) as it takes place in 399 BC, whereas the audience of the *Theaetetus* are listening to a slave reading a record of a conversation. That conversation took place in 399 BC, on the day before the conversation in the *Sophist*, but the reading which we are listening to is being given some thirty years afterwards.[17] To meet this point Ryle supposes that the *Theaetetus* was originally written as a direct dialogue, like the *Sophist* and the *Statesman*, and that the short preface which turns it into a reported

---

[16] When pursuing this view, Ryle tends to overlook the fact that the *Sophist* and *Statesman* announce a further dialogue, the *Philosopher*, as completing the business on which they are engaged. In fact there are indications that Plato intended all *four* dialogues to be taken together with one another. (See e.g. Cornford (1935), p. 168.)

[17] It is plausibly conjectured that the battle in which Theaetetus met his death was in 369 BC. (However, this date is of no help in establishing the relative chronology of the dialogues, since we have no such dates for other relevant dialogues.)

dialogue was a later addition. This is not in itself particularly improbable: one might naturally suggest that the preface was added upon the occasion of Theaetetus' death.[18] Anyway, the point is a minor one, for I am mainly concerned with the view that the *Theaetetus*, *Sophist*, and *Statesman* were composed in quick succession, and not with Ryle's further claim that they were to be presented orally to the public as a connected trilogy.

A more important difficulty for Ryle's view is the fact that the *Theaetetus* is written in 'natural' Greek, while the *Sophist* and the *Statesman* have been smoothed into special hiatus-avoiding Greek. Ryle explains this (pp. 295–300) by supposing that all three were originally written in natural Greek, and delivered together in this form. But only the *Theaetetus* was favourably received by the audience, and so it was the only one to be released to the public as a book. The *Sophist* and the *Statesman* remained upon Plato's shelf, and in his old age, when he was past creative writing, he 'polished them up' by removing the many instances of ordinary conversational hiatus that they originally contained.[19] This conjecture is in some ways attractive, for it does seem so very odd that Plato should have decided to ornament what is meant to be a conversation with the device of avoiding hiatus, a device recently introduced (by Isocrates) to promote the smooth flow of an orator's address. It is not particularly surprising to find this device used in the *Timaeus* (and *Critias*), or in the *Laws*, for they are basically monologues rather than dialogues, but the decision to treat genuine conversations in the same way does seem strange. If we can assign it to Plato's dotage, it may appear more comprehensible.[20]

But whether or not Ryle is right in his conjecture about the lack of hiatus, still his overall hypothesis cannot be correct, for he has overlooked many points of difference between the *Theaetetus* and the *Sophist*. I mention a minor point first. Both dialogues devote considerable space to what they each call the problem of how there can be such a thing as a false belief. Now admittedly it is not in fact

[18] This is not Ryle's suggestion. He supposes that the trilogy was written some ten years after 369 BC, and invents quite a different reason for adding the new preface. (Cornford argues, p. 15, that the flattering description of Theaetetus in 143d–144d would not have been written while Theaetetus was still alive, but I see no strong reason to agree. One might compare *Phaedrus* 278e–279a, on Isocrates.)

[19] Ryle adds that Plato also inserted, at *Statesman* 286b–287b, a comment on its unfavourable reception.

[20] Ryle extends the same hypothesis to the *Philebus*, which is also a conversation pruned of hiatus.

quite the same problem that is attacked on each occasion: the *Sophist* is more concerned to explain how there could *be* such a thing as a falsehood, while the *Theaetetus* is puzzled over how one could *believe* it. So it is not altogether impossible that Plato should have thought it worth while to devote thirteen pages of the *Theaetetus* to an inconclusive discussion of its problem, while he already envisaged the much longer and successful discussion of the *Sophist*. But the fact remains that each introduces its problem in the same way, and yet the *Sophist* never acknowledges in any way that its main topic is one that was discussed 'yesterday'. (To be sure, the visitor from Elea, who is the main speaker in the *Sophist*, would not have known that it was. But young Theaetetus would not have forgotten overnight, and Socrates and Theodorus were both there to remind him if he had.) This demolishes Ryle's view that the two dialogues were designed to be delivered on successive days to the same audience, and makes it quite difficult to believe that they were composed in quick succession.

But anyway, there are many other pointers to this. No one can fail to notice that the *Theaetetus* has the life and sparkle of many of Plato's earlier writings. The participants are deftly characterized, there are many touches of humour and a little by-play (e.g. when Theodorus is being persuaded to answer for his friend Protagoras), and above all we have a genuine conversation. Theaetetus and Theodorus do not just say 'yes' or 'no' as expected, but have a real contribution to make to the discussion. But there is no such effective dramatization in the *Sophist*, which is from a literary point of view flat and uninspired. There has been a distinct falling off in Plato's dramatic powers between the two.

In fact the *Theaetetus* is in other ways too very similar to an early dialogue. First, the topic is set by the question 'What is knowledge?', and very many of the early dialogues are also discussions of a 'What is X?' question, though the middle dialogues seldom approach their topic in this way. Next, although various answers to this question are proposed during the course of the dialogue, Socrates manages to reject them all, which again is exactly what happens in one early dialogue after another. Further, we begin with Theaetetus giving us a 'many' instead of a 'one' (146d), as in almost every early dialogue with a similar question, so giving Socrates an opportunity to make clearer how he wishes his question to be understood. Then immediately afterwards we find Socrates explaining that he is quite incapable of answering the question himself, which again can be paralleled in very many early dialogues. In fact we get a memorable picture here of Socrates as the intellectual midwife with no children of his own, which is entirely in keeping with the Socrates we meet in the early dialogues, but surely quite incongruous when one remembers the very detailed and positive doctrines put forward by the Socrates of, say, the *Republic*.

The explanation of these similarities is surely not that the *Theaetetus is* an early dialogue, contrary to all the chronological evidence we have noted, but it may perhaps be that Plato feels himself to be in much the same situation as when he wrote the early dialogues. Those early dialogues are not constructed as expositions of, or arguments for, any particular doctrines. Certainly there are themes which frequently recur, e.g. that no man does wrong on purpose, and there is a cluster of theses in which Plato shows a continuing interest, notably that all the virtues are essentially a matter of knowledge and so not really distinct from one another. But one of the salient features of these early dialogues is that they are constantly critical; they are designed to develop difficulties for these interesting theses, rather than simply to recommend them, and they invariably end negatively with the conclusion that no satisfactory answer has been reached. Many answers have been proposed, but each has (apparently) been refuted by close and detailed argument. But towards the end of this early period we begin to find something more positive (e.g. in the *Gorgias* and the *Meno*), and in the middle dialogues Plato's confidence blossoms. There is no doubt that in the *Phaedo*, the *Symposium*, the *Republic*, and the *Timaeus* Plato is definitely recommending a number of doctrines on a variety of topics. He now thinks that he has found the solution to his problems, and Socrates' sceptical questioning has been left far behind. (Accordingly, in the *Timaeus* he is removed from his position of chief speaker.) But the late dialogues open with a recognition that something has gone wrong. In the first part of the *Parmenides* Plato shows himself aware that the theory of forms is not after all the panacea for all problems, but involves serious difficulties of its own. This is a severe blow to all the great theories of the middle period, and it appears that everything is now back in the melting-pot again. So Plato reverts once more to the Socratic approach, and again undertakes a critical examination of some key concepts in philosophy. The *Theaetetus* is, I suggest, an examination of knowledge undertaken in much the same spirit as the examinations of courage, piety, virtue, and so on, that we find in the early dialogues. That is, Plato is no longer confident that he does know the answer to the question that he raises, and Socrates is appropriately reintroduced as chief speaker. This newly recaptured scepticism does not last for very long. The *Sophist* evidently does think that it has finally unravelled the tangle of problems with which it deals, and the same confidence is also found in the *Statesman* and the *Philebus*. But the *Parmenides* and the *Theaetetus*, it seems to me,[21] both belong to a period of doubt and self-questioning, when Plato was *not* looking forward to the renewed conviction that we find in the *Sophist*.

What are we to say, then, of the last sentence of the *Theaetetus*? The hypothesis that it is a later addition, added when Plato wrote— or began to write—the *Sophist*, is difficult but perhaps not impossible. What makes the hypothesis difficult is that Plato's dialogues were clearly issued to the public in book form,[22] and it is not easy to see how he could add a sentence to a book that was already published. But he *could* presumably make the addition to his own copy, which would have been preserved in the Academy, and if later editors had access to this they would certainly have preserved the addition, since the opening of the *Sophist* so evidently demands it. Alternatively, it is just possible that the last sentence of the *Theaetetus* is there almost by accident. The *Philebus* may be taken as referring to the possibility of a discussion 'tomorrow' at 50d6–e2 (compare 67b11–13), but there is no reason to suppose that Plato did plan a continuation of that dialogue. It is also possible that the *Cratylus* envisages a discussion 'tomorrow' at 396e, and again the same comment would apply. So perhaps when the *Theaetetus* ends by looking forward to 'tomorrow' Plato has as yet no definite plans on what 'tomorrow' might contain. Perhaps he put in the forward reference just on the off chance that it might prove to be useful, and it is somewhat accidental that, in this case, it did.

---

[21] I shall not argue for this way of looking at the *Parmenides*. For some justification in the case of the *Theaetetus* see chapter VII, section 1.
[22] See e.g. *Letter* ii. 314c, *Letter* xiii. 363a.

2. BACKGROUND: KNOWLEDGE AND THE FORMS

Plato's position in the middle dialogues is that only forms can be known. To understand why he came to hold that position we must first consider what he took forms to be, and why he supposed that there were such things. But I shall be as brief as possible on this aspect of our topic, since I have already given it some attention elsewhere.[23] However, it is worth beginning a little further back with an early dialogue, the *Meno*, where Plato is beginning to pay some attention to the notion of knowledge. Although the *Meno* has nothing to say about forms (as Plato later understood them), it does introduce the theory of recollection for the first time.

(i) *The* Meno *and Recollection*

The *Meno* begins by asking 'What is virtue?', and Meno offers various answers which Socrates has no difficulty in refuting. But when Socrates proposes that they co-operate on a joint search Meno replies with this pretty problem: 'But how will you look for something when you don't in the least know what it is? How can you propose something you don't know as the object of a search? Or again, even if you did come right up against it, how would you know that what you have found is the thing you didn't know?' (80d). Now Meno presents this problem as a problem for all inquiry whatever, even, for example, for the inquiry into who it was that murdered poor Smith. Similarly, Socrates proposes his answer, that learning is really recollection, as if it applies to all learning whatever, even to the discovery that the bullet that killed Smith came from Jones's gun. But presumably neither of them means to be taken so generally. In context the question is 'How do you set about the search for a correct definition of virtue? And how do you recognize that a suggested definition is correct?'. This is certainly not a silly question, nor one that is easy to answer.

In fact Socrates does not try to answer the first part of the question, but he does propose an answer to the second part, which is that once upon a time, before birth, we all did know what virtue is, so the problem is to recapture that knowledge. His idea is, presumably, that if only we could manage to formulate a correct account of virtue, that would somehow jog our memory, and so we would

---

[23] See my *Plato's* Phaedo (1986), esp. pp. 94–101, 194–207.

remember what virtue is and thereby recognize the account as a correct one. To demonstrate that this kind of thing is possible, Socrates then in effect[24] points out that it is possible to discover the solution to a geometrical problem by using only facts that one knew beforehand, and that one certainly can recognize the solution as correct. He evidently thinks of this as a matter of 'drawing the knowledge out of oneself', and infers that it must have been within one from the start (85c–d). Perhaps he is also relying on a parallel between the feeling one has when one grasps a solution and the feeling one has when one succeeds in remembering: in each case it 'clicks into place' as something evidently right, and carries conviction with it.

This recognition that sometimes one can draw knowledge out of oneself seems to be, in our terminology, a recognition that some knowledge is a priori: we can attain it without relying on perception. Certainly, a priori knowledge does seem to call for an explanation, and perhaps it was not altogether a foolish idea to suggest that it is possible only because of something that is innate in us. Nor is it at all surprising that Plato should regard mathematical knowledge as a priori, and hope that we might attain a similar a priori knowledge of what virtue is. But does he suppose that *all* genuine knowledge is a priori? Certainly, Socrates makes no distinctions, and on the surface he commits himself to the view that *all* learning is recollection. It is also true, as we shall see, that in later dialogues Plato does so restrict the notion of knowledge that only a priori knowledge will qualify. But I doubt whether we should read that implication back into the *Meno*.

A little later on, the *Meno* does propose two marks to distinguish knowledge from true belief. One is that true belief is apt to run away and leave you, whereas knowledge is stable because it is firmly tied down. The other is that the thing that ties knowledge down is 'working out the reason' (αἰτίας λογισμός, 97d–98a). Presumably the idea is that you do not count as knowing something unless you can explain why it is so, whereas a true belief need not be accompanied by any such explanation. Now the *Meno* at once adds that this process of 'working out the reason' *is* recollection, apparently implying that it must be something one can do a priori, but it does not explain why. After all it would seem that there could be perfectly good explanations, based on experience, of facts which

---

[24] This brief summary is rather generous to the text.

themselves were known only by experience. But there is a way of ruling out such apparent explanations, namely by setting the standard of what is to count as an adequate explanation so high that nothing that empirical science could provide will be able to meet it. This is just what the *Phaedo* does, during its discussion of explanations (αἰτίαι) at 95e–102a. But again it is doubtful whether we should read this back into the *Meno*, which gives no account of what an explanation must be. Worse, the *Meno* very clearly ignores its own account of what distinguishes knowledge from belief. Just before drawing this distinction it has claimed that knowledge and true belief are equally effective in practice as guides to action, giving as an example that one who knows the road to Larissa, because he has travelled it himself, will be no better as a guide than one who merely has a true belief about it (97a–b). But if I count as knowing the road to Larissa because I have travelled it (and can remember it), this is evidently not a piece of a priori knowledge, and apparently it does not even satisfy the requirement that I must be able to explain what I know. Clearly I can be familiar with the road, and in this sense know it, without in any way being able to answer the question '*Why* does this road get to Larissa?'.

To sum up, then, there are certainly hints in the *Meno* that all genuine knowledge must be based on recollection, and so is a priori. But one of the *Meno*'s own examples implicitly denies this thesis, and so it seems fair to conclude that it is not yet an established feature of Plato's thought about knowledge. When we turn to the *Phaedo* things look rather different, but the *Phaedo* relies upon the theory of forms, and we must first say a word about this.

(ii) *Forms as Paradigms*

Plato inherited from Socrates a belief that it is crucially important to be able to answer such questions as 'What is courage?', 'What is justice?', 'What is beauty?', construed as questions which ask for the *one* thing that is common to the *many* instances, cases, or examples. Now sometimes there is no great difficulty in answering a 'What is X?' question of this sort—for example, 'What is shape?' may be answered by saying that shape is the limit of a solid—but with the cases which actually interested Plato it seemed to be very difficult indeed. I conjecture that Plato asked himself what the source of the difficulty was, and came to the conclusion that the trouble lay in the instances themselves. For interesting values of 'X', there are not even any unambiguous *instances* of X. For example, whatever is beautiful will also turn out to be, in some ways or in some circumstances or in some settings, not beautiful. Similarly whatever is just will also be unjust, whatever is good will also be bad, in much the same way—Plato supposes—as whatever is large (compared with one thing) will also be small (compared with another), whatever is double (one thing) will also be half (another), and whatever is one (finger) will also be many (joints). But if every case of X is also a case of non-X, there then seems to be a problem over how we ever grasp the concept of X-ness at all, for surely the *usual* way of coming to grasp a concept is by being shown standard examples of things to which it applies. Yet we have just said that in these interesting cases all the examples available to us are radically defective, and it is very difficult to see how one could come to grasp a concept from examples which illustrate its opposite just as much as they illustrate it itself. So this leads Plato to posit forms as examples to which the concept does apply without any ambiguity or any need for qualification. They just exemplify it, without also exemplifying its opposite, or indeed any other concept at all. And the theory is that we must be 'in touch' with such an unambiguous example in some way, for otherwise we could not grasp the relevant concept.

But here we must add a further sophistication. In *one* sense we all know what beauty is, in so far as we evidently do attach some meaning to the word 'beautiful'. But in another more demanding sense we do not know what beauty is, for we are quite unable to *say* what it is in any way that reveals the one thing common to the many instances. So in the *Phaedo* the theory of recollection appears in this complex way. Before being born into this world we all had some acquaintance with the form (i.e. perfect example) of beauty, which we do in some way recollect, for otherwise we would not grasp the concept at all. But this recollection cannot be clear to our consciousness, for otherwise we would be able to say what beauty is, which we cannot. So the position is that we have a dim recollection and not a clear one, and the philosophical enterprise of trying to say what beauty is is to be pursued by trying to bring that dim recollection more clearly into view. The task is to expose more clearly an understanding that must be already latent within us, and trying to collect examples of beautiful things from the world around us will not help us in the slightest.

On this line of thought, then, forms are—as I shall say—perfect paradigms, posited to resolve a problem about how we understand our language. Moreover, it has clear implications about how one gets to know the forms. When we are learning language in the first place, it is our perception of the defective examples in this world that originally triggers the required recollection, but once that has happened our experience of this world has no further role to play. So the *Phaedo* complains that the senses never yield knowledge, and are merely a hindrance to it, evidently because they will not yield knowledge *of the forms*. But it is now perfectly clear that this knowledge is the only thing that Plato will count as knowledge, perhaps because he is still connecting the notion of knowledge with the demand for an explanation (though the *Phaedo* does not make this connection explicitly), and he does now put severe restrictions on what he will count as an adequate explanation.

The bulk of the *Republic* understands forms in much the same way as the *Phaedo* (though with more emphasis on their role in mathematics), and it too wishes to confine knowledge to the forms. This is explicitly argued at the end of book v, where it is claimed that only the philosopher can properly be said to love knowledge, on the ground that only he concerns himself about the forms. Other people do not recognize the forms, but concentrate their attention on what they can perceive, and for that reason they can only be said to love belief (474b–476d). The argument is that knowledge and belief are different, since the one is liable to error but the other is not, and from this it is inferred that the two therefore have different objects. But it is agreed that knowledge is of what is, and that it will not do to say that belief is of what is not, so the object of belief should be between being and not being. And this indeed proves to be the case with those things that the lovers of sights and sounds concern themselves about, for the many beautiful things are also ugly as well as beautiful, so the right thing to say of them is that they both are and are not (sc. beautiful). The intended contrast must be that the form genuinely is (sc. beautiful), and that is why it can be known (to be beautiful?) while its perceptible instances cannot (476e–480a). Now there are various problems with the detailed interpretation of this argument, and however it is interpreted it must be admitted that it is not very satisfactory. But at least it does show clearly enough that the original contrast between forms as perfect paradigms and perceptible things as defective or ambiguous paradigms is now also associated with another contrast between knowledge as the special province of the philosopher and belief as the state of ordinary men. But let us leave knowledge aside for a while, and return to the forms.

(iii) *Forms as Universals*

Unfortunately, Plato's view of the forms was never as single-minded as my account so far has suggested. As well as conceiving of them as perfect paradigms he at the same time, and inconsistently, thought of them as universals. Thinking of forms as perfect paradigms, he speaks of particular things as resembling them but falling short of them, as being (imperfect) images or copies of them, and so forth. But thinking of forms as universals he speaks of particular things as sharing in them, or participating in them, or of forms as being present in particulars. On this latter conception, the form itself *is* the one thing that is common to the many examples of it, whereas on the former conception it is itself an example (though a perfect one). Right from the beginning, i.e. from the *Phaedo* onwards, Plato thought of his forms in both ways at once, and this of course is what lies behind the famous problem of 'the third man' posed in the *Parmenides*. It also leads to some uncertainty over what forms there are.

Thinking of forms as perfect paradigms, the argument to show that there must be such things depends upon the premiss that ordinary perceptible paradigms are not available (since every case of X is also a case of non-X). Plato evidently thinks that this premiss holds for moral and aesthetic concepts, for mathematical concepts (e.g. the numbers and the geometrical figures), and for what we would call relational concepts such as being large or small, double or half, and so on. But one would not expect it to hold everywhere, and at least for *most* of the *Phaedo* and the *Republic* the population of the world of forms seems to be fairly restricted. But things are different when we come to the discussion of imitation in *Republic* x (595a–608b). This is evidently an appendix to the main work, and it is not altogether consistent with the earlier discussion of education at 376d–403c. It also takes a rather different view of forms, leaning more to the view that they are mere universals, as Socrates announces that 'We are accustomed to posit one form for *any* set of many things that are all called by the same name' (596a). Immediately he introduces the form of a bed, the form of a table, and the form of a bridle, which are certainly not the kinds of forms we have been accustomed to. Similarly in the *Cratylus* we have the form of a shuttle, and apparently of every kind of tool (including the form of a name—names being regarded as tools for distinguishing objects). Again in the *Timaeus* we have forms of man and other animals, of the four elements, and—it would seem—of every natural object.

It appears from *Parmenides* 130b–e that Plato recognized this to be an extension of his original ideas, and it is clear to us that the justification for it in *Republic* x is one that simply construes forms as universals. But Plato himself has not yet separated the idea of forms as universals from his conception of them as perfect paradigms, for throughout *Republic* x, *Cratylus*, and *Timaeus*, he continues to use the language of resembling and copying, and the word 'participation' hardly occurs. Indeed we find a new role for the form as a paradigm, and that is to explain our ability to manufacture things according to a preconceived design. The idea is that when a craftsman sets out to make a bed (*Republic* x. 596a–b) or a shuttle (*Cratylus* 389a–c) he has in mind what the finished product is to be like, and can reject some of his creations as not up to standard. He can do this, Plato supposes, only because he is working with an eye on the form: his products are thus modelled on the form, and his attempt is to get them to resemble the form as much as possible. In the *Timaeus* this line of thought is extended further to objects that exist by nature and not by human manufacture, on the ground that they also were created by the Supreme Craftsman, namely God, and he must have kept his eye on the relevant forms when doing so. (In *Republic* x God had been credited with the creation of the forms themselves; in the *Timaeus* this suggestion is dropped in favour of the general thesis that all creation requires a pre-existing model.)

On this expanded theory of forms it is no longer very plausible to say that knowledge of the forms is the special province of the philosopher, or that it is to be pursued by ignoring the evidence of the senses. And it turns out that Plato does drop these claims in *Republic* x and the *Cratylus*, when considering the manufacture of such ordinary articles as beds, bridles, and shuttles. But he does not say, as one might expect him to, that the craftsman who keeps his eye on the form knows what it is. Instead he distinguishes between the man who makes the article and the different man who uses it, and ascribes knowledge only to the latter (*Republic* x. 601c–e, *Cratylus* 390b–d). Presumably the idea is that the user will know not only what a good bridle ought to be like, but also *why* it should be like that, so only he counts as having a full understanding of bridles. But there is no suggestion that it is only the philosopher who can achieve this understanding, or that it is to be done by recollecting a pre-mundane experience.

In fact the theory of recollection does not appear anywhere in the *Republic*, and there is one passage which appears to deny it (though it is not clear whether the denial was intended).[25] However, the theory does reappear in the *Phaedrus*, where it is again connected with our ability to understand language (249b–c), and there may be a hint of it in the *Timaeus* at 41d–e. There we are told that when human souls were first created, and before they were embodied, each was placed in a star 'as in a chariot'[26] and shown 'the nature of the universe' (τὴν τοῦ παντὸς φύσιν). We are not told why it was necessary for each soul to be allowed this view of 'the nature of the universe', but it *may* be that the point is that it will enable the soul to recollect what it has seen.

Anyway, whether or not the *Timaeus* reverts to the theory of recollection, it certainly does revert to the view that sense-perception cannot yield knowledge. It tells us very forcibly, and several times, that no knowledge can be had of the topic that it itself is concerned to expound, namely the nature of the physical world, and that its own theories cannot therefore be reckoned as more than a probable opinion. At the same time, the *Timaeus* brings us a new argument for the existence of forms, which both justifies the extension of the world of forms and restores the old link between forms and knowledge.

(iv) *Forms and Knowledge in the* Timaeus

The new argument is one that Aristotle was more familiar with, and this is the way that he introduces Plato's theory of forms:

[25] At x. 585a–b ignorance in the soul is regarded as an emptiness which is *not* the result of an emptying.

[26] If (the first half of) the *Phaedrus* was written before the *Timaeus*, then we might see the phrase 'as in a chariot' as designed to remind us of the image of the soul in the *Phaedrus*, and hence of the theory of recollection that goes with it. (The same word, ὄχημα, is used at *Phaedrus* 247b2.)

After the systems we have discussed came the philosophy of Plato . . . In his youth he became familiar with Cratylus, and with the Heraclitean doctrines—that all sensible things are always in a state of flux and there is no knowledge of them—and these views he retained even in later years. On the other hand Socrates was busying himself with ethical matters, and—neglecting the natural world—he sought for what was universal in these ethical matters, being the first to direct attention to definitions. Plato accepted his teaching, but held that the problem applied not to sensible things but to entities of another kind, for this reason, that the common definition could not be a definition of any sensible thing as they were constantly changing. Things of this sort, then, he called forms, and said that sensible things were all named after them: for the many existed by participation in the forms that had the same name as they. (*Metaphysics* A6. 987a29–b10; cf. M4. 1078b9–17)

In Aristotle's view the theory of forms arises simply by combining the Heraclitean view that all sensible things are in flux with the Socratic demand that definitions be permanent and unchanging. As I have explained, I do not think that this is altogether a correct account: Socrates did have quite a lot to do with the early stages of the theory, but Heraclitus is not very important at this stage. Later Heraclitus does become important, but Socrates has rather dropped into the background. The argument that Aristotle sketches was certainly used by Plato, but it is first sketched tentatively in the *Cratylus* and nowhere given in detail before the *Timaeus*. It is essentially this: there is such a thing as knowledge, so something is known; but whatever is known cannot change, whereas sensible things are constantly changing; hence there are non-sensible objects of knowledge, and these are what we call forms. Notice that this new argument removes the limitation that affected the old one. We said that that old argument could be applied only where ordinary perceptible examples were inadequate to yield a grasp of the concept involved, but according to the new argument they will *always* be inadequate: for any value of 'X' whatever, it will always be true that any perceptible example of X will later *become* an example of non-X. So on the one hand we are forced to extend the world of forms, and on the other hand the possibility of knowing anything about sensible particulars can be ruled out. Admittedly there is nothing very new in the claim that sensible things change whereas forms do not (e.g. *Phaedo* 78b–80b, *Republic* vi. 485b), but this point has not previously been used as a ground for affirming that there are forms.

In the *Cratylus* the new argument is put rather tentatively. For much of that dialogue Socrates has been flirting with Heraclitean etymologies, but he ends on a more serious note, admitting that his conjectures on the history of language can hardly settle the important question whether Heraclitus was actually right. Turning to this question (at 439c) he deliberately sets aside the issue of whether the *perceptible* beautiful things are all in flux, but insists that beauty itself could not be changing, adding that if it were it could not be known. But he does not profess to have settled the matter. So we have here the main ingredients of our new argument, but it is not really pressed home. For that, we must turn to the *Timaeus*, where Plato is much more dogmatic. (And I shall quote from the *Timaeus* at some length, in order to illustrate the importance of the question whether it precedes or follows the *Theaetetus*.)

Timaeus begins his account of the universe with this general principle:

In my opinion, the first thing we must do is to make this distinction: what is it that *is* always and has no becoming, and what is it that is always becoming but never *is*? The first is to be grasped by intelligence (νόησις) with reason (μετὰ λόγου), and it remains always the same; the second is to be believed (δοξαστόν) by belief (δόξα) with unreasoning perception (αἴσθησις ἄλογος), and it is coming into being and passing away but it never really is. (27d–28a)

This uncompromising distinction between what is or exists and what merely becomes (i.e. is in flux), and its equation with the distinction between what is properly intelligible and knowable and what is merely believable and perceptible, is adhered to throughout Timaeus' speech. No reason is here given for making the two distinctions so firmly, or for supposing that they coincide, but language is used which seems to refer us back to the *Republic* (e.g. 29c). The opposition between being and becoming is sharpened in 37e–38b, where it is claimed that the verb 'to be' (in its present tense) should only be used of what is eternal and completely changeless, and this point is put to use a little later, where Timaeus is discussing the nature of the four elements and their relation to space (48e ff.).

In order to introduce the concept of space Timaeus says he must first raise some difficulties about fire and the other elements:

It is difficult to say with any conviction or certainty which of these elements should really be called water rather than fire, or which of them should be called any of them rather than all of them. (49b)

His reason is that the elements are constantly changing into one another, so

> how can anyone definitely affirm, without disgrace, that any of them *is* some one thing rather than another? It cannot be done. Much the safest course is to speak of them like this: anything we see to be continually changing—as for instance fire—must not be called 'this' (τοῦτο) but rather 'suchlike' (τοιοῦτο). . . . Nor must we speak of anything else as having any permanence by trying to indicate it with the words 'this' and 'that'. They slip away and will not abide these expressions, or any others which show them as stable and as being. (49d–e)

Timaeus' idea seems to be that one cannot pick out any (percept-ible) subject of which one can say that it *is* fire, for any such subject will soon change into something else, and to say that it *is* fire is to attribute fieriness to it in perpetuity. The solution he suggests is that we only permit *space* to figure as a subject of our assertions, and we replace 'this is fire' by 'this *space* is *fiery*'—and this contrast between a substantival and an adjectival use of the notion of fire is no doubt what he is getting at in his distinction between 'this' and 'suchlike'. One expects him to add not only that we should use adjectives rather than nouns to describe how space is characterized, but also that we should use the verb 'becomes' rather than 'is' to do so. In fact he does not say this directly, but simply avoids using any part of the verb 'to be' in connection with his word 'suchlike'. (That is, he uses locutions such as 'we should call it suchlike and not this', 'we should speak of it as suchlike', and so on (49e–50b).) Later, when particular adjectival forms are introduced as appropriate expressions to be used of space, they are parts of verbs. Thus we may talk of a part of space which 'has been made fiery' or 'has been made moist' (τὸ πεπυρωμένον μέρος, τὸ ὑγρανθέν, 51b4–5), or we may describe it as 'being fierified' or 'being moistened' (πυρουμένη, ὑγραινομένη, 52d5). These expressions again avoid the verb 'to be' (in Greek), and are perhaps intended to suggest 'becomes' in its place.

Anyway, it is claimed that, because of the perpetual transmu-tation of the elements, there is nothing in this world which can properly be said to *be* fire. All we have in this world is space, which may be called 'fierified' here and there, according as it receives, imprinted on it, an image of what really *is* fire, viz. the form. But do such forms exist at all? Upon this Timaeus pronounces as follows:

> If understanding (νοῦς) and true belief are two distinct things, then there

certainly are separate forms, imperceptible to us, and only to be grasped with the mind (νοούμενον). But if, as some think, understanding and true belief do not differ at all, then we must take it that whatever we perceive through the body is entirely certain. But the two should in fact be reckoned distinct, since they have different origins and different natures. The one originates in instruction, the other in persuasion; the one is accompanied by a true account (λόγος), the other has no account (ἄλογον); the one is not to be moved by persuasion, the other may be; and finally, whereas all men must be said to share in belief, understanding belongs to god, and only in small measure to men. In consequence we must agree that one kind of being is a form, which stays always the same, uncreated and indestructible, . . . not visible or in any other way perceptible, and it is this which it is the task of the intellect (νόησις) to consider; the second kind resembles it, and has the same name as it, but is perceptible, created, always in motion . . . and this is apprehended by belief with perception. [And the third kind is space.] (51d–52a)

It is to be observed that the general structure of the argument here is the same as it was in *Republic* v. First it is claimed that there are marks which allow us to distinguish between knowledge or understanding on the one hand and mere belief on the other. Then it is inferred (tacitly in the *Timaeus*, and explicitly in the *Republic*) that the two must therefore have different objects. The object of belief is equated with the object of perception, though no good reason is given for this step in either dialogue. But it is claimed in both that the objects of perception are unsatisfactory as objects of knowledge, for they are not unambiguously (in the *Republic*) or unchangingly (in the *Timaeus*) what we call them. Both dialogues then infer that the objects of knowledge must therefore be something else, namely forms. But whereas the *Republic* aims to stress the point that it is only forms that can be known, and takes their existence for granted, the *Timaeus* is concerned to conclude that there must therefore be forms. (And hence the *Timaeus* is on weaker ground, since it needs the additional premiss that knowledge is indeed possible. In fact it apparently needs to argue that there can be knowledge of all those forms that the changeable objects of perception so fleetingly exemplify.)

(v) *Conclusions*

This argument to show that forms are the only objects of knowledge can of course be resisted at many points, but perhaps the most fundamental error is the way in which it employs the notion of an *object* of knowledge or belief, as if what is known or believed is always a thing or entity, to be indicated by a name, rather than stated in a that-clause. The verb 'to know' can certainly be followed by a direct object, as when we talk of knowing a person, or a place, but this should not be confused with the use by which we talk of knowing *that* something-or-other is the case. (In other languages the distinction is marked by two separate verbs, e.g. in French by *connaître* as opposed to *savoir*, or in German by *kennen* as opposed to *wissen*.) It is only in the second use that knowledge can properly be contrasted with belief, for the verb 'to believe' cannot be followed by a direct object in the same way, but must govern a that-clause. It may perhaps be partly for this reason that Plato tends to slip from belief to perception, where the direct object construction is again available. But more seriously Plato seems to have been led into thinking of knowledge as *very like* perception, except that it is done 'with the mind' rather than 'with the senses'. This difference ensures that the two are directed to different objects—intelligible ones, or perceptible ones, respectively—but in other respects they are apparently taken to be very similar. Of course we do commonly use verbs of perception, such as 'seeing' or 'grasping', in a metaphorical way to describe knowledge and understanding, but Plato seems to have taken these metaphors far more seriously than he should have done.

I do not wish to suggest that Plato always and consistently thought of knowledge as directed to objects (as *connaître* is) rather than to facts or propositions. We have noted that early on, in the *Meno*, he connects knowledge with the ability to explain or give reasons, and of course it is facts and not objects that are explained. Again, in the *Phaedo* and the *Republic*, when he is describing how the philosopher is to seek for knowledge, he tells us that it must be done by using hypotheses, which are surely propositions rather than objects,[27] and the procedure is to ascend from one hypothesis to another that is 'higher', apparently in the sense that the higher hypothesis explains or gives a reason for those beneath it. It is also true that when he does speak of knowing an object (*connaître*?) he

---

[27] But note *Republic* vi. 510c, where it said that mathematicians proceed by 'hypothesizing the odd and the even and the figures and three kinds of angle . . . making them hypotheses, as if they were known, but giving no account of them'. It is difficult to see what *propositions* are in question.

evidently connects this very closely with knowing what that object is (*savoir*). The Greek language has an idiom whereby one may be said to 'know a thing, what it is', in which the two notions are directly run together, and it is not unreasonable to say that it is this combination of notions that Plato seems standardly to have in mind in the middle dialogues when he speaks of knowing forms. The combination is reflected in his constant demand that if you know a thing then you must be able to *say* what it is, to give a suitable 'account' (λόγος) of the thing (e.g. *Phaedo* 76b, *Republic* vii. 533c, *Timaeus* 51e, and often elsewhere).

In the early dialogues it is often not very clear what exactly the relation is supposed to be between knowing X and being able to say what X is,[28] but in the *Phaedo* the position would seem to be this. The task of knowing the form is the task of recollecting one's previous experience of it in full clarity, and then when we have the form clearly in view we will somehow be able to read off a suitable account of it from what we can see. Or perhaps, if we have stumbled across a suitable account somehow, that will jog our memories and give us a clear view of the form we seek. Then we shall be able to verify from what we see that the account is indeed correct. Although recollection is not assigned a similar role in any of the other dialogues we have been considering, still in the central books of the *Republic* the picture appears to be much the same. The famous similes of the Sun, Line, and Cave evidently treat knowing as a kind of vision of the forms, culminating in the vision of the form of the good,[29] and the whole task of education is described as the task of turning the soul's gaze in the right direction. (But it is never explained how the correct employment of hypotheses will yield this vision.) On the other hand in *Republic* x and the *Cratylus*, where much less exciting forms are under consideration, looking at the form is explicitly distinguished from knowing what it is, and in those dialogues there is no reason to say that knowledge is construed as a kind of vision. We may also note that the *Timaeus* offers it as a distinction between knowledge and belief that knowledge comes from instruction (διὰ διδαχῆς), as opposed to persuasion,[30] and this is not a phrase that suggests vision, but seems rather at odds with the *Republic*'s account of what education is. Nevertheless the

---

[28] See White (1976), pp. 19–22, for some discussion of this.
[29] Compare the vision of the form of beauty at *Symposium* 210a–211b.
[30] Cf. *Theaetetus* 198b1–5, 201a7–b3.

Timaeus still retains the *Republic*'s view that knowledge and belief are chiefly to be distinguished by the fact that they have different *objects*, in the one case forms and in the other perceptible things, and that is the essential point that I wish to fasten upon.

If one does think of knowledge as primarily directed towards objects, then it will be very tempting to infer that the objects in question cannot be the same as those we perceive. This is obviously so if one thinks of knowledge, properly speaking, as limited to what can be known a priori, as the *Meno* rather suggests (but not very consistently) and the *Phaedo* certainly affirms. And although Plato may later have abandoned the theory of recollection that was his first way of distinguishing a priori knowledge, he does not seem to have abandoned the strict conception of what genuine knowledge is that went with it. Indeed I think it likely that *Republic* v wishes to endorse such a strict conception when it distinguishes knowledge from belief on the ground that knowledge is not liable to error (ἀναμάρτητος, 477e6). This point is offered as a ground for saying that the two are different capacities or faculties (δυνάμεις), and hence have different objects, and this inference would be quite unreasonable if all that was meant was that we do not call a belief knowledge when it is in error. So I think it likely that Plato's thought is that knowledge cannot be mistaken in the sense that what knowledge is of is something we cannot be mistaken about. That is, in Aristotle's useful (because ambiguous) phrase, knowledge is of 'what cannot be otherwise'. We, of course, are familiar with this view as a (contentious) view about knowledge *of truths*: a truth that can be known must be a truth that cannot be otherwise, i.e. a necessary truth. But if we think rather in terms of objects then we obtain the conclusion of the *Timaeus*: an object that can be known must be an object that cannot be otherwise, and hence an object that cannot change. No perceptible object satisfies this condition.

To sum up, then, there are two fundamental mistakes which run all through Plato's middle dialogues. The first is a mistake in the theory of meaning, which leads him to construe forms as perfect paradigms. The second is a mistake about knowledge, which leads him to think of knowledge as primarily knowledge of objects (*connaître*), the objects in question being forms viewed as perfect paradigms. Then, since knowledge evidently contrasts with belief, belief is also construed as if it were primarily directed at objects, though in fact there is nothing which stands to *connaître* as belief stands to *savoir*. And perhaps because of this Plato is led to equate belief with perception, since at least there are objects of perception. So we have on the one hand perception (= belief), the bodily sense-organs, and the changing sensible objects which form the realm of becoming; on the other hand we have knowledge, the mind, and the unchanging forms which form the realm of being; and in each case the relationships are conceived as running parallel. Apart from a slight hesitation in *Republic* x and the *Cratylus*, this broad dichotomy is constant throughout the middle dialogues: it is introduced in the *Phaedo*, retained and further elaborated in the *Republic*, and made the basis of an argument for forms in the *Timaeus*. I have illustrated it mainly from the *Timaeus* partly because that is where it appears as an argument for forms, and partly also because the *Timaeus* lays greater stress on the idea that *being* applies to forms whereas *becoming* applies to perceptible things; but most importantly because this very clearly shows the importance of the question of the relative dates of the *Timaeus* and the *Theaetetus*.

If the *Timaeus* precedes the *Theaetetus*, then we should not be surprised to find that the arguments of the *Theaetetus* tend to the *destruction* of this aspect of the theory of the middle dialogues, just as the arguments of the *Parmenides* appear to show that there is something wrong with its more logical aspect. Both dialogues may record a period of self-criticism. But if the *Theaetetus* precedes the *Timaeus* then we can be sure that, even if it does seem to contain criticisms, Plato must in the end have decided that the criticisms were not serious. What we surely cannot do is to suppose that the *Theaetetus* has simply no relation to the doctrines of the middle period; that would be incomprehensible.

Indeed the *Theaetetus* first discusses the claim that knowledge is to be identified with perception, and without the background of the middle dialogues it must seem strange that Plato thought this claim even worth considering. Is it not *obvious* that we know a good deal about things that we have not perceived, and indeed about things that could not in any ordinary sense be perceived? Moreover, the introduction to the dialogue seems designed to bring out just this point, for we are told that young Theaetetus is a mathematician, and has been engaged in the theory of *irrational* numbers. Surely he could not be supposing that he can *perceive* that certain ratios are irrational? Yet surely he would count this as something he *knew*?

The claim that knowledge is perception might well seem to have been refuted already by 147d–148a, before it is even put forward. Why, then, does Plato go on to treat it at such length?

One suggested answer arises at once from the *Timaeus* passage just quoted (pp. 25–6): if there are forms then knowledge and belief-or-perception will be distinct, but if there are not then there will be nothing else for knowledge to be except perception. It may be, as e.g. Ross and Cornford suppose, that essentially this thesis underlies the *Theaetetus*, and that Plato wishes to demonstrate that knowledge cannot be identified either with perception or with belief because he thinks that it must then follow that there are forms. Alternatively, it may be that this thesis underlies the *Theaetetus* in a somewhat different way, by being itself refuted as over-simple. The thesis is an illustration of Plato's tendency to construe knowledge as *very like* perception, though directed to a different object, and perhaps he has now come to see that that is a mistake. Perhaps the reasons he will give for denying that knowledge *is* perception are principally of interest because they also show that knowledge is not *like* perception either. But it is now time to set aside such a priori speculations, and to come to grips with the *Theaetetus* itself.

3. THE QUESTION 'WHAT IS KNOWLEDGE?' (143d–151d)

After the little preface in which Euclides and Terpsion agree to have the dialogue recited to them, there is some conversation between Socrates, Theodorus, and Theaetetus which is designed to introduce us to the characters. Theaetetus is at the time a young and promising pupil of Theodorus, and he has at least touched on philosophical questions: he has noted that there is a question over what knowledge is (148c), and—as we later learn—he has 'often' read Protagoras' book *On Truth* (152a). Theodorus is an established mathematician, with a certain reputation in his subject (143d–e, 145a), but little inclination to venture outside it (146b). As for Socrates, he is here introduced as an intellectual midwife, with no children of his own, but skilled at bringing others' thoughts to birth and then testing them for truth. (Unlike more ordinary midwives, we are told that Socrates has *never* had an intellectual child of his own (149c and 150c–d).) As well as introducing the characters, this opening conversation also introduces the theme of the dialogue, namely the question 'What is knowledge?', and it is worth pausing for a few remarks on this. (Ironically the question is introduced[31] at 145d as a 'small point', but is later at 148c admitted to be not so small.)

As in many early dialogues, Theaetetus first tries to answer the question by giving a list of examples of knowledge, namely geometry, astronomy, harmonics, and arithmetic, and again the crafts or skills (τέχναι) of cobbling and so on (146c–d). These he calls 'knowledges' (ἐπιστῆμαι), presumably thinking of them as the various branches of knowledge. As Socrates justly observes, the principle behind his list is to catalogue the various things that there is knowledge of (146d–e). But this is not the sort of answer that Socrates wants, and he makes three complaints about it. First he says that he was not asking for an enumeration either of the things that there is knowledge of or of the several different 'knowledges' (146e). (He does not, apparently, object to the view that there are as many different 'knowledges' as there are different things known.) What he is asking, he says, is the different question 'What is knowledge itself?', which he evidently construes as a question about the *one* thing common to all the various examples. Next he says that the answer is anyway absurd, for since cobbling just is the knowledge of how to make shoes one cannot know what cobbling is unless one already knows what knowledge is (147a–b). And finally he claims that this kind of answer is needlessly long-winded, for one short formula is all that is needed, just as one can say what clay is simply by saying that it is earth mixed with water (147c).

Perhaps the most interesting complaint here is the second, which in effect maintains that such an answer would be *circular*. But in fact this is a mistake on Socrates' part, and there is no circularity involved in trying to explain a concept by giving a list of examples.[32] The point can be seen clearly if we look at Socrates' own illustration. It is obviously quite possible for someone to be familiar with, say, potters' clay without having ever met any other kind of clay, and without having any understanding of the *general* concept of clay. Such a person will not, of course, know what is meant by

---

[31] Knowledge (ἐπιστήμη) is here somewhat rashly equated with wisdom (σοφία), but I pass over that, as it is of no importance to the rest of the dialogue.
[32] The same mistake occurs at *Meno* 79b–c.

saying of this stuff *that it is clay*, but he may still know what potters' clay is in the ordinary sense that he can recognize it when he sees it, and knows the kind of thing that it is used for, and very possibly can manipulate it himself. No doubt a potter's child is often in this position. And if you wish to explain to this child what clay, in general, is, there is nothing wrong with giving as an example this stuff that he is already familiar with. (But, no doubt, one would need to give *other* examples too.)

In a similar way it is conceivable—though not, I suppose, very likely—that someone should know what cobbling is (e.g. through his own training and experience), and indeed should know what geometry is (in the same way), without having yet attained to the general concept of knowledge. Again such a person will not know what is meant by saying that cobbling or geometry is a branch of *knowledge*, and he will not understand the description '*knowledge* of how to make shoes'. But that does not prevent him knowing what cobbling is, at least in the ordinary sense of that expression. It does, no doubt, prevent him from *saying* what cobbling is (in any way that would satisfy Socrates), and this alerts us to a further point, which may, I think, be fairly regarded as a further mistake, underlying the first, and much more important than it.[33]

Socrates speaks as though he and the others do *not* know what knowledge is, but here it is necessary to distinguish between what one might call two levels of knowledge. In an ordinary sense, we all know perfectly well what knowledge is: we know what the word means, and we can use it perfectly well for everyday purposes. Moreover, we can recognize examples of knowledge, and recognize that other purported examples are not knowledge. Briefly, we *have got* the concept of knowledge. But what we cannot do is to *say* what knowledge is, in one single and unified account: we cannot give any suitable *analysis* of this concept. Now Plato in earlier dialogues has constantly taken the attitude that one does not count as having genuine knowledge of what something is unless one can give a proper account of it, and he appears to be taking the same attitude here. He is insisting on the higher level of knowledge (sometimes called 'explicit' knowledge or 'articulate' knowledge), and we need not criticize him for this. But it is important to recognize that there is *also* such a thing as the lower-level knowledge ('tacit' or 'inarticulate'), and one reason is this. A lower-level understanding of one

[33] I suspect that it also underlies the famous puzzle at *Meno* 80d.

concept may perfectly well be used when giving an explicit account of another.[34] Thus to understand the account of clay as earth mixed with water, all that is required is an ordinary and everyday understanding of what earth is and what water is (and what mixing is); there is no call to say that we need an explicit account of earth and of water before we can give an explicit account of clay. And to come back to the question of what knowledge is, there is in principle no reason why one should not rely upon the learner's ordinary and lower-level understanding of geometry and cobbling when using these as examples to impart a lower-level understanding of what knowledge is. Plato is no doubt right to say that a higher-level understanding of what knowledge is cannot be imparted in this way, but that is because—as he conceives of a higher-level understanding—it cannot be imparted by examples anyway. It is *not* because the examples cannot be understood until we have first understood what they are examples of.

The charge of circularity, then, is a mistake, but in the long run this particular mistake does not seem very important. One can agree that a list of examples does not provide an adequate answer to Socrates' question, even though there is nothing circular about it. This is just because the list of examples does not by itself tell you what it is that is common to all the examples. But underlying it is the deeper mistake of failing to recognize that we have two distinct levels of understanding to reckon with, and that in *one* sense we all have a perfectly good understanding of what knowledge is. I do not believe that Plato has seen this point fully. He cannot, of course, be wholly unaware of it: his remarks at 196d–e, which are surely intended to be humorous, show well enough that we must have *some* understanding of what knowledge is in order to be able to *begin* upon the inquiry into what it is. But still, there is an awkwardness that remains. As I have already remarked, because in *one* way we do already know what knowledge is, we can very properly test a proposed analysis of knowledge against agreed examples, as Plato evidently does at 201a–c and 207d–208b. The point is that we are *already* in a position to tell whether a suggested example of knowledge is an example or not, even though we cannot yet state any proper definition of knowledge. But this means that our problem is not at all the same as the mathematical problem that Theaetetus and his friend Young Socrates solved so successfully,

---

[34] Compare pp. 239–40 below, on the infinite regress of analyses.

and Plato is quite wrong to give this as an example of a successful inquiry into what something is (147d–148b).

Put in modern terminology, what seems to have happened is that Theaetetus noticed that no (whole) number which is not a square number has a rational square root, so he introduced the *new* concept of a *power* (δύναμις)—i.e. in modern terminology, a surd—to apply to all those numbers[35] whose squares are whole numbers but not square numbers. The *point* of introducing this concept of a power is that every power is irrational, and the mathematically interesting task would be to prove this. We are not told that Theaetetus proved it, but no doubt he did. Essentially, then, this is an example of a mathematical generalization: it is already known that $\sqrt{2}$ is not rational, $\sqrt{3}$ is not rational, $\sqrt{5}$ is not rational, and so on up to $\sqrt{17}$; and we now show more generally that *no* power is rational. To state this generalization it is convenient to introduce this new concept of a power, which is done by explicitly defining it in terms of familiar concepts. If this is right,[36] then the example illustrates the introduction of a new concept and not the analysis of an already familiar concept. Thus Theaetetus could hardly tell, *before* he had defined 'power', whether some number was a power or not. But by and large we can tell, before we have defined knowledge, whether some suggested example is an example of knowledge. This, as I say, goes some way towards explaining how it is possible to test a proposed analysis of knowledge for correctness: checking an account against agreed examples is an important weapon in Socrates' art of midwifery (150b–c).

Unfortunately, it appears that this weapon by itself will not be adequate. For one thing, some suggested examples of knowledge may be contentious, and we may feel that in order to decide them we need *first* to agree on an analysis of knowledge. Another problem is that it seems to be possible for some suggested analysis to fit *all* the examples, but still not be a correct analysis, if the fit is merely 'accidental'. (Thus if, in conditions of perpetual drought, it turns out actually to be true that the only wet earth there is is clay, and vice versa, nevertheless it would still be a mistake to give 'wet

---

[35] In orthodox Greek mathematics there are, strictly speaking, no irrational *numbers*; rather, there are *lengths* (and other magnitudes) that are not commensurable with a selected unit length. Hence the apparently tortured phrasing of our passage.

[36] The phrasing of 147d3 does rather suggest that the concept of a 'power' was not Theaetetus' invention, but was already in use. But if so, then Theaetetus' achievement was nothing to do with definition. It was simply a generalization of a proof.

earth' as the *analysis* of 'clay'.[37]) So this brings us to the question of what other conditions a successful analysis is supposed to satisfy. What would count as a fully correct answer to Socrates' question 'What is knowledge?'? But I shall not make any serious attempt to answer this question. Plato would no doubt say that a correct analysis must state what it is for something to *be* knowledge, or in other words that it must give the *being* or *essence* (οὐσία) of knowledge.[38] We might prefer to say that a correct analysis should tell us what it *means* to say that something is knowledge. But it is not at all clear that this difference of terminology would amount to any significant difference in practice, since the notions of *essence* and of *meaning* are both rather vague,[39] and I shall not try to give any precise formulation of them. That is, I will not propose any analysis of analysis, or any explicit account of what an explicit account should be. But perhaps we can just say this: an analysis should fit not only the actual examples, but also all possible examples, at least where there is no serious doubt as to how those examples should be classified. So if the account of knowledge is that knowledge is XYZ, then it should be not just true, but also necessarily true, that all examples of knowledge are examples of XYZ, and vice versa.

Let us now pass to a different question about the desired analysis of knowledge: is there any reason to suppose that *there is* an answer to the question 'What is knowledge?' of the kind that Plato desires? To judge from the early and the middle dialogues, Plato used simply to take it for granted that it must always be possible to give an analysis of *any* concept. In his language, it is possible to come to know any form, and knowledge of a form always involves the ability to 'give an account' (διδόναι λόγον). But if we require that such analyses should not be circular, then this appears to be an impossibility. Some concepts may be analysed in terms of others, and these others may perhaps be analysed in terms of yet further concepts, but the procedure cannot be carried on *ad infinitum* without eventually going round in circles; for the number of concepts available at any

[37] This is a captious objection to what Socrates says at 147c. The Greek word in question (πηλός) covers all kinds of mud, and not only what we call clay.

[38] Cf. *Euthyphro* 11a.

[39] Recall that Locke, in his *Essay Concerning Human Understanding*, distinguished between what he called *real essence* and *nominal essence*, and he argued that meaning should be identified with the latter. But more recently Kripke (1976) and Putnam (1975) have argued that meaning should be identified with the former.

time is presumably finite. We must, then, eventually come to 'simple' concepts that we cannot analyse any further[40] (at any rate, not without inventing new concepts for the purpose). What guarantee do we have that the concept of knowledge is not itself a simple and unanalysable concept? None that I know of. Yet ever since the *Theaetetus* philosophers have shared Plato's faith that *there is* an analysis to be found. I suspect this is largely because the idea with which our dialogue closes, that knowledge is to be analysed as true belief plus something else (which may perhaps deserve to be called a '*logos*'), has seemed for centuries to be an extremely promising starting-point. But unfortunately it is still not clear how the continuation should go.

But I must at once qualify that suggestion. Philosophers nowadays would be very wary of accepting Plato's apparent faith that there is some one account which fits absolutely *all* kinds of knowledge. On the contrary, it is usual nowadays to accept at least[41] a tripartite division of knowledge, into (*a*) knowing *that* (something-or-other is the case), (*b*) knowing *how* (to do something), and (*c*) knowing an *object* (e.g. a person, a place, and so on). Contemporary investigations usually focus in particular on knowing *that* (French *savoir*), and it is here that an analysis of the pattern 'true belief plus . . .' seems so promising. But the *Theaetetus* appears to be discussing this pattern of analysis as an analysis of knowing an *object* (French *connaître*), where it is much less plausible. The distinction between *savoir* and *connaître* is not marked by different words in Greek,[42] any more than it is in English, and throughout the *Theaetetus* it will be a constantly recurring problem to determine which notion Plato is speaking of. But for the present we can just make this observation: the question 'What is knowledge?' is introduced as asking for some one account which fits all varieties of knowledge, including both *savoir* and *connaître*, for we are given no

---

[40] The *Theaetetus* may contain some recognition of this point, in the theory put forward as 'Socrates' Dream'. I postpone comment until I come to that passage.

[41] One may also wish to distinguish between 'tacit' and 'explicit' knowledge (as on p. 33), and many other distinctions may be suggested.

[42] This is perhaps something of an exaggeration. Of the three main Greek verbs for 'to know' (ἐπιστᾶσθαι, εἰδέναι, γιγνώσκειν) the first very seldom takes as a direct object the name of a person or place, while the last very frequently does. (Lyons's book *Structural Semantics* (1963) provides a wealth of data on how in fact Plato uses these, and related, terms.) But I think it is clear that, when Plato is explicitly thinking about what knowledge is, he does not notice any differences between the several verbs in question.

hint of any restriction on how 'knowledge' is to be understood. In that respect, most contemporary philosophers presumably do *not* share Plato's faith that there is some one analysis to be found.

PART A

KNOWLEDGE AND PERCEPTION

II

THE THEORY THAT PERCEPTION
IS KNOWLEDGE

1. THEAETETUS AND PROTAGORAS (151e–152c)

There are various ways of understanding the thesis that knowledge is perception, and it will be useful to begin by making a few points about our ordinary use of the verbs 'know' and 'perceive'. I have already mentioned the distinction between knowing a thing or object (French *connaître*), and knowing *that* something-or-other (French *savoir*). For example we speak of knowing a person, say John Smith, and of knowing something *about* him, say *that* he is bald. The relation between these two kinds of knowledge is somewhat problematic, and we shall have to say more about it later. An entirely similar grammatical distinction applies to the verb 'perceive' (and similarly 'see', 'hear', 'feel', etc.): we speak of seeing John Smith and of seeing that he is bald, of hearing John Smith and of hearing him approach, and so on. These points apply just as much to Greek as to English, for Greek makes no more distinction between *savoir* and *connaître* than we do, and verbs of knowing and perceiving can each take either a direct object or the equivalent of a that-clause (i.e. a participial construction, an accusative and infinitive, or ὅτι).

Theaetetus' first statement of his thesis (151e) rather suggests that he is equating knowing an object with perceiving that object, in view of the present infinitive αἰσθάνεσθαι. ('It seems to me that a person who knows something is perceiving the thing he knows.') This does tend to suggest that what Theaetetus has in mind is contemplating, or keeping steadily in view, *the object* one is knowing. However if this was the original idea, Socrates does not respect it, for he immediately goes on to speak of the same wind appearing hot to one man and cold to another, and it is clear that what is here in question is knowing or perceiving *that* the wind is hot (or cold). Presumably, then, Theaetetus' suggestion is to be understood as being—or at any rate as entailing—the suggestion that to know that *P* is the same as to perceive that *P*.

Yet we soon discover that it is not quite this. Of course from '*a* knows that *P*' it follows that *P*, and similarly from '*a* perceives (sees, hears) that *P*' it again follows that *P*. But on the face of it this does *not* follow from 'it appears to *a* that *P*', and yet it is this latter which Socrates in fact takes to be what Theaetetus intends. This becomes clear in 152b–c, where Socrates quite explicitly equates perception (αἴσϑησις) with mere appearance (φαντασία), remarking that they are 'the same in the case of that which is hot and everything of that sort'. Moreover from 157e and following it is plain that Theaetetus is supposed to be claiming that what we might naturally call *illusions* are in fact examples of knowledge, simply because they are appearings, though one could quite plausibly say that they should not properly be classed as *perceptions*. So Theaetetus' equation is in fact specified as an equation between '*a* knows that *P*' and 'it appears to *a* that *P*'.

This resolves one possible ambiguity with the word 'perceive'. We sometimes use this word in such a way that a man can correctly be said to perceive (see, hear) something *x* even though he does not recognize *x* as *x*, and even though *x* fails to register in his consciousness at all. (For example, I might say 'I suppose I must have seen it, for it was right in front of me and the light was perfectly good, though I was not *aware* of it at the time'.) But more normally '*a* perceives (sees, hears) *x*' is taken to imply that *a* recognizes what he perceives *as x*. (Thus in the same circumstances I might have said instead 'I know it was right in front of me, but I simply didn't see it'.) It is fairly clear that Plato is employing this latter sense of 'perceive' throughout most of the first part of the dialogue. This is a fair inference from the way in which he here switches from 'perceive' to 'appear', for it would be distinctly odd to say that *x* *appeared* to one, if in fact *x* failed to register in one's consciousness at all, and pretty odd if *x* was not in fact thought to be *x*, but something else. Thus, where a little further on Plato talks of a perception of white, it is surely implied that the percipient does *believe* that he is perceiving white, for otherwise it would seem extremely strange to identify this perception with knowledge of any sort.[1]

---

[1] But I shall argue that the final argument of the first part of the dialogue rejects this view, and claims that perception by itself yields *no* beliefs.

The relevant sense of 'perception', then, is one which entails a belief or judgement, at least in so far as I am not said to perceive a so-and-so unless I judge that it is a so-and-so and I am not said to perceive that *P* unless I believe that *P*. This much we can gather both from the examples given and from the way in which perception is equated with appearance. Unfortunately the equation with appearance, which resolves one ambiguity, at the same time introduces another ambiguity in the opposite direction; for it is quite legitimate to say 'it appears to me that *P*' even when this 'appearance' has nothing to do with perception in the literal sense, but only indicates belief (or at least, an inclination to believe). This wider use of 'appears' will figure later, in the refutation of Protagoras, but we do at least begin by restricting attention to what one might call genuinely perceptual appearances, as Socrates perhaps means to indicate when he says that appearance and perception are the same 'in the case of that which is hot, and everything of that sort' (152c1–2).

Theaetetus' first suggestion, then, is in effect interpreted as the suggestion that if *a* knows that *P* then *a* perceives, or at least seems to perceive, that *P*, and conversely. The implication in one direction (from knowledge to perception) is not immediately pursued, and the implication in the other direction (from perception to knowledge) is at once exchanged for something simpler. It is agreed that if *a* knows that *P* then it must be true that *P*, i.e. knowledge is of what is the case (τὸ ὄν) and is never false (ἀψευδές)—this is surely the simplest and easiest way to take 152c5–6—and so the claim that we finally settle down to consider is that what appears to a man (to be true) in perception in fact *is* true. This is justly represented as Protagoras' view,[2] and the general line on which it is to be supported is easily enough seen from the opening remarks about the wind. The wind, let us say, feels cold to you but not to me. So we might at first think that one of us must be wrong: the wind itself cannot actually be both cold and not cold. But Protagoras' reply (152b5–7) is that that is a mistaken way of looking at it: in itself the wind is neither cold nor not cold—it makes no sense to attribute either property to the wind in itself—and all we can say is that it is indeed cold *to you*, and not cold *to me*. There is no opportunity here for any kind of error in perception.

2. PROTAGORAS AND HERACLITUS (152d–153d)

Socrates at once goes on to couple this Protagorean thesis with the flux doctrine of Heraclitus.[3] He says somewhat playfully that this was a *secret* doctrine of Protagoras, no doubt because everyone knows that there is not a hint of it in Protagoras' own works. Further, it seems fairly clear that Plato is not putting this idea forward as a piece of sober history, any more than he puts it forward as a piece of sober history that Homer held this 'secret' doctrine of flux (152e). But he certainly writes as if we are to understand that the flux doctrine does somehow lie behind Protagoras' position, and that the flux doctrine is needed to provide a justification for that position. Yet the connection between the two is by no means straightforward.

Up to 152c Socrates has apparently been intent on developing the admission that the same wind *is* hot (to *a*) and *is* cold (to *b*). This is the point that, at first sight, he wishes to generalize at 152d when he first introduces the secret doctrine as claiming that 'nothing is *one* thing just by itself [e.g. hot?], and you can't correctly speak of anything either as some thing or as qualified in some way'. To begin with, then, what seems to be happening is that we are being offered new Protagorean grounds for the old Platonic view that any case of X will also turn out to be a case of non-X. The new ground is that a given thing may be both hot and cold, since it feels hot to one man and cold to another; and this is set alongside some examples that Plato has often used before, that a given thing may be both big and small, or both heavy and light (when compared with different things). Indeed a page or so later Plato takes up these old examples again, and discusses them in detail (154c–155c; I say more of this passage shortly). So, we are now offered cases of a thing which is both X and non-X, either because it seems X to one man but not to another, or because it is X compared to one thing but not to

---

[3] Heraclitus lived in Ephesus, and was considerably earlier than Protagoras. (He is said to have flourished *c*.500 BC.) A number of short and pithy fragments survive from his writing(s), but they are not very clearly or directly concerned with the doctrine of universal flux, though that is the doctrine that Plato standardly credits to him.

another, and it would not have been very surprising if Plato had gone on to add as a third example that a thing may be X at one *time* but not at another, for this indeed was how the flux doctrine appeared in the *Timaeus*. But what actually happens is not this at all. Our text introduces the idea of flux as if it were the *explanation* of the claim that nothing is either one thing or qualified in one way, saying 'The fact is that, as a result of movement, change, and mixture with one another, all the things which we say are—which is not the right way to speak of them—are coming to be; because nothing ever is, but things are always coming to be' (152d7–e1). This doctrine, then, summed up a few lines later as the doctrine that 'everything is the offspring of flux and change' (152e7), is presented as the heart of the 'secret doctrine', and it is apparently offered as the *explanation* of such facts as that a thing that is hot is also cold, a thing that is large is also small, and so on. But this is plainly nonsense. Things may flow as much as you like, but no amount of *change* will explain why the wind is *simultaneously* hot (to a) and cold (to b), or how the same thing can be *simultaneously* both big(ger than x) and small(er than y). Nor is there any satisfactory explanation of this point.

It may be tempting to say just that Plato has fallen into some kind of muddle here, and this suggestion might be reinforced by noting that his later discussion of the dice (154c–155b) contains a suspicious feature. The fact that 6 dice are both more (than 4) and less (than 12) is evidently a case of the *simultaneous* presence of (apparent) opposites. It does not in any way depend upon temporal change. But Plato presents it as if it did, because he speaks of the 6 dice being more *when we put 4 beside them*, and less *when we put 12 beside them*, and seems to imagine us doing first one and then the other. That is why he assimilates this alleged problem to the problem of how Socrates can be first larger and then smaller than Theaetetus without himself changing in size. To deal with this latter problem we must indeed qualify the general principle on becoming which he presents in 154c8–9, and offers premises for in 155a2–b2: while it is true that nothing can become larger *than it was* without undergoing increase, it is not true that nothing can become larger *than something else* without undergoing increase. Of course in either case the alleged problem disappears as soon as we specify what the comparisons are comparisons with, but the awkward point remains that the problem about the dice is *not* really a problem about becoming at all, though Plato has presented it as if it were.

It may possibly be relevant to this suggestion that Heraclitus himself seems to have held *both* the doctrines that every case of X is also simultaneously a case of non-X, *and* that everything is in a perpetual flux.[4] So perhaps Plato was led to associate the two doctrines because it appeared that Heraclitus had so associated them. Quite apart from this, we can certainly say that Plato's own earlier writings seem to suggest that he saw some connection between them. In the *Phaedo* (at 74–5) and *Republic* v (at 479–80) he argues for the existence of forms from the premiss that perceptible things *simultaneously* manifest opposite properties, but his usual characterization of the difference between the two is in terms of change: forms are unchanging and perceptible things are constantly changing (e.g. *Phaedo* 78d–e, *Republic* vi. 485b). Moreover the *Timaeus* recasts the argument, so that its premiss is that perceptible things change from one opposite property to another (51d–52a, above pp. 25–6), and Plato may not have been fully aware that this was a different basis for argument. But, if so, then all that we can say is that Plato was mistaken, for the two doctrines are actually quite distinct. Although both can plausibly be represented as claiming that 'nothing is ever *one* thing just by itself' (for any case of X is also a case of non-X), they have quite different considerations in view. Protagoras is claiming that everything is relative to someone (appears X to one man, but not to another), while Heraclitus—as we are currently understanding him—is claiming that everything is changing, and so is X at one time but not at another. It does not seem that Heraclitus' view could in any way support, explain, or justify Protagoras'. What, then, is Heraclitus doing in our dialogue at all?

Well, first let us notice that we may be misinterpreting the 'secret doctrine' which is supposed to link Protagoras with Heraclitus. Heraclitus is traditionally cited for the view that everything is (always) changing, but that is not quite the same as the claim that our 'secret doctrine' in fact advances. Rather, the 'secret doctrine' is represented at 152d–e as the doctrine that everything comes to be *as a result of* change—it is an 'offspring' of change—which would

---

[4] There is in fact ample documentation of the first, the so-called doctrine of the 'unity of opposites', in the fragments of Heraclitus that we possess (e.g. fragments 4, 9, 13, 37, 61), while for the second we are almost entirely dependent on the testimony of Plato and Aristotle.

not appear to be quite the same thing. We might hope to gain further illumination from the 'indications' (σημεῖα) that are at once offered as favouring this doctrine (153a–d), but that hope is disappointed, for these 'indications' are evidently playful.[5] But the 'secret doctrine' and its implications are restated several times in the fuller development of the theory that follows, and to understand what exactly the doctrine is we must follow through these more detailed expositions. However there is no denying that the more detailed expositions are actually thoroughly confusing. I therefore propose to digress at this point, and to speculate in a somewhat a priori fashion on the reasons which *might* lead one to say that the thesis of Protagoras in some way requires a doctrine of flux to support it. When we have considered some possible alternative views that Plato *might* be advancing, we can then return to consider the text in more detail, to see what view he actually *is* advancing.

3. A PRIORI CONSIDERATIONS

Let us begin by noting two different ways of taking what Protagoras has to say about the wind. Our object is to maintain the claim that every perceptual judgement is true, and one point that threatens this claim is that it appears to be possible for two people to disagree on a perceptual judgement, as when the wind feels hot to one and cold to the other. This is a case of *simultaneous* perceptual judgements, apparently about the same thing (namely the wind), which seem to be in conflict. In order to resolve the conflict we have two possible tactics, which at first sight seem equally effective. Each may be put by saying that the judgements are not really about the wind in itself, but about how the wind appears to the person making the judgement. However, this can be understood in two ways. On one way of taking it we construe it as admitting that there is some one object, the wind, which you and I are both judging about, but what each of us is judging about it is how that same wind is *related* to himself. So I am concerned with how the wind is related to me, and you are concerned with how it is related to you, and that is why our judgements are not really in conflict after all. Let us call this the solution by relativity: our judgements do concern the same object,

[5] In fact the 'indications' seem rather more relevant to the view that change is good than to the view that it is universal. (Cf. *Cratylus* 411c ff., 436e ff.)

but say quite compatible things about it, for the predicate of the judgement should in each case be regarded as relativized to the person making it. A different solution is to say that the judgements are not really about the same object: my judgement concerns the-wind-as-it-is-for-me, and *this* object genuinely is hot, but your judgement concerns the-wind-as-it-is-to-you, which genuinely is cold. On this approach, there simply is not such a thing as the wind *itself*. I have my private wind, the wind for me, which is what I am judging about, and you have your private wind, the wind for you, which is what you are judging about, and there is no common object, the wind, for us to disagree on. Let us call this the solution by private objects. Either of these kinds of solution is available, but—as we shall see shortly—it is a mistake to try to combine them both.

Now let us come to the question of how Protagoras' doctrine is related to Heraclitus' doctrine of flux. We begin once more from the observation that what we are trying to do is to maintain the claim that every perceptual judgement is true. One difficulty for this claim, as we said, is that it appears to be possible for two men to disagree with one another on a perceptual judgement, when each *simultaneously* makes a judgement, attributing incompatible predicates to the same subject (e.g. the wind). But it also seems possible that one man should disagree with *himself* at another time, as for instance when I at first judge that the wind is not cold, and then (on further exposure to it) I change my mind and decide that it is cold after all. Here again it looks as if we have two conflicting perceptual judgements about the same object, which threatens to upset the claim that all such judgements are true. And again we have the same two kinds of solution open to us. We may employ the approach of relativity to the different judgements which the same subject makes at different times, allowing that there is indeed a constant object, the wind, but maintaining that my two judgements about it do not conflict with one another, since one concerns how the wind appears to me at one time, and the other concerns how the wind appears to me at another time. It may very well be that this appearance has changed, not because there has been any change in the wind, but because there has been a change in me. (I have got colder.) Alternatively, we may adapt the private object approach, by further distinguishng temporal objects, namely the wind (for me) at one time and the wind (for me) at another time. These are different objects, and my first judgement is made about the one, while my second judgement is made about the other, so again the appearance of conflict is resolved.

Now if one sticks firmly to the approach in terms of relativity, there is no obvious temptation to be led from these considerations to anything resembling the doctrine of Heraclitean flux, as that appears in our dialogue. A given object (the wind) may present a different appearance to one man and to another, or at one time and at another, but there is no particular reason to say that it will *always* appear differently, to every observer and at every time. However I shall indicate in a moment that there are some problems with the simple approach in terms of relativity, and if we think instead in terms of private and temporal objects then it may seem quite natural to suppose that these objects have only a *momentary* existence. It is true that there is nothing in the argument sketched that actually requires this. There is no reason why we should not say that for so long as my private wind feels the same to me, it is still the same wind. All that the argument requires is that a wind, continuously perceived, cannot be *guaranteed* to remain the same wind with the same perceptual qualities, for any specifiable length of time. But the general outline of the picture rather encourages one to think that there will be some *uniform* answer to the question 'how long does one of these private and temporally limited objects endure?', and once that is granted then it is clear that the only possible answer is 'only for a moment'. That is, *some* of these private objects must be admitted to exist only for a very short time, so if they are all on a par with one another then we shall say that the same is true of them all.

Now this conclusion could certainly be put as the conclusion that the objects of perception are perpetually changing, in so far as one such object is always being succeeded by a different one. (But notice that 'different' here means '*numerically* different'; there is no reason to suppose that the successor will also be *qualitatively* different, unless, by a confusion, that is thought to follow from numerical difference.) This may reasonably be regarded as a *kind* of flux theory, and it does certainly seem to ensure that there can be no conflicts between perceptual judgements. For each such judgement concerns an object private to the perceiver, and one that lasts no longer than the judgement itself. Thus no one else is in a position to contradict it, and the perceiver himself cannot ever perceive the same object again, and so cannot ever have that ground for revising the judgement.

I add as a footnote that this flux theory just outlined does not strictly entail the Protagorean thesis that all judgements of perception are true. It ensures that no perceptual judgement can be contradicted by another *perceptual* judgement, but that obviously does not imply that it cannot be contradicted at all, or even that we can never have any grounds for revising our perceptual judgements. To establish the Protagorean thesis one would have to argue directly that it is impossible to make a mistake about what one is currently perceiving, and that certainly does not *follow* from the claim that no one else can perceive it, and nor can I ever perceive it again. So this flux theory does not entail the Protagorean thesis, and equally it is not entailed by it (as I pointed out when developing the theory). What it does is to remove *one* ground for objecting to the Protagorean thesis.

Now I began this discussion by saying that Plato *may* have conceived the relationship between the Protagorean doctrine and the Heraclitean doctrine in some such way as this. But I confess that there is no positive evidence to suppose that he did, and there is quite good evidence for supposing that he did not. A minor problem is this. The crucial point of the flux theory just outlined is that the objects of perception are *numerically* different, from one perceiver to another, and from one moment to another. So long as they are numerically different, it does not matter at all whether or not they are also qualitatively different, and of course the natural view will be that they often stay qualitatively the same for quite extended periods of time. But, as we shall see, Plato's own account of the theory seems to start from qualitative change, claiming (most implausibly) that *this* never ceases, and thence inferring (fallaciously) to a succession of numerically different objects of perception. But this also brings to light a more important problem, which is that Plato's own account *also* infers to a succession of numerically different observers. Not only the things perceived, but also the things that perceive them, are denied the status of enduring objects and construed as a succession of different and changing objects. But the flux theory I have just outlined provides no motivation for this step.

This problem is no doubt connected with another. The theory I have outlined could certainly be referred to as the doctrine that everything *is changing*, but that seems not to be how, in the end, our dialogue understands its own 'secret doctrine'. Instead this doctrine seems to be summed up as the doctrine that everything *is change*, which clearly has very different implications. It is some time before this version of the doctrine emerges. The flux doctrine is standardly represented in Plato's writings as the doctrine that everything is (always) changing (πάντα κινεῖται, or πάντα ῥεῖ, as at 183c2–3 of our dialogue), and its initial introduction in 152d7–e1 seems quite compatible with this: 'As a result of movement, change, and mixture with one another, all the things we say are—which is not the right way to speak of them—are coming to be; because nothing ever is, but things are always coming to be.' The point here seems simply to be an application of the doctrine of the *Timaeus*, that one should not use the present tense of the verb 'to be' of *things which change.*[6] But we get a notably different statement a little later at 156a5, which is not that everything is *undergoing* change but that everything *is* change: there is not anything else other than change, so in particular there are not any *things which change*, but only changes. Why might Plato have thought it relevant to propound such a startling doctrine about what there is? Consideration of this point leads to a rather different line of thought.

Let us take up again the approach to Protagoras' thesis in terms of relativity: all my perceptual judgements are true because they merely report how things appear to me at the time, which is a matter of how those things are *related* to me. Thus if I perceive a stone, and it looks white to me, then I will judge accordingly and no one will be in a position to contradict me, just because my judgement merely reports what relation the stone then bears to me. On this account, *all* that I can perceive, and all that I can know about through perception, is the way that that object is related to me, which is quite compatible with that same object's being quite differently related to you. Thus I perceive that it appears as white to me, that it appears over there to me, that it appears as a stone to me, and so on. You perhaps perceive that it appears brown to you, that it appears just here to you, and that it appears as a piece of bread to you. But now, what is this 'it' which appears in one way to me and in a very

---

[6] Cf. pp. 24–5 above.

Knowledge and Perception

different way to you? It would seem that we cannot tell—or anyway, that we cannot tell purely by perception.

The problem appears very clearly if we consider a situation in which, as we would *ordinarily* say, I was suffering from a hallucination, and there was not actually any genuine object that was appearing to me as a white stone. Nevertheless I was surely 'being appeared to', for certainly it appeared to me that there was a white stone. And if this 'appearance' has to be treated in the same relational way as all others then we must presumably say that there was some 'chunk of reality' which appeared to me as a white stone, though it appeared to others simply as empty space. But if one and the same 'chunk of reality' can appear to one man as a green field full of mushrooms, to another as a procession of pink rats, to another as an explosion of bright stars, and to another as nothing at all, then the question of what it is like in itself will seem utterly baffling. The point here is that the 'it' which appears to me in a case of hallucination surely does not have any independent existence of its own, though that is not something that I can tell simply by inspecting my own perception.

But the point can be made without bringing in the case of hallucinations, for even in the case of perfectly ordinary perceptions, where there is an 'it' that appears to me, our theory is that all that I can perceive is how it appears to me, and not what it is 'in itself'. But presumably it must *be* something 'in itself', if it can interact with me to produce the appearings. To put the point in another way, the theory is that I can tell by perception that it appears white to me, and that it appears as a stone to me, and so on. But I cannot tell by perception what this word 'it' refers to, or even whether the word manages to refer to anything at all. According to the theory that appearance is always a relation, there must always *be* something that this 'it' refers to, for a relation cannot hold but hold between no things; but according to the theory itself it cannot be perception that assures me of this. All that I can perceive is how the thing is related to me, and although it could not be thus related to me unless it existed, I cannot tell by perception that it does exist. For to say that it exists is *not* to say how it is related to me.

Moreover, the theory we are considering is symmetrical as between the objects perceived and the subjects that perceive them, so exactly the same considerations apply to both. According to this theory, what one can know about through perception is a relation, which in fact holds between oneself and some object. But *neither* term of this relation is itself known through perception. Just as I do not perceive the object 'in itself', but only how it is related to me, so equally I do not perceive myself, but only how I am related to it. Perhaps it is a fact that the object does exist, and perhaps it is also a fact that I exist, but neither of those facts can be known by perception, for neither of them are relations. Thus the theory requires the existence both of the object-in-itself and of the perceiver-in-himself, and if it is not to be an utterly mysterious theory it will allow that each has its own intrinsic nature, which explains why they relate together as they do. But it cannot allow that either the existence or the intrinsic nature of either of these participants in a perception can itself be known by perception.

Is this a genuine difficulty for the Protagorean thesis we are trying to support? Well, at first sight it looks as if one could continue to say that perceptual judgements do report relationships between objects and observers, and that they are all true, while admitting that the objects and observers are not perceived. Rather, they are known about in some other way (possibly as an essential part of a 'scientific' theory that yields the best explanation of why our perceptions are as they are[7]). Of course it will follow that knowledge and perception cannot be identified, for we are now admitting that some things, viz. the objects and observers, are known but not perceived. But, as I shall argue later (pp. 96–7), it seems probable that Plato's discussion is never concerned with this point. He is concerned always with the claim that whatever is perceived is known rather than with the converse claim that whatever is known is perceived. If that is right, then this objection to Protagoras—or rather to Theaetetus—is one that does not really affect the question that is actually at issue. But on further reflection we see that there is a genuine difficulty here. If perceptual judgements are judgements about items which are not perceived (but known in some other way) then in what sense are they to be regarded as the deliverances *of perception*? It appears that to get at the genuinely *perceptual* content of such a judgement, the reference to an object and to oneself will have to be removed, and this of course will mean that the whole form of the judgement must be recast. It cannot report a relationship between things which it does not refer to.

---

[7] This is roughly the line taken by Russell in his *Problems of Philosophy* (1912), at any rate with respect to objects, if not observers.

How, then, should we construe a judgement of perception? What is it about? Well, the obvious suggestion seems to be that it is simply about a perception. And what is a perception? It is presumably an *event*, or an *occurrence*, or a *happening* of some kind. One might not unreasonably say that it is a coming-to-be, or indeed a change. But it is important here not to be misled by the normal associations of the word 'change' into supposing that where there is a change that is because one or more independently existing objects are changing. On the contrary, the present suggestion is that a perception is a change which is not—or anyway is not perceived as being—a change *of* any objects. Is this, perhaps, the point of the radical Heraclitean thesis that only changes exist? In context, the point will be to maintain that only perceptions exist, and there are no people to perceive and no objects to be perceived. Or rather, we may allow that in a sense there are perceivers and perceived objects, but they do not exist independently of those changes that are perceptions. On the contrary, perceivers and perceived objects should be construed simply as collections of perceptions.

The version of this theory that is nowadays most familiar to us is that known as 'neutral monism'.[8] According to this, the only things that exist in their own right are the events that are perceivings (or better, appearings). These events can be described as it were from the viewpoint of the perceiver as (apparent) seeings, hearings, touchings, and so forth. Or they can equally be described as cases of being seen, being heard, and being touched. But it is the same events that are being described from either perspective. The theory is thus a monistic theory, in so far as it claims that there is only *one* kind of thing that has an independent existence, namely the events of perception. And it is a neutral theory, in so far as it claims that these events, taken in isolation, cannot be called either mental or physical. But the same events yield both physical objects and mental objects (i.e. minds) when they are collected together in different ways, for what we call a mind is in fact just the collection of all those perception-events that we would ordinarily call perceptions that that mind has, and what we call a physical object is just the collection of all those perception-events that we would ordinarily call perceptions of that physical object.

---

[8] It may reasonably be credited to Hume (in the *Treatise*), but for a more explicit version one looks rather to Russell. He looks favourably on this theory in his *Lectures on Logical Atomism*, and adopts it in his *Analysis of Mind*.

It would appear that if Plato is meaning to advance some such theory as this, then his own version of it is not such a neutral and monistic one. He constantly maintains a duality between what he calls a perceiving (αἴσθησις) and a perceived thing (αἰσθητόν), which he refers to as the 'twin offspring' of any perception. This may have seemed the more natural to him, because it is clear that he took a dualistic view of the physical nature of an act of perception. On the account that he gives both here and in the *Timaeus* (45b–46c, 67c–68d) something that we may call a ray of sight flows outwards from the observer, while a ray of colour flows outwards from the object seen, and perception occurs when the *two* rays, travelling in opposite directions, meet and coalesce in some way. Of course we are now trying to describe this occurrence in a way which does not presuppose the independent existence of objects and observers. Moreover, if indeed we are now trying to confine attention to what we are actually aware of in perception, then no speculation on the physical mechanisms involved should be allowed to form part of the account. But perhaps, if Plato's own theory of the physical mechanism was a dualistic one (unlike ours), that would make it natural for him to retain a dualistic element even when his concern is with the different question of what could be said to be known in perception: there is on the one side a seeing (corresponding to the visual-ray streaming in one direction) and on the other side a being seen (corresponding to the colour-ray streaming in the other direction), but each depends for its existence on the other, for neither takes place unless the rays intermingle in a suitable fashion.

On this account, the apparent dualism in the theory that Plato presents is really something of a mirage. For a seeing and a being seen are simply the same event, even if this event does consist in, or arise from, the intermingling of two distinct streams. But of course it may be that, like many generations of philosophers after him, Plato did think that one was aware of a distinction between perceiver and perceived object within the act of perception, and that this distinction must somehow be maintained even though we are now trying to make the existence of the perceiver and the perceived object depend on the existence of the perception, and not vice versa. In that case the perceived objects will presumably be something like what we now call sense-data, or what I earlier called 'private and momentary objects', which will exist only while they are perceived, and will have no properties that are independent of their being perceived. Then, just as these sense-data have only a momentary existence, one might expect that the things that perceive would equally have only a momentary existence, lasting no longer than the perception itself. This would lead *us* to talk of 'momentary selves', but on the theory that Plato develops it is the sense-organs—the eyes, the ears, the tongue—that do the perceiving, so his version might be expected to invoke momentary eyes, ears, and tongues. In each case, the idea would be that both the thing perceived and the thing that perceives depend for their existence on that very perception itself, so that a judgement of perception, which mentions these things, still does not have any content that goes beyond what is perceived in that perception. But the result will no longer be a 'neutral monism', since the act of perception is now analysed as an interaction between two objects, a momentary perceiver and a momentary thing perceived. Thus perceivers in the ordinary sense will on this version be collections of momentary perceivers, while objects in the ordinary sense will be collections of momentary things perceived.

However, it is worth noting three points about this theory. First, the momentary perceivers and perceived things may well be said to be constantly *changing*, in so far as each is perpetually giving way to the next, but it is not very natural to say that they are themselves *changes*. It would still appear to be the events of perception, and not the things that participate in those events (if any), that are most naturally called changes. Second, if we have begun by thinking in terms of private objects (sense-data) there is not much reason to be led into any view about the nature of the perceiver. For on this approach a judgement of perception will naturally be taken simply as a description of a sense-datum; there is no pressing reason to suppose that it need mention a perceiver at all. (It may, for example, be thought of as having the form of 'white here now'.) It is when we have begun by thinking in terms of relativity, so that a judgement of perception is at first taken as reporting a relation between perceiver and perceived object, that it will seem natural to treat the perceiver and the perceived object symmetrically when the initial theory is revised in order to accommodate the objection we have been considering. Finally, Plato's own theory is at first sight curiously asymmetrical. On the one side we have events of perceiving, such as a sight of whiteness, and on the other side we apparently have not an event of being perceived, i.e. an appearing to be white—or, according to Protagoras, a being white—but a thing perceived, namely white colour. So we seem to be offered a contrast between events on the one side and (momentary) things that appear in those events on the other. This would then lead to the view that perceivers are collections of events (changes) while things perceived are collections of the sense-data that are the immediate objects of perception—objects which are indeed short-lived, but still seem to be objects rather than events.

I would not wish to say that such an asymmetrical theory is any more obviously open to objection than are either of the two symmetrical theories just sketched. But the asymmetry is nevertheless curious, in view of the fact that Plato often professes to be treating the two sides of his duality in a symmetrical way. And I am therefore inclined to think that he does intend us to think of things perceived—i.e. colours, sounds, tastes—as the events that are more properly called the appearings of colour, or sound, or taste, even though this is not what his language at first suggests. For only in this way are they reasonably said to be changes, rather than things which change. But in that case his theory really is the theory of 'neutral monism', viewing everything whatever as either events of perception or collections of them, however much he appears to insist on a duality.

However, in this present section I am not yet trying to look at Plato's own account in any detail. Rather, I have aimed to set out, more or less a priori, some possible ways in which Plato *may* have viewed the relationship between the Protagorean thesis that all perceptual judgements are true and the Heraclitean doctrine of universal flux. According to the first suggestion, the main point is to remove the objection that I may come to revise a perceptual judgement in the light of further experience of the same object, and the objection is removed by the claim that one never does perceive the same object more than once. This is because the objects of perception are perpetually changing, but the *relevant* claim here is that the objects are very short-lived: it would be quite unnecessary to add—what is anyway utterly implausible—that no one of them is ever qualitatively similar to any other. According to the second suggestion, the main point is that the relativity of perception (or rather, of appearance), which our Protagoras begins by insisting upon, will not do by itself. It appears to lead to a position in which a perceptual judgement is taken to be a judgement about things which are not themselves perceived, which is surely very paradoxical. The remedy, then, will be to remove the observer-in-himself and the object-in-itself from the content of the judgement of perception. *One* way of doing this will be to claim that judgements of perception simply report on the character of perceptual events, and do not mention any objects that figure in those events. *One* way of securing this result will be by claiming that only perceptual events exist in their own right, and other things are to be regarded as merely collections of these. Events may not unreasonably be regarded as changes, so the claim can be put as the claim that only (perceptual) changes exist. If this is what the 'secret doctrine' amounts to, then again it is not strictly entailed by the Protagorean thesis that all judgements of perception are true, but it is *one* way of meeting some objections that the thesis naturally invites. (Equally, it does not entail the Protagorean thesis for the same reason as before: it gives us no direct reason to say that a judgement about a perception-event cannot be mistaken.)

But I now leave these a priori speculations in order to look more closely at how Plato himself develops the 'secret doctrine' and its implications. We have four main passages to consider, namely 153d–154b, 155e–157c, 157e–160a, and the final summary at 160a–e. As will emerge, the doctrine seems to differ from one passage to another, and all of them contain very puzzling features. I consider them in order.

4. FIRST STATEMENT: 153d–154b

To recapitulate briefly, Socrates has opened his discussion by developing the point that the wind is hot (to óne person) and is cold (to another), implying that we should not ask what it is in itself (152a–c). He then states the 'secret doctrine' as the doctrine that everything is the offspring of flux and change (152d–153d), apparently as explaining his opening point. In our next passage he appears to be trying to tell us how the one explains the other, changing to the example of seeing a white colour.

The white colour, he claims, cannot be located *in* the eye, and cannot be located outside it either (i.e. *in* the object seen, presumably), or assigned any place at all. This is a consequence of the secret doctrine, for—he says—to assign it any place would be to credit it with being at rest, whereas that doctrine requires it to be coming to be. This comes about, he goes on, because what we call a colour is something that arises from a collision between the eye and a suitable motion; it is not to be assigned to either party to the collision, but is something that comes into being between them.[9] For if the thing perceived were itself large or white or hot, it would not give rise to a different perception when meeting a different observer, unless it itself had changed; and the perceiver himself cannot be large or white or hot for the same reason.

Now at first glance the drift of this passage seems to be as follows. We begin by admitting the relativity of perception—or rather, since we are not distinguishing between perception and appearance, the relativity of appearance. The same thing, without change in itself, can look white to one person but not to another, and the same person can, without change in himself, be 'looked white to' by one object but not by another. So the whiteness is not in either, but something 'between' them. We then get an explanation of how this can be so, namely that it is a consequence of the fact that perception is or arises from a physical interaction, and at this point the interaction is apparently construed as an interaction between persisting objects, the observer—or rather, our theory says, the eye—on the one side and (presumably) the object seen, e.g. a white stone, on the other. At any rate, it is said of these objects that they can give rise to different perceptions when interacting with different partners *without changing themselves*, so they must be construed as things capable of persisting unchanged.

This may all appear perfectly straightforward, and indeed quite unobjectionable (except, of course, for the way in which being white and looking white are surreptitiously identified, as Protagoras' doctrine requires). But how exactly is the secret doctrine being invoked in this explanation? Is the point *just* that it takes *two* things to make a perception, the perception itself being something *between* them? That would certainly appear to be the point from the way our text continues, for it goes on without a break to introduce the alleged puzzle about the 6 dice, which are both more (than 4) and less (than 12). But the right thing to say about this puzzle seems precisely to be that it takes *two* things to make a case of being more or being less, and the being more or being less is itself something *between* them. That is, the point seems simply to be that we must

---

[9] In the fuller version of 156d–e the parties to the collision seem to be a motion from the eye—rather than the eye itself—and a motion from the object seen.

recognize relations for what they are, not confusing them with properties of the related items. So the moral will be that looking white (which we are identifying with being white) is a relation. That is: if a thing looks white, it must look white *to someone*, and hence if a thing is white, then equally it is white *to someone* (cf. 160b).

But notice that if we do take the text in this way then it does not really matter to the main point being urged that the relation of looking white to (being white to) is one that arises only when a certain complex physical interaction is going on between object and observer. For clearly there is no physical interaction that need take place between 6 dice and 4 dice if the former are to be more than the latter, and there is no physical interaction that need take place between Socrates and Theaetetus when Socrates becomes smaller than Theaetetus. The only point of any importance (on this interpretation of the theory) is that the so-called sensible qualities, such as whiteness, ought not to be regarded as qualities (properties) at all, but rather as relations. Admittedly it is not entirely inappropriate to mention the physical interactions at this stage, for the fact that perception is such a physical interaction between object and observer may help us to see why it ought to be construed in this relational fashion. But obviously relations do not *have* to be constituted by physical interactions. Should we, then, say that the 'secret doctrine' is primarily a doctrine about *relations*, and is not really about motions or changes at all?

This suggestion is evidently impossible. In fact the doctrine first figures in our passage as claiming that a white colour cannot be in any definite place, since that would imply that it was 'at rest', whereas the doctrine requires it to be something that is coming to be. (More literally, it must be something that is 'in coming-into-being', ἐν γενέσει, 153e2.) This could certainly be interpreted to mean that, according to the secret doctrine, a white colour must be an event, occurrence, or happening (rather than a state of the perceiver or a state of the object perceived). Or one might perhaps take it as claiming that a white colour does not last for any appreciable time, for that is something that our passage apparently goes on to assert. At 154a2–9 Theaetetus is first persuaded that he does not know whether the way a colour appears to him is the same as the way it appears to other animals, or indeed to other men, or even whether it always appears the same to himself. But instead of remaining in this sceptical position, that he does not know, he is further led to embrace the positive conclusion that, because he himself is changing from one moment to another, so also is the way that the colour is appearing to him. It is, one has to admit, an entirely unconvincing reason for what is, on a moment's reflection, an astounding claim. The suggestion that we cannot have qualitatively similar perceptions for any length of time is flatly contradicted by common sense, and surely not needed by the Protagorean thesis that all judgements of perception are true. But it does appear to be here endorsed. What is not so clear is whether it is presented as the main point of the secret doctrine, or whether it is an extra and further claim which that doctrine at least allows for, but does not entail.

What appears to be the case so far, then, is that Socrates has begun by stressing the relational nature of perception, has introduced the secret doctrine as if it promised an explanation of this, and in our present passage is trying to indicate how it explains this. But the indication is thoroughly confusing. The secret doctrine may perhaps be being understood as the doctrine that our perceptions are radically unstable—they change character from one moment to the next—but this is a most implausible doctrine in itself, and goes far beyond what is required to explain the point that we began with. Or alternatively it may be being understood as the doctrine that a perception is an event, but in that case the event in question is here conceived of as an interaction between two persistent items that are not themselves events. In either case, the doctrine would not appear to be very relevant to the puzzle of the 6 dice which immediately follows. When at 155d5–7 Socrates asks whether Theaetetus now 'understands why, according to the doctrines we're ascribing to Protagoras, those cases are the way they are', we are not surprised to find Theaetetus replying that he does not. Neither the specific claim that whiteness is an event, nor the more general doctrine that there are only events, nor again the doctrine that things never look the same from one moment to another, seem in any way to help us in understanding the alleged puzzle of the 6 dice. What is needed for this puzzle is just to recognize relations for what they are, and that indeed is relevant to the point Socrates has been making about whiteness, but it surely cannot be what the secret doctrine is claiming. So far, then, we are left very much in doubt both as to what exactly the secret doctrine is claiming and as to why it is supposed to be relevant to Protagoras' claim.

5. SECOND STATEMENT: 155e–157c

Theaetetus having said, reasonably enough, that he does not understand, Socrates now embarks on a fuller account of the secret doctrine. At the start we have a strong hint that the doctrine is primarily a doctrine about events or happenings: it would be rejected by those crude people who suppose that there are no such things as doings, comings-to-be, or anything invisible (πράξεις καὶ γενέσεις καὶ πᾶν τὸ ἀόρατον, 155e4–6).[10] Then the doctrine is emphatically stated as the doctrine that *only* changes exist (τὸ πᾶν κίνησις ἦν καὶ ἄλλο παρὰ τοῦτο οὐδέν). At once we are told that there are two kinds of change, one active and one passive, and that their interaction generates the 'twin offspring' of a perceiving and a perceived thing, which are inseparable from one another. Both the active and the passive changes are then characterized as 'slow', apparently on the ground that a slow change 'keeps its changing in the same place, and in relation to the things which approach it, and that's how it generates' (156c9–d1). By contrast the offspring are 'quick', apparently because 'they move, and their changing naturally consists in motion' (156d2–3).[11] This is then illustrated with the example of an eye approaching something such as a white stick or stone, and thus generating a seeing of white and a whiteness, which 'move between them', filling the eye with seeing and the stone with whiteness.

The usual interpretation of this passage[12] identifies the eye and the stone with the active and passive 'slow changes' that are introduced at the beginning. (It appears from 159d that it is the stone which acts and the eye that is acted on.) This is mainly on the ground that the 'fast changes' are at first said to be generated by the slow changes, and later said to be generated by the eye and the stone. But in that case we evidently cannot take at face value the statement that the slow changes 'keep their changing in the same place'. Of course eyes and stones can move from one place to another, and if not we could not talk of them approaching one

---

[10] For the need to recognize that doings (actions) do exist, cf. *Cratylus* 386e ff. (It is not clear to me why Plato should regard them as invisible.)

[11] Perhaps better 'the nature of their change is to be in motion' (ἐν φορᾷ αὐτῶν ἡ κίνησις πέφυκεν).

[12] e.g. Cornford (1935, p. 49), Nakhnikian (1955, p. 136), Runciman (1962, p. 19), Gulley (1962, p. 78), Crombie (1963, p. 18), McDowell (1973, p. 137).

another. To deal with this difficulty it is usually suggested that Plato's point is not to deny that the slow changes can move from one place to another, but merely to say that it is not the *nature* of such a change to be a movement. It is then tempting to import the distinction between two kinds of change that is drawn later at 181c–d, and to infer that the 'slow changes' are alterations rather than movements. (But they *might* be movements which need not involve a change of place, such as rotations.) However it is really very odd to suggest that an eye or a stone *is* an alteration, and it seems somewhat weird to say that it *is* a change of any kind. We would certainly expect some elucidation, and indeed we do have more to come on this topic shortly.

But there is also a rival interpretation,[13] which is that the 'slow changes' are not the same as eyes and stones, but are genuine changes which occur *within* eyes and stones. The idea would be that the 'fast changes', which are conceived as travelling between the eye and the stone, must be generated by other changes occurring within them, and cannot simply occur spontaneously. On this view the slow changes need not last for very long; they do not have to continue uninterrupted all through the lifetime of the eye or stone, but merely for as long as the two are engaged in their transaction. And perhaps they are called 'slow', not to indicate any longevity on their part, but simply to distinguish them from their 'offspring', which are clearly described as travelling rapidly between the two partners. If we may bring in the physical account of perception given in the *Timaeus* (45b–46c, 67c–68d) these offspring are apparently conceived as streams of very tiny particles, each of which is moving very fast indeed.

But this brings us to another question: are we supposed to understand the account of perception given in this passage as in any way a *physical* theory? Admittedly, a seeing and a whiteness are certainly described as *travelling*, from the eye and from the stone respectively, in opposite directions. But perhaps, as McDowell puts the suggestion, 'we ought to understand the talk about the motion of the offspring, and its direction, as a metaphorical way of emphasizing the "directions" of the relations expressed in the sentences: "The eye sees an appearance of whiteness presented by the stone" and "The stone presents an appearance of whiteness to the seeing eye"' (1973, p. 139). McDowell himself goes on to reject

[13] Sayre (1983), pp. 212–13.

this suggestion, on the ground that when the theory is recalled and criticized at 181b–183b, the criticism begins by distinguishing movement from alteration, and must apparently be taking this distinction quite literally. It is then applied by saying that the original theory satisfied the demand that everything should be moving, but leads to problems when we insist that everything must be altering as well. It would seem to follow, then, that in our passage the talk of movement should be taken literally, as is certainly the most natural way of taking it. Crombie has suggested that there is a difficulty for this in the fact that our passage says that when seeing travels from the eye that eye becomes full of seeing, and so sees; similarly when whiteness travels from the stone the stone becomes 'filled all round' with whiteness, and so becomes white. How, he asks, can a thing become full of what is travelling *away* from it (1963, p. 21)? But the most that this suggests is that we should interpret 'becomes full of' metaphorically: to say that the eye becomes full of seeing, or the stone full of whiteness, will only be to say in a rhetorical way that the eye sees and the stone is white. But we can take *this* as a metaphor without having to extend the same treatment to all the talk of movement.[14]

First indications are, then, that the theory means to be taken seriously when it describes a seeing and a whiteness as movements, taking place in opposite directions. But it would be rash to draw too much on the clearly physical theory of the *Timaeus* to interpret our theory. For one thing, the *Timaeus* never suggests that a white stone is giving off that stream of particles which our theory calls a whiteness *only* when it is being perceived, but our theory very clearly does make this claim. For another, I doubt whether our theory would endorse the view that these movements are streams *of particles*. A particle would naturally be construed as something that *undergoes* change (e.g. change of position), but not something that *is* a change. Yet our theory wishes to claim that everything *is* a change, so here it is claiming that there are movements without wishing to say that there are things which move. The theory is, in fact, completely reticent about all the physical mechanisms involved, *except* for this one fact that it does talk in terms of

---

[14] Crombie does not himself suppose that the difficulty he mentions is decisive, and he acknowledges the force of the objection I have quoted from McDowell. (McDowell offers a literal interpretation of the eye being full of seeing and the stone 'filled all round' with whiteness, 1973, p. 140.)

movements and their directions. Should this perhaps lead us to reconsider our first verdict?

Leaving these problems unresolved for the present, let us press ahead to consider the remainder of this second exposition of the secret doctrine. Summing up the account so far, Socrates recalls that what we are maintaining is that 'nothing is hard, hot, or anything, just by itself . . . but that in their intercourse with one another things come to be all things and qualified in all ways, as a result of their change' (156e7–157a3). The phrase 'all things and qualified in all ways' (πάντα καὶ παντοῖα) reminds us of the opening statement of what was to be maintained, namely that 'you can't correctly speak of anything either as some thing or as qualified in some way' (οὐδ' ἄν τι . . . οὐδ' ὁποιονοῦν τι, 152d3–4). So far, it is clear that we have been concentrating on the question whether a thing can be said to be qualified in some way, e.g. to be hot or white, but now Socrates seems to turn his attention to the other question, whether a thing can be said to be some thing, e.g. a stone or an eye.

First he says roundly that one cannot arrive at a firm conception of the active or the passive thing, taken singly, as being *anything* (εἶναί τι).[15] In support of this he then points out that you cannot say in any absolute way that such a thing is a thing which acts, or a thing which is acted on, both because the things in question are not things which act and are acted on until they come together with one another, and because the active partner in one transaction may be the passive partner in another (that is, presumably, an eye may both see and be seen). Unfortunately the support he offers is far too weak: we may admit for the sake of argument that it is wrong to say, without qualification, that an eye is a passive thing and a stone an active thing, but it by no means follows that it is wrong to say that the one *is* an eye, and the other *is* a stone. But although the support is far too weak, there is little doubt as to what is being claimed, namely that nothing—not even an eye or a stone—'*is* one thing, just by itself, but is always coming to be for someone' (157a8–b1).

This means at least that you cannot say of anything, without qualification, that it is a stone (full stop). The best you can say is that it is a stone *for me*, though perhaps it is something else for others.

---

[15] 'To be something' is also standard Greek for 'to exist'. Is there also a suggestion here that the active and the passive thing do not *exist*, when taken singly? (Cf. Section 7, below.)

But further, you ought really to say that it *becomes* a stone (for me), because you ought not to imply that it permanently remains a stone, even for me. But this, it seems natural to say, automatically poses the problem: what is this *it* which occasionally becomes a stone to me, and becomes perhaps a piece of bread to you, and a pink rat to others? The *Timaeus* might perhaps answer that it is a piece of space, but our dialogue clearly adopts a more radical answer: there is no permanent 'it' to be referred to at all, so the word 'it' should simply be banished altogether. As a matter of fact Socrates speaks not of the word 'it' but of the words 'something', 'someone's', 'my', 'this', and 'that', which he says should all be banished as words that bring things to a standstill. (Presumably the words 'someone's' or 'my' imply the existence of a someone, or of me, as the other words equally are thought of as implying the existence of some more or less permanent object.) What conclusion should we draw?

Well, it is certainly natural to conclude in this way: it was a mistake to say, as we said initially, that the stone appears white to me (or my eye), as if the stone and I (or my eye) were more or less permanent existents, happening to be related to each other in this way for a brief moment in our otherwise independent lives. Rather, we should content ourselves with saying 'there is—i.e. comes to be, occurs—a white appearance'. We can add if we wish that it is of a stony kind, and we would no doubt wish to add—if we could think of a permitted way of doing it—that it is of a 'to-me' kind. We shall no longer talk of *what* appears, or of *what* it appears to, but simply of the appearing itself. How, then, are we to understand the usual talk of people and of stones? As Socrates explains: 'We ought to speak that way [i.e. without bringing things to a standstill] both in individual cases (κατὰ μέρος) and about many things collected together (περὶ πολλῶν ἀθροισθέντων), to which collections people apply the name of man, stone, or any animal or kind of thing' (157b8–c2). Presuming that this remark is an answer to the question just raised,[16] Socrates is here telling us that what we ordinarily regard as a single stone should in fact be viewed rather as a collection of more evanescent items, and not as one single and enduring thing at all. And if we think of a stone or a person in that

---

[16] The Greek *could* mean that we apply the word 'stone' not only to individual stones but also to collections of many stones. But that would hardly be a relevant point to make in the present context.

way then we can continue to talk of them but without 'bringing things to a standstill'.

Unfortunately Socrates does not tell us what stones and so on are collections *of*, but if we stick to the usual interpretation of the first part of our passage the only possible answer is that they are collections of the 'fast changes' previously mentioned. So the doctrine is that we should describe those 'fast changes' without mentioning any more or less stable objects that participate in them, and the apparently stable objects, which have earlier been called 'slow changes', should in fact be regarded as collections of 'fast changes'. The collection is itself said to be a change, on the ground that it is made up of a series of 'fast changes', succeeding one another with some rapidity; and it is 'slow' perhaps in the sense that the collection as a whole endures for some length of time, though its individual members do not. One would imagine that a perceiver is to be regarded as a collection of those fast changes that are perceivings, e.g. seeings of whiteness, while perceived objects such as stones are collections of those fast changes that are called things perceived, such as a whiteness (though if these are really to be changes they should be appearings of whiteness rather than whitenesses). But the text does not say this, and the point that perceivers can themselves be perceived rather destroys the suggested symmetry.

On this interpretation, the passage certainly ends by claiming that the language with which it itself began was inappropriate. This is not just because it certainly began by speaking of a perception as a transaction between such things as eyes and stones, apparently regarded as more or less stable entities, but more seriously because these entities were said to *generate* the fast changes. To begin with, then, the fast changes owe their existence to the slow changes, which produce them in pairs, whereas at the end the slow changes owe their existence to the fast changes, for they are nothing but collections of fast changes. A mere collection cannot reasonably be said to cause, produce, or generate the items of which it is composed. (This could only be taken as a way of saying that some members of the collection generated other members of it, i.e. that some fast changes generated others. But the text never suggests anything of this kind, and it would not be a very plausible suggestion either: one seeing does not bring about another.) On this interpretation, then, the causal talk of production and generation has now turned out to be misplaced, and one might therefore suppose that Plato would abandon it henceforth. But, as we shall see, he does not.

This problem is avoided by the rival interpretation which does not identify the slow changes with the eyes and stones, but takes them to be genuine changes, occurring within eyes and stones. On this interpretation we can say that the ultimate existents are these so-called 'slow' changes, which are no doubt very short-lived and called 'slow' only because they are not changes of position and involve no travelling from one place to another. Thus we can continue to say that the slow changes generate the fast changes, and we can now add without incoherence that such things as eyes and stones are really collections *of slow changes*. It will then be perfectly comprehensible to continue to speak of eyes and stones as generating perceptions, since this will simply be a short way of saying that the slow changes which make them up are changes which generate perceptions. In this way the previous incoherence may be avoided, but nevertheless the interpretation is open to serious objection, on two counts.

The first is simply that we are told so very little of the nature of these supposed slow changes. This is not particularly surprising if the slow changes are just eyes and stones, for after all they are familiar enough, and we are told more about them (namely that they are collections). But if the slow changes are in the end going to be taken to be the only things that exist in their own right, distinguished from eyes and stones which do not exist in their own right, and distinguished also from those 'movements' which are seeings, hearings, tastings, and so on, then we should surely expect to be given more detail on what exactly they are. But we are given no detail, and in fact we hear nothing more about them at all. They are not mentioned again, either in the next statement of the theory or in the final summing up. Worse, it is never even said that the collections we are talking of are indeed collections *of slow changes*. But, if Plato's doctrine is indeed as this interpretation maintains, he could hardly have failed to notice that this is a point that needs saying.

The second objection is one that applies to all interpretations so far mentioned, but with particular force to this last, for on this interpretation the 'slow changes' are completely unknown to us. They are events which *cause* perceptions, but they are not perceptions themselves and they evidently are not known to us by being perceived. Though perhaps there are changes in my eyes, ears, and tongue which *generate* the seeings, hearings, and tastings I am aware of, I certainly do not know of them by perceiving them. The same applies to those changes in the stone that enable me to see it, and those changes in the wine (if any?) that enable me to taste it. But what could be the point of introducing a whole host of quite unknown changes? Certainly, it may enable us to maintain without incoherence the purely ontological doctrine that the only things that exist ultimately and in their own right are changes, and the 'secret doctrine' Plato is trying to expound is *stated* as if it were a purely ontological doctrine. But it is *also* intimated to be what lies behind the Protagorean thesis that every judgement of perception is true, and that no such judgement can be mistaken. In order to be relevant to this thesis it must at the same time be a doctrine about what is known in perception, and so an epistemological doctrine as well as an ontological one. But the introduction of *unknown* 'slow changes' does not clarify the epistemological situation at all.

In order to support the Protagorean thesis one can see how it might at first appear to be a good idea to stress the relational nature of perception, as certainly happens at 152a–c, and again at 153d–154b (though with some extra ingredients). But one can also see how this might well seem to lead to a problem about the perceiver and the perceived object 'in themselves', for if all that can be known about in perception is the relationship between these two, then apparently they themselves cannot be known about in perception. It therefore seems puzzling that a judgement which is supposed to be a judgement of perception could even mention such things. There is thus a perfectly good motive for attempting to reconstrue the situation, and to remove the apparent reference to the perceiver and the perceived object from the content of a judgement of perception. And to achieve this it may well seem to be a good idea to say that perceivers and perceived objects are, in the end, just collections of perceptions, so that it is now the perceptions themselves that come first, and the perceivers and perceived objects are 'constructed' from these. They are things which, at first glance, we *seem* to know about through perception, and this appearance can be maintained if we say that they are really collections of perceptions. But how would it help to say that they are collections, not of perceptions, but of some obscure 'slow changes' which are supposed to *cause* perceptions? The answer must be that it would not help at all. It will not explain how we seem to know of such things as stones through perception to say that stones are really collections of 'slow changes', if it has to be added—for the same reason as before—that these 'slow changes' are again things that we do not know of through perception. On the present interpretation, then, the introduction of 'slow changes' cannot in any way assist the defence of the Protagorean thesis that we began with, and must be regarded as irrelevant to the main concerns of the dialogue.

If, as the usual interpretation has it, we construe the 'slow changes' as identical with the collections of fast changes that are perceivers and perceived objects, then at least this aspect of the objection is avoided. It is indeed relevant to the Protagorean thesis we began with to claim that perceivers and perceived objects are themselves nothing but collections of perceptions. But it is still *not* relevant to claim that perceptions themselves are 'movements' in any literal sense, i.e. movements from one place to another, for it is clear that we are not aware of them as such. It may be relevant to say that perceptions are, in a general sense, changes—that is, they are events, occurrences, or happenings—and that such changes can be construed as existing in their own right. Hence other things can in turn be construed as constructed from them. But if our problem is to get clear about what can be known in perception, then we should not allow ourselves to be distracted by speculations on the hidden physical nature of these events, any more than we should allow ourselves to postulate further hidden events as their causes. All such physical speculation is irrelevant to the support of the Protagorean thesis, and indeed tends to undermine it, since it so strongly suggests that there is more to reality than what we can perceive of it. So unless we can say that even the talk of movement and travelling should be understood in a metaphorical way in this passage, it must anyway be admitted that Plato is not confining his attention to what is strictly needed for the defence of Protagoras. But clearly it is better to posit less irrelevance rather than more, and for that reason we should, I think, prefer the usual interpretation, according to which an object such as a stone is itself a 'slow change', in so far as it is identified with an ever-changing series of 'fast changes'. However, in my judgement it would be taking charity too far to say, for the same reason, that Plato did not intend his talk of travelling in opposite directions to have any literal significance.

6. THIRD STATEMENT: 157e–160a

In the third section of his exposition of the secret doctrine, Socrates turns to the apparent objections to the Protagorean thesis that arise from dreams and illusions, for we ordinarily suppose that in such situations the way things appear is not the same as the way they are (157e–158b). He begins with a point on dreams, introducing the well-known riddle of how one can tell whether one is awake or dreaming, and easily leading Theaetetus to agree that one cannot (158b–e). This point seems to be put forward merely as a preliminary point. Socrates observes that it shows that at least we will be able to get a dispute going (158c8), but he apparently does not intend to rely on it. In this, of course, he is quite right. Even if it is conceded that we cannot tell *which* judgements are true, those we make when dreaming or those we make when awake—because we cannot tell whether we are dreaming or awake—still it does not follow that they are all true. Indeed, if we allow that they are in conflict with one another, it will follow that some of them are not true, even if we cannot tell which. We do need, then, to be told something more about dreams, and this Socrates apparently promises to do at 158e5–6. But unfortunately he does not seem to fulfil his promise.

This happens because he has coupled dreams with diseases, and his subsequent discussion focuses on the latter. He is concerned to explain how the same wine may taste sweet to Socrates when he is well and bitter to him when he is ill. But this case seems relevantly different from the case of dreams (or hallucinations) because we do not ordinarily suppose that when I dream that I am tasting wine then there *is* any wine, or anything else, that is interacting with me to give rise to this 'perception'. It is, then, a case of appearance (φαντασία) that apparently cannot be construed in the relational way that we began with, as when the wind appears hot to you and cold to me. But the case that he does choose to discuss, of the wine tasting now sweet and now bitter, certainly could have been handled simply by stressing the relativity of perception, and does not at first glance seem to introduce anything new. For all that, Socrates does have some new things to say about it. Apparently he is now trying to argue that what we ordinarily think of as one single persistent perceiver, a person, must be viewed as a series or collection of more short-lived things. This view was stated at the end of the previous passage, but very briefly and without any elaboration, and now it is to be argued for. Unfortunately, the argument that we are offered (158e–160a) is very unconvincing.

Socrates begins by getting Theaetetus to agree to the somewhat ambiguous thesis that things that are 'entirely different' are unlike, and indeed unlike in every way (158e6–159a5). On the strength of this admission he then infers that if one thing becomes like another it becomes the same as it, and if one thing becomes unlike another it becomes different from it (159a6–9). What seems to have happened here is that he has taken the opening admission as conceding that there is no distinction to be drawn between being different and being unlike, and gone on to infer that there is equally no distinction to be drawn between their 'opposites', being the same and being like. Now no doubt it would be possible to understand these claims quite innocuously, e.g. if by 'different' we mean 'different in some respect' and if by 'unlike' we mean 'unlike in some respect' (and similarly for being the same and being like). But this is not how Socrates does understand them, for in fact he takes difference and sameness to be *numerical* difference and sameness—i.e. to be a matter of whether *x* is or is not the same *object* as *y* is—whereas he takes likeness and unlikeness to be *qualitative* similarity or dissimilarity. And the two contentious claims that he actually uses are[17]

(i) If *x* and *y* are different objects, then they are dissimilar (in any respect you care to mention).

(ii) If *x* and *y* are the same object, then they are similar (in any respect you care to mention).

The first claim is unambiguously used at 160a1–3 where he argues that a thing such as the wine, when it comes together with another perceiver, will not generate the same thing, [and so will not generate a similar thing,] and so will not become similar (ταὐτὸν . . . τοιοῦτον). This is because from another perceiver it will generate another thing, [and hence an unlike thing,] and will therefore become unlike (ἄλλο . . . ἀλλοῖον). That is, two tastings of wine, just because they are two, will never have quite the same taste.[18] The second claim is used to make what seems to be the main point of this

---

[17] In symbols
(i) $x \neq y \vdash (Fx \longleftrightarrow Fy)$
(ii) $x = y \vdash (Fx \longleftrightarrow Fy)$
[18] This astonishing claim has been made before, at 154a1–4, on the (equally inadequate) ground that no one could know whether the taste was the same.

section, that Socrates when ill is not the same thing as Socrates when well. They are not the same thing simply because they are dissimilar, in that one is ill and the other is well. So what we call Socrates must actually be a series or collection of more short-lived items, indicated here by 'Socrates when ill' and 'Socrates when well'.

Now claim (i) could be put as the claim that all different things are dissimilar, and it is obviously a totally implausible claim. It also does not seem to be needed for the defence of the Protagorean thesis: all that that thesis requires is that different perceptions *may* be dissimilar, not that they *must* be. (Indeed, if we assume that they *must* be, then we reintroduce the possibility of perceptual error, for I may judge them to be exactly similar, and by hypothesis that judgement would then have to be mistaken.) It is difficult, then, to see why Plato has introduced it, unless perhaps he has failed to distinguish it from claim (ii), which could be put as the claim that all dissimilar things are different. It is claim (ii) that we need in order to argue that what we ordinarily think of as one and the same person, Socrates, is not really some one persisting thing but a collection of more short-lived items. And what about claim (ii)? Should we or should we not accept it?

Well, first it must be observed that it is a way of stating the principle that is now often called 'Leibniz's Law', viz. that if *x* and *y* are the same thing then whatever is true of *x* must also be true of *y*. This is generally held to be a correct principle about identity. On the other hand it may well seem to be a consequence of this principle that nothing can persist as the same thing through change. For when Socrates is ill it is true of him that he is ill, and when he is well it is not true of him that he is ill, so apparently there is a respect (namely, illness) in which Socrates-when-ill and Socrates-when-well differ. Indeed if we allow ourselves to say, as Theaetetus does say at 159b6–7, that we are talking of Socrates-when-ill and Socrates-when-well taken as *wholes*, then can we not quite fairly infer that the two are indeed different wholes? By the same argument, of course, Socrates asleep is not the same person as Socrates awake, Socrates outdoors is not the same person as Socrates indoors, Socrates standing up is not the same person as Socrates sitting down, and so on. More generally, Socrates at any moment is not the same thing as Socrates at any other moment, and nothing at all persists as the same thing through any length of time whatever.

Nowadays most people would say that although Leibniz's Law is a correct principle about identity, this argument misapplies it. When we are considering predicates which are true of an object at different times, then we must write into the predicate the time at which it is supposed to apply before we are entitled to invoke Leibniz's Law. Thus suppose Socrates was ill in February 399 BC but well again by March. Then the predicate 'ill in February 399 BC' is true of Socrates (full stop). It is true of him in February, but also true of him at all other times too. So also is the predicate 'well in March 399 BC'. The same thing, Socrates, has both these predicates, and now that we have built the date into the predicates in question there is no longer any reason to say that it cannot be one and the same person who satisfies both of them. That, roughly speaking, would be the modern response to this argument.

No doubt Plato would not himself have responded in quite the same way, but it seems to me unlikely that he would have found the argument any more convincing than we do. At any rate, in previous writings he has shown no discomfort at the thought that one and the same thing may have apparently opposite properties at different times,[19] and later in our dialogue he will apparently restore the natural view that it is one and the same subject that perceives now one thing and now another (p. 112 below). So I think it is a reasonable conjecture that Plato himself was quite well aware that the present argument was unsatisfactory. That is why he presents it by deliberately playing on such expressions as 'being entirely different', which runs together the ideas of having different qualities and being a different thing; and that is why he talks as if the phrase 'Socrates when ill', taken as a *whole*, names something other than the plain 'Socrates'—some larger whole which includes not only Socrates but also his attributes at the time. There is, I think, some deliberate sophistry in this argument, and perhaps the failure to distinguish claim (i) from claim (ii) is also deliberate (p. 106–9 below). But the argument may well have seemed to him plausible enough for the purpose of helping the 'secret doctrine' on its way, and reinforcing the idea that what we ordinarily think of as persisting things are really collections of more evanescent entities.

Unfortunately, it is still not made clear just what it is that

---

[19] A very clear example is *Phaedo* 102e3–5: Socrates may come to 'admit smallness' without ceasing to be Socrates. Cf. also *Symposium* 207d–e.

persisting things are taken to be collections *of*. The argument itself seems to indicate that Socrates is to be viewed as a collection of what we might call short-lived 'stages' of Socrates, such as Socrates-when-ill, Socrates-when-asleep, and so on. But we could equally take it that each of these 'stages' was in turn to be viewed as a collection, either of the perceptions that Socrates was having at the time, or possibly of the 'slow changes' within him that caused those perceptions. In either case, these collections could reasonably be regarded as 'different things', since they would consist of different members. As I have said, the obvious idea is that Socrates is a collection of the perceptions which (as we say) he has, and that the wine is a collection of those perceptions which (as we say) are perceptions of it. But the same difficulty as before still remains: throughout this passage Plato continues to speak of Socrates and the wine as coming together with one another and so *generating* perceptions, but a collection cannot properly be said to generate its own members.

For this reason one certainly wishes that Plato had returned to pay more explicit attention to the case of dreams (or hallucinations), where this talk of two things combining to generate an appearing seems out of place. When I dream that I am tasting a sweet wine, or seeing a white stone, there appears to be no 'collection' that is interacting with me to produce this appearance. And if perhaps there is a sensible quality—a sweet taste or a white colour—that could be said to be 'interacting' with me to produce the dream, still neither of these could reasonably be regarded as *travelling* in any literal way towards me from something outside me. A deeper consideration of dreams and hallucinations would surely have clarified the theory that Plato is trying to present in important ways, and would perhaps have led him to see that it was a mistake on his part to retain the ideas of generation and of travelling from what he took to be the correct *physical* account of an ordinary perception. The correct account, from Protagoras' point of view, must surely be to take the perceptions themselves as basic, and to desist from all common-sense physics. For if it is going to be impossible to be mistaken in one's judgements of perception, then the contents of such judgements cannot be allowed to go beyond what genuinely is open to perception.

The result, then, is that in this third section of the exposition we get an argument which seems mainly designed to show that apparently persisting things must really be collections of more short-lived items, but it is still not made clear what exactly these short-lived items are. The argument is introduced as depending upon the evidently false premiss that there is no distinction to be drawn between being a different thing and being dissimilar, and this premiss can in fact be split into two parts, claim (i) and claim (ii), but it is not clear whether Plato was aware of this. The more plausible claim (ii) is what is actually needed to reinforce the collection doctrine, but Plato does also invoke the very implausible claim (i), which is actually not needed for the defence of Protagoras, and seems indeed to conflict with it.

Let us now move to the final summing up.

7. FINAL STATEMENT: 160a–e

The summing up begins by recapitulating in general terms the points that have just been made about Socrates and the wine. Whenever Socrates comes to be perceiving, he comes to be perceiving something, and similarly whenever the wine comes to be sweet or bitter or anything else, it comes to be so to someone (160a8–b4). We then get a series of four statements whose interpretation is not altogether clear:

   (i) Then what we're left with, I think, is that it's for each other that we are, if we are, or come to be, if we come to be, since necessity ties our being together (160b5–7).

 (ii) Since what acts on me is for me and not someone else, it's also the case that I, and not someone else, perceive it (160c4–5).

(iii) So my perception is true for me, because it's always of the being that's mine (160c7–8).

(iv) And, as Protagoras said, it's for me to decide, of the things that are for me, that they are, and of the things that are not, that they are not (160c8–9).

The question is whether the various occurrences of the verb 'to be' in these statements should be regarded as complete in themselves, so that the verb means 'to exist' (or something similar), or whether we should always supply a complement such as 'to be bitter', 'to be perceptive of bitterness', and so on. (McDowell argues that a complement should be supplied throughout.)

The first passage, if it stood alone, would I think most naturally be taken as containing complete uses of the verbs 'to be' and 'to come to be'. The meaning is then that I and the wine *exist* (or come to *exist*) only for one another; necessity ties together our *existence*.[20] This would, after all, be a fair conclusion from the collection doctrine, for whatever exactly I and the wine are supposed to be collections of, these momentary items only *exist* in perceptual situations, as when I am seeing or tasting the wine. On the other hand, we could certainly suppose that complements are to be supplied, and the meaning is that I and the wine are respectively perceptive of bitterness and bitter only for one another; necessity ties together our being, respectively, perceptive and perceived. The main reason for wishing to take the passage in this latter way is that it then is a perfectly fair conclusion from what has gone before, as it professes to be. But equally it would not be too surprising if in fact it is introducing a new point, which is not strictly a consequence of what has just been said, but an elaboration of it.

The second passage could again be taken either way, but here it is perhaps more natural to introduce a complement. The phrase 'what acts on me is for me alone' is apparently thought of as correlative with 'I alone perceive it', and this quite plausibly suggests that it, i.e. the wine, is *bitter* only for me, while I alone perceive it *as bitter*. On the other hand it is worth noting that the phrase translated 'what acts on me' (τὸ ἐμὲ ποιοῦν) is more literally 'what *makes* me'. If we take it that this literal meaning is what is intended here,[21] then again this introduces the thought that my existence depends upon it, and naturally suggests as a correlative that its existence depends upon me. But it is not obvious that it is the literal meaning of this phrase that is intended.

However, when we come to the third passage it seems to me very difficult to avoid the suggestion that 'being' is 'existence'. We are told that my perception is true for me 'because it is always of my being'[22] (τῆς γὰρ ἐμῆς οὐσίας ἀεί ἐστιν). Now first there is a

---

[20] Cf. on 157a3–4 (above, n. 15).

[21] The same phrase occurs at 160a1. (τὸ ποιοῦν is often used by itself to mean 'the active thing'.)

[22] In place of the simple 'my being' McDowell puts 'the being that's mine'. This periphrasis is in order to assist his own interpretation, which I discuss in a moment.

problem over the genitive 'of'. This may mean that my perception is always *a part of* my being, or it may mean that my perception is always *a perception of* my being. On the interpretation I prefer we take the first alternative, and the thought is that my perception is a *part* of me: it is one of the things that make me up, because indeed I am nothing but the collection of my perceptions. (To obtain this sense, it does not actually matter whether we think of 'my being' as 'my existence' or 'my essence' – 'what I am'; in either case it effectively means 'me'.) We could obtain much the same result by taking the genitive 'of' in the other way, so that the thought is that what I perceive is always my own being, i.e. myself. But one would then wish to introduce the gloss that, more strictly, what I perceive on any given occasion is only a part of the whole collection that is me, and it seems simplest to achieve this result by taking the genitive in the first way from the beginning.

McDowell offers quite a different interpretation of this sentence (1973, p. 156). He begins by supposing that it means that my perception is always *a perception of* my being, and then paraphrases 'my being'—or, in his periphrasis, 'the being that's mine'—as if it were 'what is for me'. (Then he goes on to suppose that a complement should be supplied for this 'is', and so ends by supposing that the thought is that my perception is always a perception of something that is [whatever it is] for me.) But it is surely very forced to take the phrase 'my being' (τῆς ἐμῆς οὐσίας) as equivalent to 'what is for me', for which the standard Greek (as in the next line) is τῶν ἐμοὶ ὄντων. If our text had contained not 'my being' but something like 'the being for me' (τῆς ἐμοὶ οὐσίας), then perhaps McDowell's interpretation would be permissible. But as it is I think it must be regarded as improbable.

Admittedly, in the fourth passage we return to McDowell's preferred way of putting things, which is of course also the way that they were put at the outset (152a–c): I am in a position to determine, of the things that are [whatever they are] for me, that they are [so]. This, after all, is the conclusion which the whole discussion is designed to establish—or rather, to make plausible. (We must not forget that Plato is going on to *refute* the conclusion that he is here drawing.) As I see it, the justification that we are finally offered is that perceptions are, in fact, the ultimate reality. I am simply made up of my perceptions, and would not exist at all without them. From this it does indeed seem to follow that my perceptions must be exactly as they appear to me to be. For the reason why one at first denies this claim is that one thinks of perceptions as representing or revealing some other and independent reality, and this at once leaves room for the idea that they may be *mis*representing it. But we have now argued that there is no independent reality: there are *only* perceptions (and collections of them). Perceptions, then, cannot be misleading, for there is nothing that they might be misleading about. And if I cannot be misled by my perceptions, then (apparently) I must always be right about them. As Socrates concludes, 'If I'm free from falsehood, and don't trip up in my thinking about the things which are, or come to be, how could I fail to have knowledge of the things I'm a perceiver of?' (160d1–3). The case is indeed a plausible one.

Now I must obviously admit that my last paragraph expands considerably on what the text actually says. But if I am right in saying that the text does mean to advert to the collection doctrine, then it seems to me that the expansion is not unreasonable. It must, presumably, be in some such way as this that that doctrine is held to support the desired conclusion. But here my dispute with McDowell's interpretation is important. On my account of the passage the collection doctrine is being stated, and in fact it is the only place where it is clearly implied just what the collections are collections of. At least, it is clearly implied that Socrates is a collection of those perceptions which, as we say, he has. (So one would *expect* that a thing such as a stone should equally be a collection of those perceptions which, as we say, are perceptions of it. But nothing is directly said of this, and we are still left to speculate on whether a stone is properly to be viewed as a collection of whitenesses, hardnesses, and so on, or as a collection of *appearings* of whiteness, hardness, and so on.) By contrast, McDowell sees no reference to the collection doctrine in this final summing up, and he in fact concludes that it is really not needed for Plato's point, and that Plato would have done better to drop it (p. 157). As he sees it, the final summing up is designed only to recapitulate the simple view of the relativity of perception that we began with. But while I do not deny that the text *could* be read in his way all through (provided that we are prepared to be somewhat cavalier over the phrase 'my being' at 160c7–8), still the general conclusion that McDowell very candidly draws is distinctly unattractive. It is that virtually all of 153d–160a has turned out to be simply irrelevant. It seems to me that an interpretation which leads to that conclusion should certainly be avoided.

8. COMMENTS

There is no denying that the theory we have just worked our way through is very confusingly presented. Let us briefly recapitulate some salient points.

We begin by introducing Protagoras and his thesis that all perceptual judgements are true, and it is apparently indicated that this thesis will be defended by stressing the relativity of perception: the wind may perhaps feel hot to you and cold to me, in which case we shall say that it *is* hot to you and cold to me, and we shall not allow that it is either hot or cold 'in itself'. Then at once we get the first statement of the 'secret doctrine', stated as the doctrine that nothing ever is, but is always coming to be, and that the things that we ordinarily say are in fact come to be from motion, change, and mixture: they are the offspring of flux and change (152d–e). Taking this together with the later statement that only changes exist (156a), and using what we know of the further development of the theory, we can see that the doctrine intended must be this: the only things that exist in their own right are changes—that is, comings-to-be, happenings, or events—and what we ordinarily regard as persisting things are in fact just series or collections of these changes. In view of later developments again, we can also add—what is actually never explicitly stated—that the changes that exist in their own right are perceptions. And we can note that what is in fact going to happen is that the secret doctrine will be used to *undermine* the relativity of perception that we began with, for it will be argued that actually there are no 'things' between which perceptual relations can hold: there is no 'someone' or 'something' for which we can say 'something appears white to someone'. All this, however, is left to emerge very much later.

To begin with, we are thrown off the scent in several ways. First, the 'secret doctrine' is coupled with the name of Heraclitus, and we expect to find Heraclitus claiming that everything is *changing* rather than that everything is *change*. In fact it is claimed in subsequent expositions that no perception ever maintains precisely the same quality for any appreciable length of time, or for any two different perceivers (154a, 160a), but this (very implausible) claim seems not to be at all an important part of the theory being developed, and could easily be dropped without loss. Thus the *usual* version of Heraclitus' flux doctrine turns out to be something of a red herring. But what is even more misleading is that at its first introduction the secret doctrine is apparently offered as an *explanation* of the relativity of perception, and indeed of relational phenomena generally (e.g. the 6 dice, that are both more than 4 and less than 12), which it very obviously is not. Consequently what I have called the 'first statement' of our theory is utterly confusing.

From then on, things become rather more clear. In what I have called the 'second statement' of the theory there are certainly still some unclarities. In the opening section, it is not at first clear why— or even whether—such persistent objects as eyes and stones are called 'slow changes'; and in the closing section, when these objects are said to be really collections, it is still unclear what exactly they are collections of. In fact the claim that they are collections is stated so brusquely, and given so little elaboration, that one might at first wonder whether it was seriously intended at all. But the 'third statement' seems mainly designed to reinforce this claim, since it certainly argues that nothing can persist as the same thing through any change, and the final summing up (on my interpretation) makes essential use of it, and at last clarifies what it is that perceivers are collections of. But we still have to make two important reservations.

One is that it appears to have been a mistake on Plato's part to have thought of his theory in too physical a manner, building in as part of the theory that a perception and an appearance are two movements travelling across space in opposite directions. It would have been better to say just that they are in a broad sense changes (i.e. occurrences, comings-to-be) and not to have tried to specify their nature in any terms other than perceptual terms (i.e. as seeings, hearings, and so on). This becomes particularly clear when we note that the theory is supposed to cover those 'appearances' that occur in dreams and hallucinations, where the ordinary phys- ical mechanisms are clearly not operating. More importantly, it is not completely clear that Plato himself has seen that the introduc- tion of the secret doctrine, which turns the apparently persistent perceivers and perceived objects into collections of perceptions, does actually undermine the view of perception as a relation which he began with. Right to the end he continues to speak in terms of the relativity of perception, for example saying that the wine can only be bitter by being bitter to someone, as if 'the wine' and 'someone' named entities which have some kind of independent existence. More seriously, he continues to speak of them as *generating* perceptions, which is a quite inappropriate way of speaking if they just *are* those perceptions.

However, I think that we can be charitable over these last two points. Although it is a mistake to retain a smattering of physics in a Protagorean theory, it is quite a natural mistake, and one that does not much disturb the general outline of the theory. It would be easy enough to dispense with it. As for the tendency to speak of persisting objects *both* as things that exist in their own right *and* as things that are constructed from perceptions, this is in fact inevitable. For the truth is that the theory that we are trying to state cannot coherently be stated. The usual way of bringing this point out may be put by concentrating on the idea of the perceiver as really nothing but a collection—or, in Humean terms, a 'bundle'— of perceptions. As Hume put it, the question is 'What ties the bundle?' Putting it less metaphorically, the question is 'What entitles a perception to be classed as one of those in the collection that we call "Socrates", rather than, say, one of those in the collection that we call "Theaetetus"?' Of course the obvious answer is that a perception is in the Socrates-collection if and only if it is *Socrates* who has it. But this answer presupposes that Socrates himself is something different from the Socrates-collection, for otherwise it is entirely circular. If we are to avoid circularity, and avoid presuming that Socrates himself is something other than the Socrates-collection, then we must give some other criterion for when a perception belongs to Socrates, and one that does not presuppose that we can already identify and refer to Socrates. And although many ingenious criteria have been proposed, it would not appear that any of them are satisfactory. But perhaps the problem is even more severe when we turn from perceivers to objects perceived. How could one say which perceptions count as perceptions of just *this* stone without presupposing that we can already identify and refer to this stone? To put the point briefly, one *needs* to be able to refer to the persistent things in question in order to be able to specify just *which* momentary items they are supposed to be collections of. To apply this point to Plato's own exposition, I noted that in the 'second statement' of our theory the closing section evidently shows that the terminology used in its opening section is not after all appropriate to the finished theory. Yet Plato continues to use the 'inappropriate' terminology. This, as I have just explained, is really not particularly surprising, since *any* attempt to state the theory we are aiming for will, in the end, turn out to use terminology which that theory itself condemns. Perhaps Plato's own account falls into this problem more blatantly than some others, but it is not at all surprising that the problem is not avoided altogether, for it cannot be.

We should not be surprised, then, that there is *some* incoherence in Plato's exposition, just because the theory he is trying to expound cannot in fact be coherently expounded. But all the same there seems to be very much more confusion than there need have been, particularly towards the beginning. One naturally asks *why* the theory is presented in so confusing a fashion. Some points perhaps become clearer as we proceed. For example it emerges, from the refutation of Heraclitus that comes later, that Plato did wish to criticize the *usual* form of Heracliteanism—i.e. that everything is constantly *changing*—and that was perhaps his motive for interweaving it with an account of perception designed to validate the Protagorean thesis. But others still remain obscure to me. Why, for instance, should Plato have chosen to write as if the secret doctrine explains how 6 dice can be both more than 4 and less than 12? Apparently he knew that it does not. At any rate, Theaetetus is made to say explicitly that *he* cannot see the point (155d5–8), and it is nowhere explained to him. I have no conjecture to offer on this.

I raise one more question about this theory, only to postpone it until after we have looked at the refutations that follow. Several interpreters have supposed that Plato *believes* the theory he here sets out. At this stage I only remark that there is no reason, so far, to make any such supposition. After all, the theory is developed in support of a proposition about perception which he is going on to refute. Let us come, then, to the refutation.

III

THE REFUTATION OF THE THEORY

Having brought Theaetetus' first child to birth, Socrates now sets about testing it, and in fact he brings three separate objections. In the first he refutes Protagoras' general claim that 'man is the measure of all things', but—as he himself makes clear—this refutation leaves the heart of our theory untouched. In the second he refutes the Heraclitean claim that everything is perpetually changing, but it is not altogether obvious what effect upon our theory this refutation is intended to have, and we shall have to consider this question. In the third he turns directly to Theaetetus' claim that perception is knowledge and offers a refutation of it which hardly depends at all upon the details of the theory that has been worked out to support it.

1. THE REFUTATION OF PROTAGORAS
(161a–179c)

The refutation of Protagoras' dictum that man is the measure of all things falls into three main sections:

(i) some preliminary objections to Protagoras (161b–164c);
(ii) a speech in defence of Protagoras (166a–168c);
(iii) two important objections to Protagoras (169d–172b, and 177c–179b), separated by a digression.

Let us begin with the preliminary objections.

The first point Socrates raises (161c) is that Protagoras has no good reason for assigning special authority to *men*: he might just as well have said that pigs are the measure of all things. It is obvious that this complaint, as it stands, is merely captious. Presumably pigs are just as much the measure of what appears (and is) to pigs as men are the measure of what appears (and is) to men. Protagoras complains (at 162d–e) that this is a mere 'debating point', the kind of rhetorical trick that is effective with an ignorant audience (δημηγορία), but not in any way a genuine disproof of his position, and he is surely right to do so. We are presumably to understand that he *accepts*, as a consequence of his position, that men are no nearer to the truth of things than pigs, or any other perceivers, and that he will simply dismiss the popular prejudice to the contrary as unfounded. But in the course of making this point about pigs Socrates has carefully drawn out its implication that even among men no one is any better judge of truth than any other, and this applies in particular to Protagoras himself: according to his own theory he cannot himself be any better judge of truth than the ignorant audience he mocks. There is a genuinely serious point here, and much of the later argument centres round it.

But for the moment Socrates apparently accepts Protagoras' rebuke, and switches to a new line of attack. At first sight it appears that his tactic is to draw attention to cases where we do know something but apparently not by perceiving it, first that we know what words and sentences *mean*, but we perceive only the words and sentences themselves and not their meaning (163b), and second that we may know things by remembering them, when we are no longer perceiving them (163d). But on closer inspection it is not so clear that that is his point. The way he himself presents the objection about meaning is by pointing out that we may perceive words and sentences without understanding them, so implying that perception is not *sufficient* for knowledge. To this Theaetetus answers that we *do* know all those features of them that we *can* perceive, so the doctrine can account perfectly well for our *failure* to understand foreign languages or unfamiliar script. Socrates says it would not be proper to dispute this answer, and the point is dropped. So we never do raise what seems to be the main problem for Protagoras, viz. how to account for our *success* in understanding a known language or a perfectly familiar script. It is not clear whether the reader is supposed to see that there is an important objection here which has not been answered, or whether Plato himself has not quite seen how to put this objection properly. But another possible explanation, which I shall pursue later, is that Plato did not pursue the obvious line of objection here because it would have taken the debate in a direction in which he did not wish it to go (text to note 9, below). At any rate, this line of objection is never reopened.

When we come to the example of memory (163d–164b), it is quite clear that the objection is that perception is not *necessary* for knowledge, since memory is an adequate alternative. But even here the objection is misstated, for Socrates carelessly argues as if *sight* were the only form of perception. This is perhaps to alert us to the obvious reply for Protagoras to make: there are other forms of perception, and memory itself is one of them. It seems probable that this is indeed the reply he is allowed to give later at 166b1–4,[1] where he says: 'Do you think anyone is going to concede to you that, if[2] one is no longer experiencing (μηκέτι πάσχων), one can have present in one a memory of what one experienced (ὧν ἔπαθε), this being itself an experience (πάθος) of the same sort as the original one?' The point of the reply is presumably this: a memory is on all hands admitted to *be* an experience (πάθος) of the same sort as the original one, so obviously one cannot say that when a person is remembering he is no longer experiencing. It is true that this is not quite what Socrates did say, for what Socrates said was that when a person is remembering he is no longer *seeing*. But that is not an objection to Protagoras unless we strengthen it to: when a person is remembering he is no longer *perceiving*. Protagoras replies that when a person is remembering he certainly is *experiencing*, and we are surely to understand that he is counting all experiencing as perceiving. Given the way in which perception has been understood throughout our discussion so far—e.g. dreaming is counted as perceiving at 157e–158e—this reply seems quite sufficiently plausible. Anyway, Socrates makes no further attempt to press his point about memory. Indeed he goes on to imply, at 164c–165c, that this objection, like his first, is merely captious.

So far, then, the position is that three objections have been raised. To the first, about pigs being the measure, Protagoras has already replied that it is a mere 'debating point', and this reply appears to have been conceded, at least for the time being. To the second, about understanding languages, Theaetetus offered a reply

---

[1] Protagoras indicates at 166b that he also has many *other* ways of meeting the objection based on memory. He can claim that it is quite possible for the same person to know and not know the same thing. Or, without going so far as this, he could claim that it never is the *same* person who both knows and does not, for indeed there is not a *single* person involved at all, as the situation envisaged is one in which I see an object at one time and remember it at another.

[2] McDowell translates using 'when', rather than 'if', which tends to create confusion. (See Rowe, Welbourne, and Williams (1982).)

which was allowed to stand. It seems to *us* that this reply has missed the heart of the objection, but the text does not say this, or even hint at it with any clarity. The third, about memory, is at first treated as if it were conclusive (164b), but then Socrates shifts his position and says that we are *not* yet entitled to cry victory over Protagoras. We have been proceeding, he says, in a 'logic-chopping' way (ἀντιλογικῶς), and behaving like 'controversialists' (ἀγωνισταί) and not as philosophers should (164c). This charge is emphatically repeated at the close of the speech in Protagoras' defence (167e–168b), where Protagoras exhorts us not to argue unfairly, and in the spirit of those who will use any low trick to secure victory, but to engage in a friendly discussion, making a serious attempt to get to the bottom of his position.[3]

Explaining why the previous argument has been unfair, Socrates first says, reasonably enough, that we have not given enough thought to whether Protagoras himself could give a better reply to the objections (164e). But then he appears to give a diagnosis of why the objections have been improper—or anyway of why the last objection about memory was improper—which is somewhat surprising. He says: 'One would have to make even stranger admissions than the ones we've just had, if one didn't pay attention to expressions: as we usually don't, in our assertions and denials' (165a5–7). Apparently, we have not been paying *enough* attention to expressions (ῥήματα). But as we read on, it seems rather that our mistake has been that we have been paying *too much* attention to expressions. At 166c1–2 Protagoras seems to imply that we ought not 'to have to be on our guard against one another's attempts to chase after words' (θηρεύειν ὀνόματα); again at 166d8 he says 'don't chase after what I've said on the basis of how it's expressed' (τὸν λόγον μὴ τῷ ῥήματί μου δίωκε); and again he ends his speech at 168b7–c2 by exhorting Socrates to proceed 'not as you did now, arguing from the habitual use of expressions and words (ἐκ συνηθείας ῥημάτων τε καὶ ὀνομάτων), which most people exploit by dragging them around just anyhow, so as to cause one another all sorts of difficulties'. It seems clear that in these latter passages the charge is that we have concentrated too much on mere words, and have not paid enough attention to the thought that lies

---

[3] It is rather a nice irony that Protagoras, whose preference was for long speeches rather than the cut and thrust of debate (*Protagoras* 334–8), is here made, through Socrates' mouth, to tell Socrates how debate ought to be conducted.

behind them. I think, then, that this is also what Socrates means to say at 165a5–7. His point is that we have not been paying enough attention to expressions in the sense that we have not been paying enough attention to what they *mean*; we have not looked beyond the mere words themselves, and consequently we have taken something to be impossible—viz. remembering something but not knowing it—which is not really impossible at all. To simplify Socrates' own illustration of this mistake (165b–c), it is as if we had convicted a man of contradiction when we had led him to say that he both saw and did not see, when what he clearly *meant* was that he saw with one eye and did not see with the other. So equally a man may be led to say something which apparently implies that he both knows and does not know, but this does not convict him of error if what he *means* is that he knows in one way (viz. by memory) but does not know in another (viz. by seeing).[4]

Admittedly, it is not easy to see Socrates' further examples of 'merely verbal' objections as suffering from the same fault. He goes on (at 165d) to observe that we speak of perceiving clearly or dimly, from nearby or from far away, intensely or mildly, but we do not use these same adverbs with knowing. If the objection that could be based on such observations is to be dismissed as 'merely verbal', then this must presumably be because, although common usage does not in fact apply these adverbs to the verb 'to know', it *would* make perfectly good sense to apply them if Protagoras' theory is correct. So the line of thought would be that common usage here may seem to indicate that people in general do not subscribe to Protagoras' view, but that is no argument against it. Similarly, people in general do not think that men are no nearer the truth than pigs, but that too is no argument against Protagoras' view. What we should avoid, then, is an argument which ultimately is founded on no more than common opinion, opinion which may of course be embedded in the common and ordinary usage of words.

Apart from the complaint that the discussion so far has been 'merely verbal', the longish speech in defence of Protagoras (166a–168c) in effect makes three points. It shows that Protagoras can easily meet the objection based on memory, which Socrates had at first treated as conclusive (166a–b); it returns to the opening objection, that Protagoras' position does not seem to allow for one man to be wiser than another, and Protagoras tries to explain that it

[4] Cf. *Sophist* 256a10–b5, 259b8–d8.

does not have that consequence (166d–167d); and it exhorts us to make a serious effort to think through Protagoras' position, and not to overlook the fact that it really does seem right to say that each man is authoritative about his own perceptions (166c, 168b). Evidently we are to understand the subsequent objections, which Socrates goes on to put, as much more damaging.

By way of preliminary we have a little sparring while Theodorus is finally persuaded to answer for his friend Protagoras (168d–169c). (Socrates has been trying to get Theodorus involved for some time (162a–b, 164e–165a), but I do not imagine that there is meant to be any philosophical significance in this rather nice by-play.[5]) Then we have a general introductory passage to show that the point of Protagoras' theory which is to be attacked is its implication that no man is wiser than any other (169d–170e). At this stage in the debate, Socrates is mainly anxious to point out that we all believe that some men are wiser than others, and that we all believe wisdom is a matter of having *true* judgements. But he is not yet taking into account the line of defence Protagoras has just offered in his speech, which gives an alternative explanation of what wisdom is. Before coming to this, he produces the first of his serious objections, the 'very subtle' (κομψότατον, 171a6) argument that Protagoras' theory refutes itself (170d–171c, recalled in the summing up at 179b).

Taken strictly, the objection appears to be incorrect. Protagoras is understood to be putting forward the view that what seems to be the case to any man is the case for that man (τὸ δοκοῦν ἑκάστῳ, τοῦτο καὶ εἶναι ᾧ δοκεῖ, 170a3), i.e. that each man's beliefs are true for him. Now most people believe that this view is false, and so *ex hypothesi* it *is* false (for most people), even if it is also true (for Protagoras). But more ingeniously (171a) Socrates attempts to argue that it must also be false for Protagoras, since he will have to admit that others *believe* it to be false, and hence that it *is* false, simply because the theory is that whatever a man believes is true. However it is clear that Protagoras has a perfectly good reply to this objection. The theory is that whatever a man believes is true *for him*. So it must be admitted that the theory actually is *false for others*, and since Protagoras recognizes this it must also be *true*

[5] It may be noted that Theodorus at last agrees to answer for Protagoras, but says that he will do no more than that (169c), and yet he in fact goes on answering until the Heraclitean doctrine of flux is disposed of at 183c.

for Protagoras that it is false for others. But it does not follow that it is *false for Protagoras*. This conclusion only seems to follow if we carelessly omit the qualifications 'true *for so-and-so*' which the theory insists on, and Socrates does omit these qualifications when stating this 'very subtle' argument at 171a8–9, 171b1–2, 171b6–7. But Protagoras has been careful to retain them.

If we are to find a decent objection to Protagoras along these lines, we must first show that these qualifications are inappropriate, at least in the present case. For this purpose, two lines of argument naturally suggest themselves. One is that the considerations we first gave in favour of a Protagorean approach do not apply to the present case: we began by urging that if the wind appears cold to anyone then it is cold for him, and generally that what appears to anyone *in perception* is so for him, but our present question is not one about *perception*. That is, we have given the doctrine a wider application, extending the sense of 'appears', so that it is now taken as a doctrine about all beliefs, and not just those based on one's own perceptions. And surely even Protagoras would admit that he does not literally *perceive* that any man's beliefs on any topic are true (for that man). Another line of argument would be to point out that when Protagoras announces his theory he evidently is *not* just telling us how things are *with him*. In his own view, the theory that all perceptions—or all beliefs—are true for the man who has them is not *itself* something that is just 'true for Protagoras'. Rather, he puts it forward as something that is *true* (full stop). That is why we are expected to take notice of it, to accept it ourselves, and to think highly of Protagoras for having discovered it. In other words, the doctrine that man is the measure of all things was not actually intended, by Protagoras, to be a doctrine that applies to *itself*. Protagoras did not suppose that each man is the measure of whether man is the measure of all things, though the doctrine does apparently imply this, and the consequence is evidently unwelcome to him. He will surely not be happy to accept that, although the doctrine may be true for him, still it is, by its own admission, false for almost everyone else. But Socrates is pressing the argument too hard when he goes on to claim that Protagoras will have to admit that the doctrine has turned out to be false for Protagoras himself.

Burnyeat (1976*a*) has offered a defence of Socrates' argument, which begins from the suggestion that to say that something is 'true for *x*' is to say that it states how things are 'with *x*', or 'in *x*'s world'.

Supposing, then, that x thinks that the Protagorean doctrine is false, then according to that doctrine itself it will follow that the doctrine is false for x, i.e. that it does not correctly describe how things are in x's world. Hence if Protagoras admits—as he must—that x thinks that the doctrine is false, and if Protagoras also subscribes to the doctrine, then Protagoras should himself infer that the doctrine does not correctly describe x's world. Thus he must admit that the doctrine is false, even for him, since it is supposed to describe how things are in everyone's world.

This is an ingenious reconstruction, but the premiss that it relies on is one that Protagoras need not accept. As Burnyeat himself goes on to emphasize, his way of interpreting 'true for x' as meaning 'true of x's world' does *not* in fact treat the notion of truth as a relative notion, in any important way. On his account, a claim is taken to be 'true for x' if and only if it is a description of x's world which is true (of that world) in an absolute and objective way. It simply states *the truth* about that world, not specially *for x*, or indeed *for anyone*, but absolutely. While this is, no doubt, *one* way of finding a meaning for the odd phrase 'true for x', a defender of Protagoras need not accept it,[6] and Plato would certainly need further argument to show him that he had to. Another (related) objection to Burnyeat's reconstruction is this. His argument commits Protagoras to the view that his own doctrine is false (for him) only if what *follows* from premises that are true for Protagoras must itself be true for Protagoras. On Burnyeat's way of explaining 'true for Protagoras', that is a perfectly correct principle to rely on. But it is a principle that cannot be accepted by anyone who wishes to equate what is true for a person with what that person believes, for people do not always believe everything that follows from what they do believe.

A little thought about this argument, then, shows that 'relative truth', or 'truth for a person', is not at all a straightforward notion, and the view that it is the only kind of truth there is is certainly obscure. Moreover, one who puts forward such a view does not in fact mean that it itself is only 'relatively true' or 'true for him', and so he is in fact in an untenable position. But Plato's first attempt to

[6] How else should 'true for x' be understood? Well, perhaps in the end it simply means the *same* as 'believed by x'. Under this interpretation, the Protagorean thesis, as stated, is merely a tautology. But it does not lose its *point*, for its *point* may then be restated simply as the claim that there is no such thing as (objective) truth is supposed to be.

say why must, I think, be criticized as too swift. As it stands, Protagoras has the defence that he can distinguish between 'it is true for me that it is false for others that *P*' and 'it is false for me that *P*'; and this defence is not adequately rebutted.

Let us move on, then, to the final objection against Protagoras, which is also the important point underlying the very first objection (that men are wiser than pigs), and has frequently been mentioned during the whole discussion. It is that some men are wiser than others, which seems to imply that some men are right where others are wrong. Protagoras in his speech does not deny that some men are wiser than others, but does deny that some men are right where others are wrong. The wise man, he says, is one who has the ability to 'cure' people like a doctor, and he does this by so working on them that they come to have 'beneficial' beliefs instead of 'harmful' ones, though both the beneficial and the harmful ones are equally 'true' (166d–167b). This is actually a pretty implausible account of what wisdom consists in. Socrates hints as much when he says that we look to wise men to help us when we are in trouble 'on campaigns, or in diseases, or at sea' (170a). It is because such people know about, say, boats and winds and waves that we look to them for help, not because they are skilled at persuading us into beliefs we used not to hold. But anyway, even on Protagoras' own account, the wise man is one who knows, as we do not, what is beneficial (171e), and this in turn is a special case of having right judgement about the future (178a). But Protagoras cannot account for the fact that some people are better at judging the future than others. It may perhaps be that each man is the best authority on what he *is* currently perceiving, but it is the expert and not the layman who is the authority on what the layman *will* later perceive.

Now a convinced Protagorean *could* stick to his theory even in the face of this objection. Suppose, for example, that I, who am a layman, think that the wine which tastes raw now will still taste that way in five years' time, whereas the expert thinks that—even to me—it will taste very smooth by then. And suppose that, when five years are up, I agree that it does taste smooth. Do I have to admit that he was right and I was wrong? Well, no, I do not *have* to. I can say that five years ago it *was* true for me that in five years' time the wine would taste raw, and it *was* true for him that it would not. Now it *is* true for both of us that it does not. But all these beliefs are equally *true* beliefs—true, that is, *for* the person who holds them and *at the time when* he holds them. If we relativize truth, not only to people, but also to times, the objection can still be evaded. But there is a difficulty with this defence. It indeed succeeds in maintaining (no matter how implausibly) that all beliefs are true (*for* the person in question, and *at* the time in question), but at the same time it destroys Protagoras' own account of how one man can be wiser than another. For that account assumed a distinction between what is beneficial and what is harmful, and it treated this distinction as an *objective* distinction, not relative to anyone's beliefs about it.

Let us first apply this point to the wisdom of the politician: according to Protagoras' own account at 167c, the wise politician is the one who can persuade the state to think those things just and admirable (δίκαια καὶ καλά) that are *actually* beneficial (χρηστά) rather than harmful (πονηρά). It clearly would not do to say that the wise politician persuades the state to think those things just and admirable that it *thinks* are beneficial, for presumably the state will always legislate with a view to what it *thinks* is beneficial (177e), and there is no special wisdom in persuading it to do that. Rather, the politician is envisaged as persuading the state to change its opinions on what things are beneficial, and to change them in the direction of what the politician himself believes to be beneficial, and this is *wisdom* when the politician is *right* about what is beneficial. If this is granted—and assuming (as everyone does) that not all politicians are wise—then it is implied by this account that it is possible to be *wrong* about what is beneficial. Thus false beliefs must be possible.

It should be noted that we can obtain a similar conclusion without presuming the objectivity of the distinction between harm and benefit. Although I think Protagoras is treating this distinction as an objective one, we could revise his position so that it did not do so. We could say simply that the politician aims to persuade the state to adopt a course of action which at least *will seem* beneficial, to that state itself, when it has experienced the results. And it does not matter here whether the results are actually good or not, but only that the state should believe them to be, once they have occurred. But essentially the same objection still arises: if some politicians are wise and others are not, then on this account some politicians are *right* in their predictions about what the state will think good, and others are *wrong*. Whether the task is to predict what is beneficial or merely what will seem to be beneficial, still so long as the expert is distinguished from the non-expert by getting the predictions right, it must follow that there is such a thing as getting them wrong. To avoid this result one must suppose that predictions do not enter into the matter at all. One must say, for example, that the wise politician—meaning now, in effect, the skilful orator—is just one who can persuade the state to change its views. Whether these views are changed for the better or the worse—or even for what *seems* better or *seems* worse—is now neither here nor there. On this very cynical account, wisdom in politics is simply the ability to achieve a change of opinion, and nothing more. For, as we can now go on to add, *all* views about whether the change is or is not a good thing are *equally true (for* those who hold them, *at* the time when they hold them).

But while such cynicism about politicians may perhaps seem possible, it is clearly going too far to adopt the same view about the other experts that Protagoras refers to, namely the doctors.[7] As he presents the matter, the cases are not very closely parallel, for the wise politician is imagined as one who changes the state's *beliefs*, whereas the doctor is imagined as one who changes the patient's *perceptions*, from harmful ones to beneficial ones. But it is not unreasonable to assimilate the two more closely, by adding that the way that the doctor changes his patient's perceptions is by first changing his beliefs: that is, he gets the patient to believe that some superficially unpleasant course of treatment will in the long run lead to better (i.e. more pleasant?) perceptions, and that is why the patient agrees to it. Then as before we begin by saying that the good doctor is one who is *right* about what course of treatment will lead to a better state of things—at least to one that seems better (to the patient)—and we are forced by the above argument to say that all beliefs on this topic are equally *right*. So we end up with the view that the good doctor is one who persuades his patient to accept some course of treatment or other, and it is neither here nor there whether this treatment actually cures the patient or kills him. But that is surely carrying cynicism too far.

To conclude, Plato is surely right to say that if all beliefs are equally true—which we explain by saying that they are true *for* the man who holds them, *at* the time that he holds them—then there just is no room for the concept of the expert. And this is an entirely satisfactory refutation of Protagoras, who himself claims to be an expert, and must claim some such superiority over other men, if he

---

[7] I omit the somewhat fanciful account of the gardeners.

expects us to pay any attention to his thesis that all beliefs are true. So, in a sense, one who propounds such a thesis does refute himself, for if what he says is right he has no claim on our attention.

I add a few more comments on this argument. First, it is an extremely economical argument. It is quite consistent with the claim of the theory of perception that the only physical things that exist are the events of perception, and that these are the only things we can make judgements about. It merely points out that there are at least these three different kinds of judgements about them: we can judge about what we are now perceiving, what we have perceived, and what we will perceive. Perhaps Protagoras is right in saying that our judgements about what we are now perceiving are always true. Perhaps indeed he would be right to claim that our judgements about what we have perceived are equally true. (In fact his own views on this topic seem to presuppose the unlikely theses that all such judgements are memory judgements, and that memory never misleads us; or alternatively that we never do make judgements about past perceptions, but only about present memory-experiences.) But he cannot *both* claim that all our judgements about what we will perceive are true *and* allow that some men are better than others at predicting their own and others' perceptions. And he must allow the latter if he is to continue to maintain that there is some room for the concept of the expert, and therefore if he is to maintain that he is one.

Even though the argument is so nicely economical, still it does in passing make rather an important point. It opens up a gap between perceiving and judging, and there will (in what follows) be an opportunity to exploit that gap, even in the case of my present perceptions. As Plato puts it, each person's present *experience* (τὸ παρὸν ἑκάστῳ πάθος), from which there arise his *perceptions* (αἰσθήσεις), and the *judgements* in accordance with them (αἱ κατὰ ταύτας δόξαι)—well, it's harder to show that these are not always true (179c). We now see the need at least to distinguish between the experience and the judgement. Judgements are not just the same as the experiences they are about,[8] as becomes clear when we notice that there are present judgements about future experiences, and

---

[8] So actually we cannot continue to say that the *only* things that exist are the events of perception. We must now also admit, as something different, the events of judgement.

once we have seen this we should be ready to distinguish the two even when the present judgement is about the present experience. But the implications of that point await further exploitation. For the moment we are conceding that Protagoras may be right to claim that present judgements about present experiences are always true, but pointing out that not all judgements are of this kind, so not all judgements are true.

Next it is worth observing that we *seem* already to have destroyed the claim that knowledge *is* perception, for our argument has apparently been that the expert *knows* things about the future, whereas one does not *perceive* the future. Thus some things are known but not perceived. But it is not at all clear that this is the moral Plato wishes us to draw. One might expect him to be making such a claim, for right at the beginning of the dialogue Theaetetus gave various areas of expertise as examples of knowledge, e.g. geometry and cobbling, and Socrates went on to equate knowledge with wisdom (145e). We have now argued that there are indeed such experts, and it is they who have wisdom. Hence we would apparently be entitled to infer that they do have knowledge, and hence—in view of *what* it is that they know—that knowledge is not perception. But this seems not to be a point that Plato wishes to bring out. In this passage he very seldom speaks of the expert as *knowing* what will happen. The only clear occasion is at 170b1 where the argument is just starting, though we might also add two places at the beginning and end of the argument (171e6, 179b2–3) where it is said of the non-expert that he does *not know*. But nearly everywhere else he talks of the expert having a *better* judgement, or one that is *authoritative*, or one that will turn out to be *right*, and seems rather to avoid saying that it is *knowledge*. Another point, rather more significant, is that even after our argument is concluded Plato can later say that the opening claim of Theaetetus, that knowledge is perception, has *not* yet been refuted (179c5–d1, 184a1–b6). How is this to be explained?

Well, an answer that naturally appeals to *us*, whose philosophical education probably started with sceptical arguments to show that we do *not* really know this or that, is that Plato is not prepared to commit himself to the claim that anyone *does* ever know anything about the future. After all, did not Hume demonstrate conclusively that there was no *rational* basis for *any* belief about the future? But Plato, of course, had not had the benefit of reading Hume on this topic. He was familiar, certainly, with sceptical views about morality; he had himself, in another mood, embraced a position according to which one could not know anything about the physical world at all; but I know of no reason why it should have struck him as plausible to say that while we can know what is happening now we can never know what will happen next. Scepticism specifically about the future was by no means a familiar line of thought when Plato was writing. If Plato *had* been drawn by some such thought then (*a*) one would certainly expect him to give us at least some hint of it in the present passage, and (*b*) one would expect him to avoid the few passages where he does apparently say or imply that experts know what will happen.

I think it more likely, then, that Plato was in fact quite happy with the view that the expert *knows* what is going to happen, but it is not a point that he is here anxious to stress. But this in turn must mean that he did not see it as particularly relevant to the claim under discussion. How could that be so? Well, the obvious suggestion is this: although he *states* the claim that we are ultimately concerned with as the claim that knowledge and perception are the *same*, he is actually only interested in one half of it. He is not really at all concerned to discuss whether it is true that everything that is known is perceived. Our present passage has, incidentally, made it fairly clear that that is not true, and there are lots of other ways in which one might make that clear as well (cf. p. 30). But that is not what Plato is mainly concerned with, and that is why he does not stop to point it out to us.[9] What he *is* interested in is the *other* half of the equation, stating that what is perceived is known, i.e. that a perception is *a* way of knowing, or *a* form of knowledge, though no doubt there will be others too. That is why he treats the whole equation as still standing even after this refutation of Protagoras, because the half of it that he is actually interested in *is* still standing.

What, then, has this argument with Protagoras achieved? It has cut down the Protagorean thesis to what is actually required. Protagoras did in fact announce his thesis in very general terms: man is the measure of *all* things. But what we have seen is that that is an exaggeration. At best we can say: man is the measure of what he is at the time perceiving. That is: it may be that all present-tensed

---

[9] Perhaps it also explains why he did not develop the distinction between perceiving a word and understanding its meaning in the way one might have expected him to (p. 85 above).

perceptual judgements are true (and are therefore entitled to be called knowledge), but the same cannot be extended to all judgements whatever.[10] On the contrary, some non-perceptual judgements are certainly false.

Before I move on, I should just add a postscript about the digression of 172c–177b, that breaks into the final argument against Protagoras. Protagoras is represented as maintaining first the relativity of perception, and then the relativity of everything, including *inter alia* the relativity of moral values (167c). The relativity of moral values is an idea that appeals to many who would not follow Protagoras' relativism all the way (172a–b). (For example, the claims here made about justice are made also by Thrasymachus in *Republic* i. 338e–339a.) Plato offers no formal refutation of these claims, but it would seem that the main point of the digression is to make it clear that he sharply disagrees. These claims, he implies, will appeal only to non-philosophers who have never attempted to acquire the philosopher's wider vision, and throughout this digression his language is so reminiscent of the *Republic* that it is natural to suppose that he is intending to refer the reader back to the *Republic* for a fuller account of his views. (For details of the parallels with the *Republic* see, e.g., McDowell's notes.) Now it would not be altogether misleading to say that the broad thrust of the *Republic* is to argue that to call something just is *eo ipso* to imply that it is good, and hence advantageous. So Plato's own view is that the separation of justice from advantage, which he says at 172a–b is the only way of maintaining the relativity of justice, cannot in the end be maintained. Some of his reasons are briefly sketched at 176d–177a, but he is not here attempting to develop his case in full, and I shall say no more of this.

But perhaps there is one point about this digression that deserves a further mention. In the *Republic* the argument about justice, goodness, and advantage is given a background in the theory of forms. As a matter of fact much of the argument could stand without that background, though it may be doubted whether Plato would agree with this assessment. Anyway, he does make it quite

---

[10] Our Protagoras is credited with the view that all judgements *are* judgements about one's perceptions at 167a8–9, apparently on the ground that if not they would be about nothing, which is impossible. This is apparently a foretaste of the puzzle to be introduced at 188d–189b.

clear in this digression that he has not stopped believing in the forms, for the philosopher's wider vision is explicitly credited to his concern with the *forms* of justice, injustice, happiness, and so on (175c, and possibly 176e). The same conclusion is also clear from later passages in our dialogue. But what is not very clear is how exactly Plato now conceives of the forms, or indeed whether he has a definite view on this question at all. That is a reticence which the *Theaetetus* preserves throughout. All that one can say with complete confidence is that they are still regarded as imperceptible entities (185c–e, 195d–196a). We may conclude that, for Plato, it is still important that there are forms, but also that, for the purposes of the *Theaetetus*, we do not need a very precise account of how, exactly, they are to be thought of.

2. THE REFUTATION OF HERACLITUS (181c–183b)

In 179d–181b Plato prepares for the attack on Heraclitus by spelling out the contrast between the followers of Heraclitus on the one hand and those of Parmenides on the other. He pokes some fun at the former, who, Theodorus says, are so devoted to change that they will not engage in any stable discussion. About the contrary side he is here rather brief, but later at 183d–184a Socrates does profess a deep respect for Parmenides, and declines to criticize him. (For this criticism we must wait until the *Sophist*.) The point of interest in this passage is that Socrates first proposes to discuss the Heraclitean view 'from its starting-point, the way they put it forward themselves' (179d9–e1), but when Theodorus replies that no decent statement of the doctrine can be got from its adherents it is agreed that they will instead study it 'as if it were a geometrical problem' (180c5–7). This means, presumably, that Plato is not claiming to portray the doctrine exactly as Heraclitus himself held it, but to be examining what seems to him to be its most fundamental claim. This, as we find, is taken to be the claim that everything *is changing*, rather than the claim that everything *is change*, and the latter doctrine never appears in the refutation.

Let us begin by summarizing the refutation, which goes roughly like this: First it is agreed that there are two kinds of change, namely movement (i.e. change of place, φορά) and alteration (ἀλλοίωσις), and that the Heracliteans would be bound to say that everything is changing in both these ways. This claim is then either summed up or generalized to the claim that everything is changing with *every* kind of change (181c–e).

Next it is agreed that, according to the account of perception given earlier, things come to be white, and other things come to perceive white, in virtue of a movement between the two. So this apparently satisfies the requirement that everything is in motion. But what of the requirement that everything should *also* be under-going alteration? We had earlier spoken as if 'the moving things flow qualified in such-and-such ways . . . [e.g.] that the flowing thing flows white'. But now we must say that not even this stays constant, 'but it changes, so that there is a flux of that very thing, whiteness, and a change to another colour'. But if *that* is so, it will not be possible to speak rightly of any colour at all (182a–d).

Similarly we must say that seeing is always changing into not-seeing, if everything is always changing in every way, and so there is nothing that should be called seeing any more than it should be called not-seeing. The same goes for other kinds of perception, and indeed for perception itself. So in fact it turns out, on this theory, that the claim that knowledge is perception is no better than the claim that knowledge is not perception (182d–e).

We cannot, then, support that claim by the doctrine that every-thing is changing. For if everything is changing, then in response to *every* question it is equally right to say 'it is so' and to say 'it is not so'. (Except that, more strictly, not even the words 'so' and 'not so' are available, for if they were then this 'so' and 'not so' would not be changing, as the doctrine requires. In fact, the doctrine must require a wholly new language to be stated in.) (183a–b)

So, finally, we have now got rid of Protagoras, and 'moreover we aren't going to concede that knowledge is perception, at any rate according to the line of argument that all things change' (183b–c).

There is one rather obvious point that we can make about this argument at once, before we come to more problematic issues. Although the argument begins as if it functions from the premiss that things are always changing in *two* ways—both moving and altering—in fact it requires the premiss that things are always changing in *all* ways, as is stated twice (at 182a1 and 182e4–5). For example, suppose something white is constantly changing from being (or looking) dull white to being (or looking) glistening white.

This surely satisfies the requirement that it is always undergoing *some* alteration, and we can allow for the sake of argument that it is always in motion as well. But this clearly does not imply that it must be changing *colour*. The point is even more obvious with the later examples. Thus a seeing may be continually changing from being a seeing of one colour to being a seeing of another, but this does not imply that it must be changing from *being a seeing*. The implications that Plato seeks to extract can only be got from the premiss (which he twice acknowledges in parentheses) that things are changing in *all* ways. But it is, no doubt, a premiss that he is entitled to assume. At any rate, the reason he gives for committing the Heracliteans to the view that things must be changing in *both* of the two ways first distinguished is just that, if they are not, then 'things turn out to be both changing and at rest, and it will be no more correct to say that everything changes than to say that everything is at rest' (181e5–7). This same reason would apparently justify the stronger premiss that the argument in fact uses.

The basic premiss to the argument, then, is that the Heracliteans are committed to the very extreme thesis that everything is always changing in all respects. The conclusion drawn from this is that, if they are right, then nothing can truly be said at all, on *any* topic, for any claim whatever would have an equally good title to be called correct. In brief, language would be impossible.[11] In particular, it would be impossible even to state the extreme thesis about change from which we began, and from this we may infer that this thesis should be rejected. Thus what Plato is trying to argue is that if everything is always changing in all respects then nothing can truly be said, not even that everything is changing. But how is his argument supposed to work?

Let us begin with Cornford's interpretation, which is roughly this.[12] If everything whatever is in flux, then the forms are in flux. But words have meaning by standing for forms, so if forms are in flux then meanings are in flux. And if meanings are in flux, then indeed language is impossible and nothing whatever can be said. From this Cornford draws the moral that perceptible things are indeed in flux, but forms are not.

A first point to make about this interpretation is that it gives Plato

---

[11] Presumably we should not take seriously the suggestion that some *new* language might be possible (183b2).

[12] Cornford (1935), pp. 96–101.

a *good* argument. It is true that one could raise an objection in this way. Suppose that the meaning of a word is indeed fluctuating from one moment to another, but suppose also that you and I both know how it is fluctuating. Then, choosing the appropriate moment, you *could* use the word to tell me something, and I could grasp *your* (permanent) meaning by using my knowledge of the *word*'s evanescent meaning. But such a cavil is clearly of no real importance, and I think we can agree that if the Heraclitean doctrine is indeed taken to imply that words do not have more or less permanent meanings, then that is a very good reason for rejecting it. So on Cornford's interpretation we do indeed have a good argument here.

We also have an argument which fits very nicely with evidence from elsewhere. I have already rehearsed some of the evidence for crediting Plato with the view that perceptible things *are* in flux, and therefore cannot be known, and that there must therefore be some other entities, the forms, which are not in flux and can be known (chapter I, section 2(iv)). We may add that several passages can be found in which Plato apparently claims that all language presupposes the existence of forms. If the interpretation of *Phaedo* 74a–77a that I sketched earlier in chapter I (section 2(ii)) is on the right lines, then from very early on Plato held that we could not understand the word 'equal' if we had not some dim recollection of the form. The same point seems also to be made in the *Phaedrus* (at 249b–c). A similar connection, but now without the theory of recollection, is again drawn at *Parmenides* 135b, where Parmenides concludes his criticism of the theory of forms by saying

But on the other hand if, in view of all these difficulties and others like them, a man refuses to admit that forms of things exist or to distinguish a definite form in every case, he will have nothing on which to fix his thought, so long as he will not allow that each thing has a character which is always the same, and in so doing he will completely destroy the significance of all discourse.[13] (tr. Cornford)

Since the *Parmenides* and the *Theaetetus* are close to one another in date, this is good evidence for Plato's views at the time of writing the

---

[13] This translation assumes, what is not certain, that διαλέγεσθαι at 135c2 means discourse in general (rather than philosophical 'dialectic' in particular).

Theaetetus, and it too apparently claims that without forms language would be impossible. Moreover, the connection between forms and language is reaffirmed once more in the *Sophist* at 260a. It is certainly fair to say, then, that evidence from *elsewhere* can be brought in favour of Cornford's interpretation, but when we look more closely at the *Theaetetus* itself that interpretation collapses at once.

First, it is clear that our text does not claim that perceptible things *are* subject to Heraclitean flux, or indeed that anything is. Moreover, that claim has now been made to look extremely implausible. No doubt it is right enough to say that all perceptible things do change, but there is no obvious reason to say that they are changing *all the time*, from each moment to the next, and there is no reason whatever to say that they are changing *in all respects*. Once one has taken a firm grasp of the obviously correct point that a thing may be changing in one respect while remaining the same in other respects, so that change need not be an all-or-nothing affair, there is no plausibility whatever in the thesis that things are constantly changing in *all* respects. Indeed, if no restriction is put on the respects of change, the thesis is actually self-contradictory. For if a thing is changing at all times, then there is one respect in which it never changes, namely it never changes from changing to not changing. Or again, even confining attention to more ordinary aspects of change, we can create problems by stressing the idea that our thing is changing *at every moment*. For example, can one make sense of the idea that a thing may be, at every moment, changing from being at rest to being in motion and vice versa? (This would imply that the thing never remains at rest for any continuous period of time, and never remains in motion for any continuous period of time, but is in either of these states only 'for an instant'.) In brief, the flux doctrine is here stated in so exaggerated a form that it is very difficult to believe that Plato could have thought that it was true of anything.

Second, only a very superficial reading of the text could make it seem as though Plato here wished to exempt *forms* from the flux. Our argument begins by conceding that the account of perception given earlier conforms to the claim that everything is moving, in so far as an act of perception is itself a movement, viz. a flowing. (There seems to be a confusion here between being *a* movement and being *in* movement, but let us let that pass;

the concession can be regarded as merely dialectical.) But then Socrates goes on:

> Well now, if things were only moving, and not undergoing alteration, we'd be able to say, surely, that the moving things flow qualified in such-and-such ways (εἰπεῖν οἷα ἄττα ῥεῖ τὰ φερόμενα) . . . Whereas, since not even this stays constant, that the flowing thing flows white (τὸ λευκὸν ῥεῖν τὸ ῥέον), but it changes, so there's flux of that very thing whiteness (καὶ αὐτοῦ τούτου εἶναι ῥοήν, τῆς λευκότητος) and change to another colour . . . (182c9–d3)

The claim here must be that, according to the flux doctrine, the 'flowing thing' cannot be said to 'flow white' in a constant manner, but must change to 'flowing another colour'. The reference to a change in 'whiteness itself' must therefore be taken as a reference to a change in *the whiteness of the flowing thing*, for it is this flowing thing that we are requiring both to be moving and to be altering, i.e. both to be flowing and to be changing colour. It is really quite extraordinary to suppose that what Plato means to say is that we could satisfy the requirement that all things must both move and alter only if (*a*) the flowing thing flows, and therefore moves, and (*b*) the *form* of whiteness alters (so that the *meaning* of the word 'white' alters). But there is no need to saddle Plato with such an odd thought, for it is perfectly easy to understand the abstract noun 'whiteness', as it is used here, as referring to the whiteness of this or that white thing, and to say that this changes is just to say that the thing in question ceases to be white. This, indeed, is just how the noun 'whiteness' was used earlier at 156d–e, where whiteness was said to be something that moves (φέρεται, 156e1). It is *instances* or *occurrences* of whiteness that are being talked of.

I add here that the force of this reasoning is not to be evaded simply by conceding that the whiteness here in question is not a form. Thus McDowell, in his interpretation of this passage (pp. 180–4), does concede that whiteness is not a form, but he still maintains that it is genuinely *whiteness*, or *white colour*, that is being talked of. And he clearly construes this as a universal, capable (in principle) of being exemplified by many things in many places, for otherwise he presumably would not think that it is evidently correct to say that the colour white itself cannot change. No doubt universals cannot change: they cannot change their qualities (i.e. alter), but equally they cannot change their places (i.e. move), for they have no places. Similarly, they cannot properly be said to flow, but what Socrates is talking of is something that flows.[14] In fact McDowell is doubtless right in saying that our argument concerns the twin *offspring* mentioned in the account of perception, and there described as on the one hand a whiteness and on the other hand a seeing white (156b–c). But these offspring are particular occurrences of whiteness and of seeing white, thought of as coalescing streams, apparently flowing through one another in opposite directions. And it makes perfectly good sense to suppose that a 'perceptual stream' may change from 'flowing white' to 'flowing some other colour'.

I conclude, then, that despite the occurrence of the abstract noun 'whiteness' our argument should not be construed as concerned with a change in any such abstract object as the colour white, or the form of whiteness, or the meaning of the word 'white'. It is concerned with changes in particular occurrences of whiteness, and similarly with changes in particular episodes of seeing and hearing (182d8–e1). Cornford's interpretation, and McDowell's variant of it, simply do not fit the way that the argument is actually developed here (though they do, no doubt, fit with Aristotle's remark in *Metaphysics* A6, the argument at the end of the *Cratylus*, and the general stance of the *Timaeus*). But this result must be admitted to be somewhat disappointing, for we now have to admit that Plato's own argument is a thoroughly *bad* argument: it gives *no* convincing reason to say that if the flux doctrine is true then language is impossible, but goes simply like this.

Socrates opens by admitting that if the flowing thing were just flowing, and not also altering, then we should have been able to say how it was flowing, namely that it was flowing white. But as it is, he goes on, our theory insists that it must be altering as well as flowing, and indeed altering in colour. In view of this, he asks 'Can it ever be possible to refer to any colour [i.e. to anything's colour] in such a way as to be speaking of it rightly?', and he receives the answer 'no'. But clearly the right answer is 'yes'. There is nothing at all to prevent us saying 'It was white at 3.00 p.m., grey at 3.01, brown at 3.02, and so on'. That is, so long as we do have a language with stable meanings, and the ability to make temporal distinctions,

---

[14] McDowell admits that on his interpretation the colour white is said to be something that flows white, and makes some remarks on the dubious thesis that the colour white is itself something white. But he says nothing of the much more dubious thesis that the colour white moves.

there is no difficulty at all about describing an ever-changing world. On the face of it, Socrates seems to be committed to the view that if I *am* getting visual experiences which perpetually change colour, then I cannot tell you anything about them. But that is just obviously a mistake. No doubt it would be possible to fill out the argument so as to make it look rather more convincing.

For example, it may well seem that there would be a difficulty in *learning* language if our perceptual experience were very chaotic, and certainly there would be a difficulty if one man's experiences were very unlike another's, so that one trying to teach the word 'white' could never tell when his pupil was experiencing white. However, it is clear that our text gives no hint of this further line of argument, or of any other. Although it is perfectly true that the extreme Heraclitean thesis under consideration is a grossly implausible thesis, and one that no sensible person would wish to subscribe to; and although this thesis *could* validly be argued to destroy, rather than support, the claim that knowledge is perception (for if *no* fact can obtain for more than a moment, then knowledge cannot be perception for more than a moment); still, as things are, we have to admit that the argument that Plato himself uses against it is quite unsatisfactory.[15] And I see no other interpretation of the argument that would improve matters.[16]

Whatever we think of the cogency of this argument against perpetual flux, there is another problem to be considered: what is its point and relevance? Why should Plato think it worth while to refute the very extreme thesis that *everything* is changing in *every* respect at *every* moment? Why should one be interested in such a thesis at all?

First it is worth recalling that this very extreme thesis is not

[15] This is a point that seems to have been overlooked by Crombie (1963, pp. 27–33), who I think interprets the argument as I do. The same remark seems to apply to Robinson (1969, pp. 47–8).

[16] White (1976) skates over the question. Gosling (1973) gives an interpretation that I cannot understand. Owen's brief remarks (1953, pp. 323–4) seem to me quite misleading. (He apparently supposes that Plato is concerned with how to identify the *subject* of the change, but there is no concern with that question. Our subject is referred to throughout as 'the flowing thing'. And the text cannot be read as proposing whiteness as an *alternative* candidate for the subject, and then going on to reject it. Nor is Plato mainly concerned to discuss and reject the 'becoming' terminology, which does not play any role in the argument.)

actually needed by the account of perception given earlier. Indeed at one point that account itself distinguished between two different kinds of changes, called 'slow' changes and 'fast' changes. Of the fast changes we are told that 'their changing naturally consists in movement', whereas the slow changes are explicitly said to remain 'in the same place'. So at this stage it is part of the theory that some changes, namely the 'slow' ones, are *not* changing in a certain respect.[17] Similarly the 'fast' changes, the 'flowing streams' of sight and of whiteness, presumably do not *have* to be altering in quality, or at least there is no good reason why our theory should be led to claim that they are. So there seems no reason why the theory of 155e–157c should need to say that everything is *both* moving *and* altering, and in fact it appears to deny this.[18]

It is true that in the following passage at 157e–160a our theory does assert that a succession of perceptions cannot maintain the same quality, for a new perception must always have a new quality, but the only reason given for this is that there is no distinction to be drawn between being the same thing and being qualified in the same way, and surely Plato was well enough aware that that premiss is grossly implausible. As I pointed out at the time, the theory *does* have a good motivation for adopting *half* of that premiss, namely the more plausible half. The claim that if *x* and *y* are the same thing then they must be qualified in the same way can be made to seem very plausible, and can also apparently be used to show that what we call a single person must actually be a succession of different things. This can then be used to reinforce the claim that apparently persisting things are really collections. But one cannot see why our theory should be thought to *need* the other half of the premiss, that different things must be qualified in different ways. This is extremely implausible, and this is the only ground we are given for saying that one perception is never similar to another.

Moreover, we should now observe that there are two distinct ways of taking this premiss, a point which becomes clear when it is drawn to our attention that a change is always a change in some respect, and a thing may be changing in one respect but not in another. For of course exactly the same remark applies to being

---

[17] Or at least, that they do not *have* to be. (Cf. pp. 62–3, above.)

[18] A qualification is needed here: some movements are not changes of place, e.g. rotations, according to 181c7. So *perhaps* the 'slow changes' do move, though they do not change place.

qualified in the same way, or being similar: things may be similar in some respects while not being similar in other respects. Accordingly, the thesis that different things must be dissimilar may be taken as stating that different things must be dissimilar in *some* respect, or as stating that different things must be dissimilar in *every* respect. Taken in the first way, it is the thesis called 'the identity of indiscernibles' associated with Leibniz, and although it is a contentious thesis when understood in certain ways and elevated to a great metaphysical principle, it can certainly be understood as quite harmless in the present context. There is no difficulty about accepting that perceptions which are different perceptions must also be dissimilar in *some* respect. For example, they will occur at different times, or at different places, or to different people, or something of this sort. This would not prevent the perceptions also being alike in that each was a perception of exactly the same shade of colour. If we wish to deny this—and apparently our theory does wish to deny it— then the premiss being relied on is presumably the premiss that different things must be dissimilar in *all* respects. It seems in fact to be that very strong version of the premiss that is actually invoked in 157e–160a, and it is clear that that is a wholly implausible premiss. Moreover, given the *other* part of the argument, to show that there never really are things that persist through change, and that any such thing must really be a succession of shorter-lived items, it *does* have the consequence that everything is always changing in every respect. That is the thesis which our refutation of Heraclitus actually refutes. It is very tempting, then, to embrace an interpretation along these lines.

What happens in the refutation of Protagoras is that a clear distinction is drawn between the moderate thesis that all judgements *of perception* are true, and the much more extreme thesis that all judgements whatever are true. The 'refutation of Protagoras' refutes the extreme thesis, but leaves the moderate thesis still standing. Similarly, perhaps, with the 'refutation of Heraclitus'. Here again we may distinguish the extreme thesis that things are always changing in *every* respect from a more moderate thesis about change that is all that the argument actually requires. The refutation then refutes the extreme thesis, but leaves the moderate thesis still standing. According to the suggestions made in the last paragraph, the 'more moderate' thesis will be the thesis that if x and y are dissimilar in any respect then x and y must be different things, from which it follows—or anyway seems to follow—that nothing can persist as the same thing through a change. So an apparently persisting thing must really be a succession of different things, and hence a 'collection'. The suggestion, then, is that our theory needs to claim that nothing ever does persist as one and the same thing through various changes, and this part of the theory is not refuted in the present argument. But the theory does not really need to claim that apparently persisting things are always altering their qualities, and it is that extra claim that is refuted in the 'refutation of Heraclitus'. Hence the original pronouncement of Theaetetus, that knowledge is perception, is not importantly upset by the refutation of Heraclitus, and is counted as still standing when that refutation is concluded.

This interpretation is admittedly somewhat speculative. It is quite clear from our text that the discussion of Protagoras distinguishes between an extreme Protagorean thesis, which is not really needed by the claim that whatever is perceived is known, and which is refuted, and a more moderate Protagorean thesis which is needed by that claim and is not refuted. But it is not clear from the text that a similar distinction is being made in the refutation of Heraclitus. The refutation of Protagoras makes this point very clearly, while the refutation of Heraclitus, as stated, gives us no firm indication that Plato had anything similar in mind. Moreover, even if it is accepted that Plato probably did have something of this kind in mind, still it is not obvious that he drew the distinction between the extreme and the moderate Heraclitean thesis where I suggest. The extreme thesis that is (allegedly) refuted is clearly the thesis that everything is changing in all respects all the time, but one might make several different suggestions as to what is supposed to be the more moderate Heraclitean thesis that remains.[19] It may perhaps be said that my own suggestion attributes to Plato more clarity on the premises actually needed by his theory of perception than his own way of presenting that theory would justify.

Even if this interpretation is accepted, we still have not really answered the question of why the extreme Heraclitean thesis is worth discussing at all. The extreme Protagorean thesis, that

---

[19] Crombie (p. 12) takes the moderate thesis to be the thesis that all properties *result from* activity, and the extreme thesis to be that all properties are themselves in activity (i.e. changing).

absolutely all beliefs are true, perhaps deserves a place in the discussion because Protagoras himself actually held it. But, so far as our evidence on Heraclitus goes, there is no reason to say that he himself held any such extreme thesis as Plato here refutes. Did Plato perhaps think that some 'followers of Heraclitus' had actually taken the flux theory to such extremes, or anyway were committed to so doing? One thinks, naturally, of what we are told of Cratylus. According to Aristotle, he was Plato's teacher,[20] and he was so impressed by the omnipresence of flux that eventually he concluded that it was not right to say anything, and would only wag his finger.[21] Or, of course, one might just think of the Plato who wrote the middle dialogues, and in particular the *Timaeus*. But I shall come back to that suggestion in the next chapter. Meanwhile, let us proceed to the final refutation of Theaetetus.

3. THE REFUTATION OF THEAETETUS (184b–186e)

After declining to discuss Parmenides, Socrates finally turns to the investigation of Theaetetus' original claim that knowledge is perception. The argument that he gives can be distinguished into three stages. The first runs from 184b to 185e, and aims to establish that as well as the things that we perceive through one or other of the senses there are also 'common things' which the mind 'considers', or perhaps 'views' (ἐπισκοπεῖ), by itself, and not through any sense. The second runs from 186a to 186c6, and extends the list of 'common things', adding more information about them. The third runs from 186c7 to the final conclusion at 186e, and fastens on one of the 'common things' in particular, namely being. The first part of the argument has shown that perception does not 'attain being', from which it is now inferred that it does not 'attain truth', and hence that it cannot be knowledge. It is clear[22] that the conclusion Plato is arguing for is that perception *never* 'attains being', and so *never* 'attains truth', and hence is *never* knowledge.

There are many problems in the interpretation of this argument, not least the problem of what exactly Plato means when he says that perception does not 'attain being'. But I begin with a question

---

[20] *Metaphysics* A6, 987a32 (quoted above, p. 23).
[21] *Metaphysics* Γ5, 1010a11–13.
[22] Contra White (1976), pp. 185–7, nn. 11 and 15.

which affects only the first stage of the argument, where we are aiming to show that perception does not grasp any of the 'common things' (of which being is one). What, exactly, is the reason for this?

(i) *Perception and its Objects*

It will be convenient to begin with a brief summary of the first stage of the argument. It opens with the somewhat obscure question of whether, strictly speaking, we ought to say that we see *with* our eyes (dative case) or that we see *through* or *by means of* our eyes (διά, taking the genitive case). It soon emerges,[23] however, that the point that Plato wishes to make is that it is not literally the eyes that see and the ears that hear, but rather the *mind* (ψυχή) that both sees and hears, through or by means of (or indeed with) the eyes and ears. Eyes and ears are parts of the body, and they are the tools or instruments used in seeing and hearing, but it is one and the same thing, the mind, that actually does the perceiving, now with one sense and now with another (184b–e). Next Socrates introduces the principle that nothing can be perceived by means of two distinct senses, e.g. nothing can be both seen and heard (185a). Consequently he infers that if we *think* something about both a sound and a colour, this thing that we think is not *perceived* about either, because it cannot be perceived by means of sight or hearing. But we can think about a sound and a colour that they both are, and that each is different from the other, and the same as itself. Equally we can think that they are together two things, while each separately is one, and we can (perhaps) consider whether they are similar or dissimilar. By what means, then, do we grasp these things that are 'common' to the objects of different senses (185a–b)? Professing to offer a further indication (τεκμήριον) of what he is saying, Socrates unexpectedly says that if it were possible to consider whether a sound and a colour were both salty or not, one would doubtless say that we would consider this, not by sight or by hearing, but by taste. But the question is: by what faculty (δύναμις) or instrument (ὄργανον) we perceive or are shown what we express by 'is' and 'is not' and the other 'common things' (185b–c). To this Theaetetus answers that we do not perceive them by means of any part of the body; rather, the mind considers these 'common things' all by itself (185d–e). So, as Socrates concludes, 'there are some things which

---

[23] This interpretation is argued at length by Burnyeat (1976*b*).

the mind itself considers, by means of itself, and some which it considers by means of the capacities of the body' (i.e. the senses) (185e6–7).

We may begin by observing that the opening move in this argument contradicts the Heraclitean theory of perception expounded earlier. That theory had spoken always of the eyes as seeing, and the ears as hearing, and had made no mention of the mind (e.g. 156e, 159d). Moreover it had denied the existence of any one persisting thing, the same from one perception to another, but it is clear that the mind is now being envisaged as a persisting thing. (That is why it can compare its present experiences with its own past experiences, 186a10–b1.) So we may say, in terms of the previous discussion, that perceivers (minds) are now admitted to exist in their own right. One might naturally expect the same admission to be extended to the objects of perception: just as it is a single mind that both sees and tastes the wine, that both sees and feels the stone, so one might naturally expect it to be admitted that it is a single glassful of wine that is both seen and tasted, a single stone that is both seen and felt. In this vein, our dialogue will later speak of perceiving the same object, Theaetetus, by means of many different senses (192d). But here we are brought up short by the next step in the argument, which claims that *nothing* can be perceived by means of more than one sense. Why should we accept that?

Unfortunately it is not easy to reconstruct the argument in such a way that it does not rely on this very dubious principle. One might perhaps hope that all that Plato needs is the uncontroversial premiss that *some* things, e.g. colours, can be seen but not heard, and *some* things, e.g. sounds, can be heard but not seen, though there may possibly be other things that can be both seen and heard.[24] But then it will be open to us to say that the 'common things' can be both seen and heard, and indeed perceived by means of every sense. Thus, taking being[25] to be one of the common things, we shall say that we both see a colour and see that it is, we both hear a sound and hear that it is, and so on for all other objects of perception. The weaker premiss gives us no reason to suppose that such judgements as these cannot be attained purely by perception.

What seems at first sight a more promising way of reconstructing

---

[24] Burnyeat (1976*b*) tries to get by with (a version of) this weaker premiss.
[25] I discuss later what kind of being is here in question.

the argument is this. Suppose we reconstrue the leading premiss as the premiss that, if any judgement is to count as a deliverance of the senses, then it must be possible to specify some *one* sense which delivers it. That is, if I judge that *P*, and this is to count as a judgement of perception, then it must be right to say that I perceive that *P*, and it must further be right to say either that I see that *P*, or that I hear that *P*, or that I taste that *P*, and so on. (This is, it seems to me, quite a plausible principle to govern what may be counted as a 'judgement of perception'.) Now according to this principle it may well be all right to say that the judgement that a colour is—whatever that means—is a judgement of perception, for perhaps one can *see* that the colour is. Similarly one may count the judgement that a sound is as a judgement of perception, for perhaps one can *hear* that the sound is. But it cannot be a judgement of perception that they *both* are. For one cannot see that the sound is, and one cannot hear that the colour is, so one can neither see nor hear that they both are. (This latter judgement may possibly be an inference from two judgements of perception, but, by our principle, it cannot itself be a judgement of perception.) Similarly one can neither see nor hear that a sound is different from a colour, and hence one cannot perceive it. Nor for the same reason can one perceive that sounds and colours are similar or dissimilar, nor that they are together two, nor indeed that *each* of them is one. More generally, our principle dictates that one cannot *perceive* that any relationship holds between two things that are only perceptible by different modes of perception, and sharing a common characteristic is one kind of relationship that can hold between two things.

This is, I think, quite an interestingly strong argument, and it comes quite *near* to Plato's conclusion, though one has to admit that it is not Plato's own argument. It is true that his initial examples of 'common things' *can* all be read as examples of judgements which *relate* a sound and a colour, and his later remarks which connect 'common things' with *comparison* might be thought to lend further support (186a10, b8, c2). But these comparisons that he later speaks of do not seem to be comparisons between the objects of one sense and the objects of another, as they should be on this interpretation, and anyway it seems clear that the conclusion Plato wants is that any *single* judgement involving being goes beyond what perception can provide. Thus at 185c4–8 he does not ask through what faculty or organ we perceive what is expressed by 'both are', but rather how we perceive what is expressed simply by 'is', and that would be the wrong question to ask if his argument were as just suggested.

One might perhaps offer a further development of that argument which would take us all the way to Plato's conclusion. Thus one might claim that the concept of being is in fact used in just the same sense of colours and of sounds, that one who has not grasped this has not mastered the concept, and consequently that an ability to make comparisons between such disparate things as sounds and colours is presupposed in one's understanding of being. Hence one who can *only* make judgements of perception cannot judge that a colour is. But I confess that I do not see how to put such an argument rigorously, and it clearly goes beyond anything to be found in our text. Plato's own argument seems simply to be[26] that one can tell by perception that a colour is, and that a sound is, only if one can see that the colour is, and hear that the sound is. But this he takes to imply that one can both see and hear what is expressed by 'is', and he rules that out by the general principle that *nothing* can be both seen and heard. Why he felt entitled to that general principle is, at present, quite unclear.

Of course the doctrine that each sense has its own 'proper objects', and that there are no 'common objects' available to more than one sense, is now quite a familiar one. It was supported by Berkeley, in *A New Theory of Vision*, using the principle that 'the senses make no inferences', in roughly this way. We commonly say, for example, that we can both see and hear a train passing, but when one considers the basis for such a belief one finds (according to the Berkeleian approach) that a great deal of inference is involved. What strictly happens is that we hear a certain sound, and because of our past experience of sounds of this kind, we *infer* that the sound is made by a train: one does not literally hear, or see, that it is the train that is making the sound, and nothing that one can strictly *perceive* will rule out the (unlikely) hypothesis that on this occasion the train-like noise has a quite different source. Similarly, we do not strictly see the train itself: what we directly see should be described rather as a certain pattern of colours, moving in a particular way, and from this, together with our past experience of trains (or other physical objects), we *infer* the existence of a solid, material, train. By arguments such as these the Berkeleian will try to persuade us

[26] This account is rather simpler than the version in Holland (1973).

that we do not, strictly speaking, *perceive* physical objects: we see such things as colours, we hear sounds, we smell smells, we taste tastes, and we touch or feel such things as hardness, solidity, heat, cold, and so on; from these perceptions we *infer* to the existence of physical objects, but just because inference is involved it is not really accurate to say that we *perceive* physical objects. That is the first move.

The second move is more tricky. There still appear to be some sensible qualities of things which can be perceived through more than one sense, for example their size and shape, and their motion (relative to other things). Here the doctrine must distinguish what we may call visual shapes, sizes, and so on, from what we may call tactual shapes, sizes, and so on, and it must argue that we only know by *inference* from past experience that these go together. There is no contradiction in the hypothesis that something which looks round to the eye will feel square to the hand, though certainly we should be surprised to find it happen. More generally, it is conceivable that our 'visual space' as a whole should bear no stable relationship to our 'tactual space', and if that were so we simply would not believe in any 'common space' containing both visual and tactual qualities. So, finally, the argument comes out like this. The supposition that there is anything that can be both seen and touched rests upon the premiss that there is a 'common space' for such things to be located in. But we do not *perceive* that there is any such common space. We perceive our visual space (by sight), and we perceive our tactual space (by touch), and we find that the contents of the one bear constant relationships to the contents of the other, enabling us to predict with confidence from one to the other. In order to explain why these constant relationships should hold, we *infer* to the existence of a common space, containing both visual and tactual qualities, and in some cases—as e.g. with shapes and sizes—this inference carries with it the inference to a 'common quality' with both visual and tactual manifestations. But because the existence of these 'common qualities' is inferred, we are forbidden to say that any 'common quality' can be, strictly speaking, perceived. For perception makes no inferences.[27]

On some such grounds as these the principle that each sense has

---

[27] For an account of the external world on roughly these lines see e.g. Russell's *Our Knowledge of the External World* (1914), chs. 3–4. (But in that book Russell prefers to 'construct' the external world rather than 'infer' it.)

its own 'proper objects', and no others, might possibly be defended. (Obviously, I do not commit myself to the cogency of the defence.) The fundamental premiss on which it rests, that perception makes no inferences, is—I imagine—one that Plato would find entirely acceptable. (Indeed, one might reasonably say that it is implied by his final argument at 186c–d.) But he does not state the premiss here, where it is needed, and in fact he does not even appear to admit that any argument is required. Part of the explanation may be that he has not seen all the objections that may be raised; there are relatively few sensible *qualities*, such as shape, which we ordinarily suppose can be detected by more than one sense, and he may have simply overlooked this point. But it is difficult to believe that he has just *overlooked* the obvious fact that we all assume—in our unphilosophical moments—that the same physical object can be perceived in several different ways. And if he has not overlooked this point, but is consciously denying the common-sense view, we would surely expect some argument. But we do not get any.

   The explanation for this may perhaps be that Plato is continuing to assume part of the Heraclitean theory developed earlier. We have seen that in one respect he is certainly rejecting that theory: the perceiver is no longer being viewed as nothing but a bundle of perceptions, but is now claimed to be a mind existing in its own right. But perhaps he is still retaining the view that a physical object is nothing but the collection of those perceptions that we call perceptions of it. In that case it is no doubt fair to say that two perceptions which are ordinarily called perceptions of the same object are, more strictly, perceptions of different things; for one is a perception of one ingredient in the collection, and the other is a perception of another ingredient. But it is not at all clear that Plato would himself wish to subscribe to this view of physical objects as mere collections—I shall discuss this question in the next chapter (pp. 151–5)—and there is anyway an alternative explanation, lying closer to hand.

   We noted that, when he was concluding his argument against Protagoras, Socrates incidentally drew a distinction between (*a*) the experiences (πάθη) that are present to one, (*b*) the perceptions (αἰσθήσεις) that arise therefrom, and (*c*) the judgements (δόξαι) in accordance with them (179c). Later in the present argument he will again distinguish between the experiences (παθήματα) that one has, and the reasonings (ἀναλογίσματα, συλλογισμοί) that one employs about them[28] (186c–d). But on this occasion he apparently identifies perceiving with the having of experiences (186d–e)—and, incidentally, he will go on to connect reasonings with judgement. Perception, then, is a matter of having experiences which have travelled through the body to reach the mind,[29] and moreover Plato appears to say that it is the experiences that are perceived. But unfortunately the crucial sentence is ambiguous. McDowell translates: 'There are some things which both men and animals are able by nature to perceive from the moment they're born: namely, all the things which direct experiences to the mind by means of the body' (186b11–c2). But, as McDowell notes, the usual translation of this sentence is different, and the second half would generally be rendered: '. . . namely, all those experiences which reach through the body to the mind'.[30] On the usual translation, it is the experiences themselves that are perceived, whereas on McDowell's translation it is those 'outer' things that transmit the experiences.

It must be admitted that either translation is possible. McDowell's reason for preferring his version is that 'it is an odd view that we perceive our experiences' (p. 111), and perhaps this is an odd view when applied to sight, but it is not so odd with some of the other senses, and anyway it has always been a very popular view amongst philosophers. Besides, one may surely counter McDowell's point by observing that it is equally 'an odd view' that we cannot both see and touch the same thing. But Plato certainly does assert this latter 'odd view', and it is precisely the former 'odd view' that is needed to explain why. So I think it much more likely that the usual translation is correct, and that Plato does suppose that, strictly speaking, we perceive only our own experiences. Thus what I perceive by sight are, strictly speaking, disturbances (παθήματα) which reach my mind via the eye, and what I perceive by hearing are disturbances which reach my mind via the ear. Given this approach, it will seem obvious that I cannot, strictly speaking,

---

[28] I here beg the question against McDowell, who thinks that the reasonings are not 'about the experiences' but 'about what is perceived', which he takes to be something different.

[29] *Philebus* 33d–34a gives the same account.

[30] ὅσα διὰ τοῦ σώματος παθήματα ἐπὶ τὴν ψυχὴν τείνει. The question is whether τείνει is here a transitive or an intransitive verb. (The parallel passage in the *Philebus* uses a (different) intransitive verb, but it does not directly say what it is that is perceived.)

perceive the *same* thing both by sight and by hearing, for the same disturbance cannot reach my mind via both routes. (If it could, then I could not tell whether I was seeing or hearing.) Of course later in the dialogue Plato will speak, as we all do, of perceiving ordinary objects (such as persons), and not of perceiving those changes in our sense-organs that are caused by them and that penetrate to the mind. But officially this will be, for him, a loose usage of words. Here he is trying to be accurate about what, exactly, we do perceive, for his argument that perception is not knowledge will depend upon it.

Notice that if this interpretation is correct then the assumption that Plato is relying on, and taking to be obvious, is an assumption about the *objects* of perception, and not the *judgements* that perception is capable of delivering about those objects. It thus does not require the Berkeleian defence of the doctrine that nothing can be both seen and heard that I sketched earlier, for the Berkeleian defence was primarily concerned with the judgements that can properly be credited to perception. It did claim that no object could be perceived by more than one sense, but it also presumed that to perceive an object is at the same time to recognize it as having this or that property, and so went on to argue that no property can be perceived to hold of an object by more than one sense. (For example, one cannot both see and feel *that* an object is square, since sight can only detect visual shapes and touch can only detect tactual shapes.) But Plato's assumption, as I interpret him, is simply about the objects that one can perceive. We have not yet raised the question of what can be perceived *about* those objects. However, this claim is controversial, as we shall see.

(ii) *Grasping the 'Common Things'*

So far it has been argued that any object which we can perceive (when perception is taken strictly) can be perceived only through one sense. The objects of perception may thus be taken to be such things as colours, sounds, tastes, smells, 'feels', and so on, thought of as particular instances of colour, or whatever, that are present to the mind. Since it would be impossible to specify any one sense which presents to the mind such 'objects' as being, sameness, or difference, we can now infer that these 'objects' are not perceived.

According to what I think we may call the orthodox interpretation of Plato's argument,[31] it then continues in this way. Before I can make any judgement to the effect that something is, or is the same as itself, or is different from something else, I must in some way grasp these (abstract) objects—being, sameness, and difference. This is achieved by the mind, operating 'by itself' and independently of perception. The idea is that in order to grasp any judgement one must first grasp the 'terms' employed in it, and it cannot be perception that provides us with our grasp of such terms as being or sameness or difference. Hence perception cannot yield any judgements in which these terms occur.

On the other hand, Cooper (1970) has argued that there is no warrant for attributing to Plato any such theory about what it is to grasp a judgement. On the account that he prefers, to grasp a 'common thing' is not to be in any relationship to an abstract object, such as being, but is just to make a judgement of a special kind, e.g. the judgement, concerning something, that it is. These judgements are special because what they predicate of their subjects can be predicated of items that are perceived by any sense. They contrast with judgements whose predicates can only be applied to items perceived by a single sense, e.g. the judgement that something is salty, which is a judgement that can only be made about tastes (or things tasted). Thus on Cooper's account the contrast which Plato intends when he distinguishes 'common things' from others is essentially a contrast between two different kinds of *judgement*, whereas on the usual account it is a contrast between two different kinds of terms that can occur in a judgement, namely those that are perceived and those that are apprehended by the mind without any assistance from perception.

This dispute is important because of its implications for the interpretation of the final stage of our argument. According to the orthodox account, Plato will be saying that one of the 'common things', namely being, occurs as a term in *every* judgement, and so his conclusion will be that perception by itself cannot yield any judgements *at all*. But if we take Cooper's view then we will have to agree that perception is capable of delivering some judgements, e.g. the judgement 'this is salty', as will emerge in a moment. For the present, however, I shall continue to postpone consideration of

[31] e.g. Cornford (1935, pp. 105–6), McDowell (1973, pp. 188–9), Burnyeat (1976b, pp. 45 ff.), Gulley (1962, p. 85).

the final stage of the argument, and review such other evidence as the text provides.

First, nothing very much can be gleaned from the verbs which Plato uses to express what it is that the mind does to the 'common things'. It is said to 'get hold of them' (λαμβάνειν, 185b8), to 'consider them' (ἐπισκοπεῖν, 185e2, 185e7), and to 'reach out for them' (ἐπορέγεσθαι,[32] 186a4). (It is also frequently *asked* how the mind 'perceives' them, but evidently the answer to this is that the mind does *not* perceive them.) Now 'reaching out for' and 'getting hold of' are clearly somewhat metaphorical expressions, and 'considering' can be taken in either of two ways: it can be used of considering a question (e.g. whether something is) or of considering, i.e. viewing, an object (being). The first of these suggests Cooper's view of the passage, but the second is quite consistent with the usual view, and so we cannot base anything upon this.

The main consideration in favour of Cooper's interpretation is the fact that Plato very frequently speaks of the mind considering or getting hold of the common things *about* this or that subject. Thus he clearly opens with the claim that the mind thinks various things *about* both a sound and a colour, e.g. *that* they both are (184a4–b6), and at once he goes on to ask through what organ or faculty the mind thinks these things *about* them (185b7–9). When this question is rephrased as the question of what faculty it is that shows us the common things expressed by 'is' and by 'is not', again the phrase 'about them' may be added[33] (185c4–7). And finally when Theaetetus says that there is no sense-organ in their case, his positive claim is that it appears that the mind by itself considers the common things *about* all objects[34] (185d7–e2). Now it seems fairly clear that to consider a common thing *about* some item must be to ask *whether* the common thing holds of that item, and to get hold of a common thing *about* some item must be to judge *that* the common

---

[32] McDowell translates 'try to get hold of'.

[33] The structure of this sentence is not clear. McDowell's translation takes the final words 'about them' (περὶ αὐτῶν) to go with the preceding phrase 'and the [other words] used just now in our questions' (καὶ ἃ νυνδὴ ἠρωτῶμεν). On his rendering, it was our questions that were questions 'about them'. But one could read the sentence as asking what faculty it is that shows us what is expressed by 'is' and 'is not' (and the others) about them, as at 185b7–9.

[34] McDowell clearly mistranslates this passage. He renders τὰ κοινὰ περὶ πάντων ἐπισκοπεῖν as 'considers the things which apply in common to everything', as if the text were τὰ ἐπὶ πᾶσι κοινὰ ἐπισκοπεῖν. But clearly our text means 'considers the common things about everything'.

thing does hold of that item. So the prevalence of these 'about'-phrases does strongly suggest, in accordance with Cooper's view, that the question that Plato is interested in is not that of how we grasp the term 'being', considered in itself, but is rather the question of how we come to judge that this term applies to this or that subject.

Now the 'about'-phrases occur explicitly at 185a4–5, 185a8, 185b7, 185b9, 185c7(?), 185d1, and 185e1. It seems natural, then, to supply these phrases also at the places where they are not explicitly included, namely at 185d2–4, 185e6–7, and 186a4. The crucial passage here is the second one. If we add a suitable 'about'-phrase to 185e6–7 then it will say: the mind considers some things, about an object, all by itself, and it considers other things, *about that object*, by means of the capacities of the body, i.e. the senses. Since it would certainly seem that to consider something by means of the senses is to *perceive* it, this passage will then say that, in some cases, one can *perceive that* an object has a certain property. Hence there are some judgements which can genuinely be called judgements *of perception*, including, no doubt, the judgement that something is salty.

One might initially suppose that the earlier passage at 185b10–c3 has anyway committed Plato to this thesis. It has by then been established that what can be thought in common about both sounds and colours is not grasped by means of sight or by means of hearing. Presumably because he wishes to emphasize that it is not grasped by *any* mode of sense-perception, Socrates then says 'If it were possible to investigate whether both a sound and a colour are or are not salty, you would of course be able to say with[35] what you would investigate it, and this would evidently be neither sight nor hearing but something else'. To this Theaetetus replies 'Of course: the capacity that works through the tongue', and Socrates agrees. This passage is odd in several ways,[36] but it does very strongly suggest

---

[35] Plato slips into using the dative case, which he had begun by saying was not an accurate locution.

[36] On the usual interpretation, Socrates thinks that one cannot investigate whether a colour is salty, because one cannot taste a colour. But if one cannot investigate the question, it appears to follow that one does not know the answer, which seems an absurd result. For, in context, to be salty is to taste salty, and we surely know that colours do not taste salty because we know that they do not taste at all. But a curious question which arises is this: *how* do we know that colours cannot be tasted? Is it by the faculty of taste? If so, then should we admit that something common to both sounds and colours is discerned by the mind, operating through the tongue, viz. that neither of them can be tasted, so neither is salty?

that with objects that *can* be tasted one can tell by tasting, and hence by perception, whether or not they are salty. However it *may* be that Socrates wishes to *correct* this impression with his next remark, which pointedly asks about the faculty by which we discern what is expressed by 'is' and 'is not'. *Perhaps* he is thinking of the 'is' and 'is not' which figure in the very judgements 'this is salty' and 'this is not salty', and so is pointing out that, after all, perception alone cannot deliver such judgements. Whether this is the right way of understanding the notion of being in our argument is a question I am still postponing, but for the moment it is enough to observe that this is a possible way of understanding our text. Hence 185b10–c3 *need* not be taken as admitting that perception can frame the judgement 'this is salty'. If that admission is to be found in our text, then it is at 185e6–7, provided that that passage contrasts two kinds of judgement, and not two ways of grasping *objects*. And apparently it will do this, if a suitable 'about'-phrase is to be supplied.

We are given more information about the 'common things', and how the mind 'considers' them, in the succeeding passage 186a8–c5. If we now take this passage too into account, then I think it must be admitted that Cooper's interpretation appears, at first sight, to receive further support.

In 186a2–7 it is agreed that the things already introduced as 'common things'—namely being, likeness and unlikeness, sameness and difference— are indeed things which the mind reaches out for by itself. Socrates then suggests adding to this list 'beautiful and ugly, good and bad',[37] and Theaetetus agrees. But what Theaetetus offers as a reason is that they are things 'whose being the mind considers in relation to one another, calculating in itself things past and present in relation to things in the future' (186a9–b1). This is somewhat unexpected, since the reason we expect to be given is of course that beauty and goodness are *common* to objects perceived by different senses. No doubt this is a point that could perfectly well be maintained,[38] but it is clear that it is not the point that is being maintained. Socrates interrupts with 'Hold on' (ἔχε δή), which

[37] I do not understand why Socrates (ungrammatically) says 'beautiful' rather than 'beauty'. (Despite McDowell's translation, he has used the abstract nouns 'likeness', 'sameness', and so on, just above.)

[38] *Hippias Major* 297e–299c explicitly makes this point about beauty (and *Symposium* 210a–212a adds that beauty is by no means confined to the objects of the senses).

might be taken as a signal that Theaetetus has said the wrong thing.
As McDowell suggests, he may perhaps be warning Theaetetus not
to muddle the present argument with the previous argument against
Protagoras, where indeed a judgement that something is good was
taken to be—or anyway to depend on—a judgement about the
future. But as we read on that interpretation becomes implausible,
for Socrates himself goes on to stress the notions of comparison and
calculation. It seems rather that Theaetetus has said very much the
right thing, and Socrates asks him to 'hold on' while he gets that
point more firmly made.

The hardness of what is hard, he says, and the softness of what is
soft, are things that the mind perceives by the faculty of touch, 'but
their being, and that[39] they both are, and their oppositeness to one
another, and the being in its turn of this oppositeness, are things
which the mind itself tries to decide for us, by reviewing them and
comparing them with one another' (186b6–9). Some things we
perceive, he goes on, namely the experiences[40] that reach through
the body to the mind. We do not have to learn to do this: we can all
do it from birth, and so can other animals. But on the other hand
'the calculations (ἀναλογίσματα) about these things, with respect to
being and usefulness, are acquired, by those who do acquire them,
with difficulty and over a long time, by means of a great deal of
troublesome education' (186c2–5). The stress here is very clearly on
the contrast between merely having experiences and reasoning
about them (as again at 186d2–3), and evidently it is the latter which
is now being thought of as what the mind does 'by itself'.

To judge from these passages, whatever it is that we do when we
'consider a common thing about something', it is no easy task: it
requires 'a great deal of troublesome education'. But one would not
suppose that any long and troublesome education is needed before
we can judge of something that it is hard, or that it is salty. Here
again, then, I think we must say that a first view of these passages
rather strongly suggests that perception *is* capable of making such
simple judgements as these, where it would not appear that reasoning and calculating and comparing are in any way involved. Another
feature of these passages, that points in the same direction, is
this. When our argument first introduced the problem about the

---

[39] McDowell translates 'what they both are'. I discuss this alternative translation
below (pp. 139–40).
[40] See p. 117 above for a justification of this paraphrase.

'common things', it looked as if the problem was to say how we grasp or *understand* either those things themselves or the judgements involving them. But the present passage is surely not saying that we need reasoning and calculation in order to *understand* these judgements, i.e. in order to know what they *mean*, but rather that we need reasoning and calculation in order to find out whether they are *true*. But if the problem was never viewed as a problem about understanding at all, then it seems unlikely that Plato would at any point have been concerned with how the mind grasps such abstract objects as being, sameness, and difference. For it is clear that that theory is an attempt to explain how we *understand* the propositions which employ such notions; it is not designed to tell us how we can sometimes know that they are *true*.

Nevertheless, it is clear that these considerations in favour of Cooper's interpretation are not conclusive. To deal with the last point first, it may perhaps be that Plato's argument *began* with the problem of how we understand judgements that attribute 'common things' to perceived subjects, even if he has now allowed himself to get side-tracked into the different question of how we can sometimes tell that they are true. Nor is it impossible to suppose that, in his view, a long and arduous training is required before one can make even such simple judgements as that what one is perceiving is hard, or is salty. Notice first that, according to the account of what a judgement is that is given later, it always is preceded by reasoning and calculation. Socrates says:

It looks to me as if, when the mind is thinking, it's simply carrying on a discussion, asking itself questions and answering them, and making assertions and denials. And when it has come to a decision, either slowly or in a sudden rush, and it's no longer divided, but says one single thing, we call that its judgement. So what I call 'judging' is speaking, and what I call 'judgement' is speech; but speech spoken, not aloud to someone else, but silently to oneself. (189e7–190a6)

This passage shows well enough that Plato is inclined to exaggerate the mental preliminaries that are needed before any judgement can be reached. But, more importantly, it also shows that he took one of the prerequisites to be mastery of a language. Perhaps, then, the long and troublesome education that he refers to is the process of learning to talk. After all, this does take time, and only humans can do it. And one might note that, if this is his point, then the stress that he lays on comparisons is entirely apposite. One cannot learn to apply even such simple words as 'hard' and 'salty' without grasping the relevant similarities between all hard things and all salty things.

The orthodox interpretation can, then, explain these passages about the difficulty of applying 'common things' while still supposing that they are applied even in such simple judgements as 'this is hard' or 'this is salty'. As for the point with which we began, that our text so often speaks of the mind 'considering' or 'getting hold of' the common things *about* this or that subject, it must be admitted that this locution indicates the formulation or affirmation of a judgement. But of course the orthodox interpretation does not deny that Plato's argument depends upon the fact that we do make such judgements, and on any view one would expect him to begin by drawing attention to them. But according to the orthodox interpretation his point is that we could not grasp such judgements unless we could first grasp the terms they contain, and these terms have to be grasped 'in themselves', and not 'about' any particular subject. This is not a point that our text stresses because, according to the orthodox interpretation, Plato took it to be completely obvious: one cannot grasp the judgement that, say, a colour is unless one also grasps what is meant by 'is', which is a matter of having some kind of access to the object that this word means, namely being. And, after all, the 'about'-phrases are *not* found everywhere. In particular, there is no 'about'-phrase in the crucial passage at 185e6–7, where we have a contrast between what the mind considers all by itself and what it considers through the senses.

The arguments for Cooper's view, then, are not conclusive, and there is, as we shall see, a great difficulty in reconciling this view with the final stage of our argument. Besides, there are also some considerations which tell in favour of the orthodox view, even before we come to the final stage of the argument. But they too are hardly compelling.

I mention a small point first. At 185c5–6, where the words 'is' and 'is not' are quoted as words for common things, a literal translation of the text makes it say that you *give the names* 'is' and 'is not' to common things (ἐπονομάζεις). If Plato is inclined to think of 'is' as a name, then of course he will suppose that to understand the word is to grasp the thing that it names. But one cannot build very much on this; there is no reason to suppose that this use of the verb 'to name' is meant in any strict way, and the apparent implication may not have been intended.[41]

A more interesting point is this. It is obvious that when Plato says that the mind considers common things 'by itself', he means this to contrast with 'by means of the senses'. On Cooper's account, when the mind judges, about some colour that it perceives, that the colour is—or that it is the same, or different, or like, or unlike, some other perceived colour—then it is said to be operating 'by itself'. But if what it is doing is making a judgement about a thing that it perceives, then is it not strange to find this activity characterized as independent of perception? Clearly, it could not make such a judgement unless it did perceive the subject it is judging about.

To this it may certainly be replied that Plato evidently does, in our passage, count judgements about perceived things as judgements which the mind forms 'by itself'. The calculations and reasonings which are mentioned in 186c–d are explicitly said to be *about* the things we perceive, and although they are not explicitly said to be done by the mind 'by itself', this is evidently what Plato means. For he does say that that is where knowledge is to be found, and he sums up at 187a by saying that knowledge is to be looked for, not in perception, but 'in whatever one calls what the mind is doing when it's busying itself, by itself, about the things which are'. There is no doubt, then, that Plato does count judgements about perceived things as formed by the mind when operating 'by itself', which apparently means 'without the assistance of the senses'. But all the same one must acknowledge that this terminology is distinctly odd. One might naturally suppose that it is only what we would call a priori judgements that could be credited to the mind operating all by itself, but that is evidently not what Plato intends.

On Cooper's interpretation one simply has to accept that Plato's terminology is unexpected, and one can say no more. On the orthodox interpretation there is something one can add. The main point of the argument is that there is something which the mind really does do entirely by itself, and without any assistance from perception: it 'considers' being, and the other common things, in the sense that it grasps what is meant by 'is' and similar expressions,

---

[41] Plato incidentally distinguishes names (ὀνόματα) from verbs and other expressions (ῥήματα) in the early *Cratylus* at 424e and 431b, and in this dialogue at 206d. But he does not give the distinction any work to do until the later *Sophist* (261d ff.), and at *Cratylus* 385c he apparently counts all words as names.

not 'about' any particular objects but simply in themselves. This *purely* mental achievement is not itself the formation of any judgement, but it is a prerequisite to all judgements involving the terms in question. If these judgements, as wholes, are also credited to the mind acting 'by itself' that is something of an exaggeration. For the other terms to those judgements may be supplied by perception, and it would be more accurate to say that the judgements presuppose a purely mental activity rather than to assign them entirely to that activity. But on this account the exaggeration is perhaps more explicable.

Finally, it is worth adding a brief comment on what exactly Plato's argument is, as Cooper conceives it. On the orthodox account, it is straightforward: perception can only put us in touch with objects that are special to whatever sense is involved, but being is not a special object of this kind, so perception cannot put us in touch with being. But we cannot grasp any judgement containing the word 'is' without being in touch with being, and hence no such judgement can be credited to perception. That is, as I say, a nice straightforward argument. But on Cooper's account the argument should not be phrased as an argument about *objects* at all, but as an argument about how we are led to make judgements with different predicates. It claims that we can tell by perception that something is hard, or that something is salty, but perception will not tell us that something is (whatever that means). Accordingly, the premiss must be taken as a premiss concerning the predicates in question. It must be something like: one can tell by perception that an object is so-and-so only when there is only one sense by which one can tell that a thing is so-and-so. Now (*a*) it is difficult to see any justification that Plato might have appealed to in support of this premiss,[42] and even more difficult to explain why he should have felt entitled to assert it without any argument at all. (Plainly, the claim that the only objects that we perceive are our own experiences would not justify it.) Moreover (*b*) it needs a good deal of charity to see *this* premiss as the one that Plato is himself trying to state at 184e8–185a2, where all that he says is 'if you perceive something by means of one power [i.e. faculty], it's impossible to perceive that same thing by means of another. For instance, you can't perceive by means of sight what you perceive by means of hearing, or vice versa.' Plato's own way of stating his premiss is undeniably in terms of the objects

[42] The argument that I indicated on pp. 113–15 might perhaps serve the purpose.

of perception, and it does not introduce judgements of perception at all.

I would maintain, then, that even while we are still confining our attention to the first stage of the argument, there are points to be made in favour of the orthodox interpretation. But there are also, as we have seen, points to be made in favour of Cooper's interpretation, and at this stage neither of them can be ruled out. But when we come to the final stage of the argument, which I now proceed to, we shall be able to be rather more definite.

(iii) *The Final Argument (186c7–e12)*

The final stage of our argument goes through extremely quickly. It is taken to be established in the earlier stages that one does not 'attain being' (οὐσίας τυχεῖν) by perception, from which it is now inferred that one does not 'attain truth' by perception. But one cannot know what one does not attain the truth of (186c7–d1). From this it is inferred that perception cannot be knowledge. Filling in a little more detail, Socrates adds that knowledge is not to be found in our experiences, but in our reasoning about them, because it is only in the latter that we can 'contact being and truth' (οὐσίας καὶ ἀληθείας ἅψασθαι). But it is the former—i.e. having experiences— that we call perceiving (186d2–e5).

I shall consider three main ways of interpreting this argument. The first, which I shall continue to call the 'orthodox' interpretation, is presented in different versions by Cornford (1935) and by Burnyeat (1976*b*). The second is designed to harmonize with Cooper's interpretation, and I shall include here the interpretation offered by Crombie. The third is McDowell's interpretation, which—so far as I know—exists only in McDowell's own version.[43]

(a) The 'orthodox' interpretation

According to this interpretation, the main point that Plato is making is that having experiences is one thing, and making judgements about them is another. His argument is that in order to make any judgement one must grasp the notion of being, for every judgement involves this notion. Moreover, only judgements can be true, and only what is true can be known. Thus perception never yields knowledge just because, by itself, it never yields any judgement. To

---

[43] Sayre (1983, p. 213), agrees with McDowell's translation of 186b6. But he does not offer a general interpretation of the argument.

put the point in a different way: perception is not the right *kind* of thing to be knowledge, because one perceives objects but does not perceive *that* anything. Knowledge, on the other hand, is always knowledge *that* something, since what is known must be true and what is true is always *that* something. In accordance with this conclusion, the next suggestion raised is that knowledge is belief or judgement of some kind (δόξα), because that is at least the right *kind* of thing to be knowledge, whereas perception is not.

On this interpretation, how should we understand the claim that every judgement involves being? On Cornford's account (1935, pp. 102–8), being is here to be understood as existence, and this is certainly the most natural way of taking the passage that first introduces being as a common thing. When Socrates says 'Now take a sound and a colour. First of all, you think just this about them: that they both are' (185a8–9), it is natural to suppose that he means to be indicating a *complete* thought, and is not leaving part of this thought unexpressed. In that case the thought must be that they both exist, and so Cornford's view is certainly not without support. The leading premiss to Plato's argument will then be that every judgement involves the notion of existence, perhaps in the sense that it presupposes the existence of all the terms it contains (so one cannot make the judgement without also judging that its terms exist).[44] But there is a crushing objection to this view to be drawn from 185c4–7, where Socrates tells us that not only does 'is' apply to a sound and a colour and indeed to everything whatever, but so also does 'is not'. On Cornford's account, this must mean that it is true of everything not only that it exists but also that it does not exist (and Cornford actually translates the passage in this way, p. 104). But this is evidently absurd. Existence may well be said to apply in common to everything, but we can hardly say the same of non-existence.

It therefore seems that the better version of this interpretation is that presented by Burnyeat (1976*b*, pp. 44–50), according to which the 'is' that every judgement involves is the copula. We can say of everything whatever that it *is* something-or-other and *is not* something-or-other-else. To deal with the point made in the last paragraph, that in some places it is more natural to take the 'is' in

---

[44] This thesis was at least familiar to Plato. He makes use of it in the second part of the *Parmenides* (most notably at 160b–164b) and in the *Sophist* (at 237b–241b). But he uses it to generate puzzles, and one would hesitate to say that he *endorses* it in those dialogues.

question as a complete 'is', meaning 'exists', we may reasonably say that Plato has not yet seen any need to distinguish between the two.[45] Or perhaps he is presuming, as would be quite natural for any Greek speaker, that the use of 'is' to mean 'exists' is actually an elliptical use of the copula. It is a standard Greek idiom to express 'exists' by 'is something' (ἐστί τι). In any case, the main idea behind this line of interpretation is that every judgement will contain the verb 'to be' in some form, no doubt usually as a copula.

On this interpretation it will be natural, but not strictly necessary, to put a slightly special gloss on 186b, where it is said that the mind perceives the hardness of what is hard, and the softness of what is soft, by means of touch, 'but their being, and that they both are, and their oppositeness to each other . . . are things which the mind itself tries to decide for us'. This sentence must presumably be taken to be speaking of the being of hardness and softness, and not of the being of the hard and soft things, since it is the qualities hardness and softness that are opposite to one another, and not the things that have those qualities.[46] But it is not difficult to suppose that the sentence is elliptical, and we should understand that what the mind decides is the being of hardness 'about the hard thing', or (in other words) that hardness is 'about the hard thing'. This will then be a roundabout way of saying that the mind decides, concerning the hard thing, *that it is hard*. On this account, the relevant 'is' in this passage is the copula, just as it was at 185c (referring back to the judgement 'this is salty'). One could also suppose that when being was first introduced as a common thing at 185a that sentence too was elliptical in the same way. It speaks of the thought that a colour is, and may perhaps mean this as the thought that a colour is, *about* some perceived object, i.e. the thought that that object is that colour. But it is not strictly necessary for this interpretation to regard either or both of these sentences as elliptical. The main point is that 185c shows that the 'is' that Plato is talking of does at least include the copula, and that is why it is reasonable for him to claim that every judgement contains an 'is'. But is this, in fact, a reasonable claim?

The thought that every judgement may be expressed by using the

---

[45] He appears to draw the distinction explicitly at *Sophist* 255c12–13 (but the interpretation of that passage is controversial).

[46] On the other hand it is at best *instances* of those qualities, regarded as 'experiences in the mind', that are perceived in the previous line.

word 'is' as a copula is one that is entirely familiar to us, but the reason why it is familiar to us will not explain why it should have seemed evident to Plato. It is essentially a medieval doctrine, deriving from Aristotle's claim (which the medievals accepted) that all valid reasoning could be represented in his system of syllogistic logic. Aristotle's syllogistic concerns itself with four forms of propositions, namely the forms 'All S is P', 'No S is P', 'Some S is P', and 'Some S is not P'. In all cases we can say that we have a subject-term S, a predicate-term P, and a copula. (We also have the signs of 'quality' and 'quantity' which are 'All', 'No', 'Some', and 'Some . . . not'.) It was soon realized that we must also add singular propositions, of the form '*x* is P' (where '*x*' refers to some particular thing), but evidently that does not disturb the general pattern 'subject–copula–predicate'. So, if this system of logic is really to be adequate to represent all valid reasoning, it must be possible to represent all (simple[47]) propositions as having one of these forms, and the pattern must be universal. But Plato, of course, did not have the benefit of a medieval education in logic, and so would not have had *this* reason to suppose that every judgement contains an 'is'. Would he have had any other reason?

Well, perhaps the thought is quite a natural one. On the one hand one might point to the fact that in the next section of the *Theaetetus*, where Plato is discussing the possibility of false judgement, every judgement that he considers does have 'is' as a copula. On the other hand one might point to the later *Sophist*, where he explains that every judgement contains at least one name (ὄνομα) and one verb (ῥῆμα), and gives as examples of simple judgements 'Theaetetus sits' and 'Theaetetus flies' (261d–263a).[48] These do not contain an explicit 'is', and one has only to reflect for a moment to see that there are very many simple sentences which do not contain an explicit copula. But it is also very natural to think that they can easily be re-expressed so that they do contain one. Aristotle, in what is always regarded as a very early work, remarks that there is

---

[47] It was recognized that more complex forms could be built up by combining the simple forms mentioned by means of such connectives as 'if . . . then . . .'. But this aspect of logic was by and large neglected.

[48] The *sense* of the Greek sentences cited is no doubt the sense of the English sentences 'Theaetetus is sitting' and 'Theaetetus is flying'. That is, they are straightforwardly present-tensed sentences about what Theaetetus is now doing, rather than about what he does habitually. But in Greek the straightforward present tense does not require the copula.

no difference (in Greek[49]) between saying 'a man walks' (ἄνθρωπος βαδίζει) and 'a man is walking' (ἄνθρωπός ἐστι βαδίζων), and the moral that he wished to draw was, apparently, that one can always presume that an 'is' is present (*De Interpretatione* 12, 21b9–10). It is possible, then, that this point was common ground in Plato's Academy, even as early as the time when he was writing the *Theaetetus*.[50] If so, that would satisfactorily explain why, according to the present interpretation, Plato could simply take it for granted that every judgement contains an 'is', without offering any discussion in support.

This interpretation, then, is certainly a possible one. The most notable difficulty for it that has emerged so far is probably that, if Plato is simply concerned to point to the difference between having experiences and making judgements about them, then it is somewhat strange that he should wish to stress the great trouble and difficulty that we have in learning to make judgements, and the calculations and reasonings that are required. For we can all make judgements about what we perceive, and we have no recollection of a time when this was difficult. But I have indicated (on p. 124, above) that this objection can be met. However I should also mention at this point what may well seem to be another problem for this interpretation, namely that it attributes to Plato more clarity on the nature of knowledge than the rest of our dialogue justifies. In particular, it takes him to be identifying knowledge with knowledge *that* (*savoir*), and distinguishing it from any state of mind that is directed simply at *objects*. But one has to admit that, in that case, many features of the discussion in the second part of the dialogue are highly surprising.

Without discussing this latter problem any further at present, let us first inquire what other interpretations of this argument are available.

(b) Cooper's interpretation

If we accept Cooper's interpretation of the opening stages of our argument, then we cannot suppose that its final stage claims that perception cannot furnish judgements. For the point of Cooper's

---

[49] The previous note applies also to the Greek sentence translated as 'a man walks'.

[50] The *Theaetetus*—or anyway its preface—was written after 369 BC, which is when Theaetetus died. Aristotle joined the Academy in 367 BC, as a young man of eighteen.

interpretation is that perception is capable of providing certain judgements, namely judgements which attribute to a perceived object one of the 'special' properties that are in the field of some one particular sense. What perception cannot judge of, according to him, are the 'common' properties which are not the province of any one sense. Why, then, should it be said that perception cannot 'attain truth', and for that reason is not knowledge? For presumably it *can* 'attain truth' concerning the 'special' properties that it is competent to deal with, and there seems to be no obvious reason for denying these truths the status of knowledge.

One suggestion that Cooper makes (pp. 141–4) is that these judgements of perception, though perhaps true, do not count as knowledge because they are not exercises of *skill* or *wisdom*: there is no scope here for assigning any special role to the *expert*. Now it is certainly true that when the question 'what is knowledge?' was introduced in the first place, knowledge and wisdom were equated (145d–e). It is also true that the final refutation of Protagoras was much concerned with the notion of the expert, though in fact there was very little stress upon the point that the expert has *knowledge* of what will happen (pp. 92–5 above). It is also not unreasonable to suggest that when Plato lays so much emphasis on calculations and reasonings, 'with respect to being *and usefulness*', what he mainly has in mind is the problem of attributing the common things beauty and goodness, which may well be a matter that calls for the expert. But at the same time the argument that he actually offers is one that focuses on being, and not on usefulness, goodness, or beauty. And he connects being, not with wisdom or expertise, but simply with truth. In fact the concepts of wisdom, and of the expert, simply do not occur in those passages that carry the burden of his argument here, and there is no reason to suppose that they are at all relevant to that argument. What Cooper must provide is an explanation of why perception, though it does furnish judgements, still does not reach being, and hence does not reach truth.

Cooper's proposal here is that the judgements that perception can provide do not reach being because they do not aim to tell us how things actually *are*, but only how they are perceived as being. The contrast, one might say, is essentially the same contrast between appearance and reality as lay behind the long discussion of Protagoras, which forced us to admit that the way that things appear to a man is not necessarily the same as the way they really are. In that earlier argument the point was made only in respect of judgements about the future, but we shall now extend it to judgements about the present as well. Perception can tell us how things currently appear (e.g. as hard, or as salty), but it does not 'reach being' in the sense that it does not reach reality, as opposed to mere appearance. A rather similar suggestion emerges from Crombie's discussion of our passage (1963, pp. 13–14, 26). Crombie, of course, was writing before Cooper, and does not therefore consider Cooper's claim that perception is capable of yielding some judgements. But he does suppose that Plato's view is that being and truth are to be reached only in judgements concerning what we call 'the external world', and that these go beyond the immediate deliverances of perception.

On Crombie's account, Plato's own theory of 'the external world' is the Heraclitean theory developed earlier, when pruned of some unnecessary extravagance.[51] He takes this to be an unstable amalgamation of what we now call the phenomenalist theory, according to which a physical thing just is the collection of our perceptions of it,[52] and the causal theory, according to which the physical thing is the cause of those perceptions. But for present purposes the distinction does not matter, for in either case it may be said that in order to form a judgement about a physical thing we must begin by noticing a *pattern* or *regularity* in our experiences. Whether the physical thing *is* that pattern, or *causes* that pattern, it is in any case the pattern that must be noticed if we are to have any access to it. This is the role that Crombie assigns to the reasonings and calculations, and in particular to calculations of 'things past and present in relation to things in the future' (186b1). The idea is that the judgement that what I am seeing is (say) a frog automatically commits me to many assumptions about the kinds of perception that would have been available in the past, and that will be available in the future, both to me and to others. For a frog either is or causes a particular kind of collection of perceptions, and the judgement that my present perception is one that belongs to a collection of this kind inevitably goes beyond anything that can be read off from the perception itself. That is why it is credited to reasoning. So Plato's position is this. The judgement 'that is a frog' does claim to 'attain

[51] I discuss this claim in the next chapter.
[52] It would be usual, these days, to include *potential* perceptions, as well as actual ones.

being', can be true, and may therefore be known. But it cannot be credited to perception. What one can credit to perception are judgements such as 'there is now a green and spotty appearance', and this does not even claim to 'attain being', and so is not even a candidate for being known.

But there are several strong objections to any interpretation along these lines. The first and most obvious one is the one with which I began: if perception is permitted to yield judgements—perhaps such judgements as 'there is now a green and spotty appearance'—why is it not admitted that it can 'attain truth'? In fact there is no obvious ground for saying that it cannot 'attain being', at least about those objects (one's present experiences) or those properties (the properties special to particular senses) with which it is competent to deal. And there is of course no difficulty over presenting its judgements as judgements that contain the verb 'to be'. (Cf. 'There *is* now an appearance, which *is* of such-and-such a kind'.) But even if we grant that perception does not count as 'attaining being'—because the most that it attains is 'appearing'—still if it can make judgements at all then obviously it can make true ones. Indeed, at 179c Socrates explicitly envisaged the possibility that all judgements which were strictly about one's present perceptions were bound to be true. So, on the present interpretation, the final stage of his argument is open to an obvious objection. He asks 'Is it possible that someone should attain truth if he doesn't even attain being?', and on this account the correct answer is '*Yes*, namely in his judgements of perception'. But this objection seems so obvious, that it is surely better to avoid an interpretation that leads to it if we can.

There is another potent objection, which we may put by asking how this interpretation is supposed to connect with the emphasis upon 'common things' that is Plato's own way of presenting the argument. With Crombie's version of the interpretation, one can see how it *could* be connected with Plato's point about 'common things', for physical objects are themselves 'common things'. (A frog, for example, can be seen and heard and smelled and touched and tasted.) That, it may be said, is why perception by itself cannot form any judgements about them. But if we look at Plato's own examples of 'common things' they are: being, sameness, difference, likeness, oneness or manyness, goodness, and beauty. Though it may not unreasonably be argued that a thing such as a frog *is* a 'common thing', it is quite obvious that it is not the kind of 'common thing' that Plato is in fact thinking of. In fact the argument that Crombie presents him with, contrasting particular perceptions with the physical objects that we either construct from them or more riskily infer from them, is a modern argument, familiar to readers of Locke, Berkeley, Hume, and their successors. But there is no reason to suppose that it was familiar to Plato, who—I imagine— was entering this area for the first time when he attempted to formulate a Heraclitean theory of perception. Anyway, even if it was familiar to him, it clearly is not the argument he is presenting here. In what he says himself there is no hint of a distinction between judgements that are about experiences and judgements that are about something else, namely physical objects. There is a distinction between experiences and 'common things', but these 'common things' are not either physical objects in particular or 'the external world' in general. They are concepts of a special and rather abstract kind.

I therefore abandon Crombie's version of this interpretation, and come back to Cooper, who is by no means so specific. On his account, the relevant distinction is just that between what *seems* or *appears* to be the case (φαίνεται) and what *is* the case (ἔστι), and it may perfectly well be the very same subject which is judged (by perception) to *appear* in a certain way and which is judged (by the mind, operating 'by itself') to *be* in a certain way. It may still be said that there is scope for reasoning and calculation to be what intervenes between my initial judgement as to how things appear and my final judgement as to how things are. For example, suppose that I am tasting something and that my first judgement is 'it appears to be salty'. From this I can infer 'it *is* salty' only if I have reason to suppose that the conditions are not in any relevant way abnormal. (For example, I am not suffering from a cold in the head, I have not taken a drug which produces taste-hallucinations, it is not the case that my mouth is already full of sea-water, and so on.) This latter judgement, then, can well be credited to reasoning, and it will always be needed if we are to be justified in moving from appearance to reality, even with so simple a question as the question of how something tastes.

Of course, my first objection still applies: a judgement which confines itself to how things appear may surely be true, and we have been given no reason to say that these judgements are not always true. One aspect of my objection to Crombie continues to apply: there is no hint of the required distinction between appearance and reality in the argument that Plato puts. At 185b9–c3 Plato says, as Cooper interprets him, that the tongue can tell us whether something *is* salty; he evidently does not say that it can only tell us whether something *seems* salty, and that more is required in order to deduce that it *is* salty. Again, in the crucial passage at 185e6–7, we are simply told that the mind 'considers' some things by itself, and others through the capacity of the body, but there is no hint of the view that the questions that it considers through the senses are confined to questions about how things seem, in contrast to how things are. Equally, it requires a good deal of imagination to see this view as the point behind 186b2–9, where it is said that we perceive hardness but do not perceive the being of hardness. The required distinction between being and seeming simply does not figure in the argument that Plato presents, since it never mentions seeming at all.

Finally, let us come back to the question of how this line of interpretation fits with Plato's own emphasis on being as a 'common thing'. Now that Crombie's version has been disposed of, this question is quite unanswerable, for the point is that seeming is *equally* a 'common thing'. The expression 'seems to be' or 'appears to be' (φαίνεται) can be applied to items falling under *any* of the senses, just as 'is' can. Thus the whole strategy of Plato's argument would be utterly misconceived if it aimed to distinguish seeming (which perception can judge of) from being (which it cannot) on the ground that being is a 'common thing'. On the present interpretation, the fact that being is a 'common thing' is wholly irrelevant to the point that Plato is trying to make. But this surely shows that the present interpretation cannot be correct.

I conclude that the difficulties facing an interpretation along Cooper's lines are insuperable, and it is time to consider a different line of interpretation altogether.

(c) McDowell's interpretation

McDowell's interpretation is no doubt motivated by the problem for Burnyeat's interpretation that I mentioned on p. 132. Although Plato does begin the second part of the dialogue with the suggestion that knowledge might be a special kind of belief—and in fact this remains the official topic for the whole of the rest of the dialogue—still he does not appear to be thinking of knowledge *that* in the general way that Burnyeat's interpretation would lead one to expect. On the contrary, his main concern, as we shall see, seems to be with knowing *an object*, though he does apparently identify this with knowing some special truth about the object, namely knowing what that object is. There are some qualifications to be made to this outline of the topic of the second part of the dialogue, but we need not fuss about that now. At any rate, there is a great deal of truth in it. Accordingly McDowell proposes to preserve the unity of the dialogue by taking knowledge in the same way here too, at the end of the first part of the dialogue. On his account, what Plato is claiming in this passage is that it is one thing to perceive, say, hardness, and quite a different thing to know that same item, namely hardness. For to know hardness is to know what hardness is, and that is to know the being (οὐσία) of hardness in the sense of its *essence*: it is a matter of knowing the answer to the Socratic question 'What is hardness?'

Now it must certainly be granted that there is ample precedent in Plato's earlier writings for this way of taking the concept of knowledge. It must also be granted that Plato does quite often use the word 'being' in the way that McDowell suggests. (There are clear occurrences in our dialogue at 202b5, where 'the being of an account' means 'what an account is', and at 207c1–3, where 'the being of a wagon' means 'what a wagon is'.) Moreover, the line of thought here attributed to Plato is plausible enough in itself, and it makes very good sense of his stress on the difficulty of acquiring knowledge. If, as is reasonable,[53] we suppose that he would not count someone as knowing what hardness is unless he could *say* what hardness is, i.e. could produce a suitable definition of the notion (p. 33), then indeed much thought would be needed before such knowledge could be attained. It would not in fact be correct to say that this interpretation restores a unity to the dialogue, for although it may bring the end of the first part into harmony with much of the second part, at the same time it divorces it from most of the rest of the first part. Up to now, the claim that perception is knowledge has been understood simply as the claim that perception (or appearance) is always true, and it is in this form that it has been expounded, defended, and subjected to a preliminary attack (in the refutation of Protagoras). On McDowell's account, it is not *that*

---

[53] McDowell himself remains undecided on this point (pp. 191–2), but *Republic* vii. 523e–524c, might well be cited in support.

claim about perception that is finally refuted, but a quite different claim which, in fact, has never been put forward at all. But McDowell can doubtless reply that the point of the final refutation is to argue that perception does not provide the *right kind* of truths. Perhaps it is 'always true' on those matters with which it is competent to deal—this issue is simply side-stepped, on his account—but it is denied the title of knowledge because it does not provide truths *concerning essence.*

But now let us ask what positive evidence there is in favour of this interpretation. One point I have already mentioned, namely that it makes good sense of the way that Plato stresses the difficulty of attaining knowledge. Another point that one might make is that it allows us, if we wish,[54] to adopt Cooper's interpretation of the opening stages of this discussion (section (ii), above). We can concede that perception does furnish such judgements as 'this is salty' or 'this is hard' without spoiling Plato's argument. But apart from these two points, which do not, I think, carry very much weight, there is no evidence at all. McDowell attempts to manufacture some by a controversial translation of 186b6. On his reading, Socrates says:

> The mind will perceive the hardness of what's hard by means of touch, won't it, and the softness of what's soft in the same way?

> But their being, and what they both are . . . are things which the mind itself tries to decide for us.

All interpreters would, I think, agree that the clause which he translates 'and what they both are' is epexegetic: the 'and' means 'i.e.', and the clause explains what is here meant by 'being'. But the usual translation of this clause (καὶ ὅτι ἐστὸν) is 'and *that* they both are' rather than 'and *what* they both are'. Given the usual translation, there is no suggestion anywhere in this passage that the being (οὐσία) that Plato is talking of should be understood in the somewhat special sense of 'what a thing is'.

Moreover, McDowell's translation is clearly improbable. First one should note that, if this was what Plato intended, then he was writing ungrammatically.[55] This is not a conclusive reason for

---

[54] McDowell himself does not so wish (and in fact he does not appear to know of Cooper's article).
[55] If ὅτι ἐστὸν is to be taken as the indirect question ὅ τι ἐστὸν, then the dual verb ought to have a dual subject, as in ὥ τινε ἐστὸν.

rejecting the interpretation, since Plato does sometimes write ungrammatically, but it surely creates a presumption against it. But more importantly, it is obvious that this phrase looks back to the first introduction of being as a common thing, for exactly the same phrase is used at 185a9 where it is said that the mind thinks, about a sound and a colour, *that* they both are (ὅτι ἀμφοτέρω ἐστόν). Even McDowell agrees that the relevant word (ὅτι) here means 'that' and not 'what', as is abundantly clear from the parallels in 185a11 and 185b2. But there is no warrant at all for supposing that when Plato repeats the same phrase a page later, apparently making the same point again, he has actually changed its meaning, and is now making a different point. Unless he was writing very carelessly indeed, he could not have failed to notice that no reader or listener would understand what he was doing. There is, then, no positive evidence in favour of McDowell's interpretation in this passage, and one might rather say that there is evidence against it. For when being is first introduced as a 'common thing' there is no hint that it should be understood as essence, and McDowell has to suppose that this special sense of the word somehow emerges as the argument proceeds. But the truth is that it emerges only in McDowell's commentary, and not in Plato's text.

There are, anyway, much stronger objections to this interpretation. First, if Plato had wished to argue that perception does not provide knowledge of the essences of things, would it have been a good move on his part to pin his argument on the premiss that being is a 'common thing'? In what sense is an essence a 'common thing'? One might more naturally say that what a thing is is *different* from one thing to another: what a sound is is not the same as what a colour is, and it is surely highly misleading to say that what they are is something that they have in common. The most that could be said along these lines is that the 'is' which we use in saying what something is is the same 'is' whatever thing we are talking of. But that seems merely to be a point about 'is' as a copula, and there is no reason why we should not widen the claim—as Burnyeat's interpretation does—to all uses of 'is' as a copula. That is, if the argument is genuinely about a 'common thing', then it is not about *what* a thing is but about its *being* whatever it is, and there is no reason to say that this *being* applies only when we are talking of essences. It could be extended to cover a thing's *being* anything whatever, i.e. to any truth about the thing.

Moreover, it clearly *is* taken to cover all truths whatever, when Socrates asks 'Is it possible that someone should attain truth if he doesn't even attain being?' (186c6) Just as the right answer to this question appeared to be 'yes' given Cooper's interpretation of our argument, so also it appears to be 'yes' upon McDowell's account, simply because not all truths are truths about essences. Now it might be possible to argue that one does not count as *knowing* any truth about a thing unless one first knows what that thing is, i.e. its being in the sense of its essence.[56] But (*a*) the point surely needs to be argued, for it is by no means obvious,[57] and anyway (*b*) it is not what Socrates says. His claim is that one does not 'attain' truth without 'attaining' being, and although the phrase 'to attain truth' (ἀληθείας τυχεῖν) is somewhat vague, it evidently does not mean to *know* a truth. (One might perhaps translate it 'to hit on truth'; it is quite compatible with a chance encounter.) The fact, then, that Plato's own argument claims that *every* truth involves being is just as strong an objection to McDowell's version of it as it was to Cooper's.

To meet this objection, McDowell proposes to take the notion of truth in this passage in a special way. He has assumed that the argument is concerned with knowing an object, and accordingly he supposes (p. 193) that what Plato is here talking of is the truth *of an object*, understood as the truth about what that object is. But this is a distinctly unusual way of taking the notion of truth, and no reader or listener would naturally think of it in this way. In fact, upon McDowell's interpretation, it was clearly a mistake on Plato's part to introduce the notion of truth at all. He could quite easily have said that to know any object is to know what it is, and perception cannot provide this knowledge because it cannot provide any understanding of the 'is' that is involved. There was no need for him to introduce the notion of truth, and the way that he does introduce it is, on McDowell's account, gratuitously confusing. But this is a very good ground for rejecting McDowell's account. It is, after all, McDowell who has assumed that this argument is concerned with knowing *an object*. There is nothing in the text that encourages this assumption, and there is the whole of the rest of the first part of the dialogue to discourage it.

[56] Cf., perhaps, *Meno* 71a–b.
[57] Cf., perhaps, *Meno* 87d. (It appears that we know that virtue is good without yet knowing what it is.)

I therefore conclude that McDowell's interpretation will not do. It rests mainly on a mistranslation, and apart from that there is very little evidence in its favour. We cannot suppose that being, in this argument, is *what* a thing is without falsifying the premiss that being is a common thing. And once we admit that being is *that* the thing is, there is no motivation for limiting this 'is' to statements of essence, or indeed to statements of any particular kind. The perfectly general connection that Plato draws between being and truth shows clearly enough that what he is maintaining is that perception never reaches *any* truth. Only the 'orthodox' interpretation that I began with can accommodate this fact.

(iv) *A Comment*

I cannot see any other way of interpreting our argument that falls outside the three general approaches that we have considered. And since the 'orthodox' interpretation is the only one of those that appears to be tenable, I conclude that we must accept it. Plato's claim, then, is that perception *never* reaches truth, and therefore cannot be said to be knowledge of any kind. His ground for this claim is that perception cannot provide the concepts that are required to formulate any judgement at all, true or not. Should we agree with him on this point?

I think we can agree that he is right to distinguish between the mere having of experiences and the formation of judgements, either directly about those experiences ('This is a sweet taste'), or—more usually—about the things which, as we believe, give rise to them ('This wine tastes sweet'). It seems reasonable to say that virtually all animals have experiences. Even the earthworm, we imagine, feels something when it is injured, which it is natural to call pain, for that strikes us as the obvious explanation of its writhing behaviour. But it is not very natural to suppose that worms make judgements of any kind. They do not think to themselves 'I am hurt' or 'That is a pain', and cannot be said to classify what they feel in any way. None the less, we normally do suppose that they feel it. Of course this picture may be wrong in fact. It may be that worms react to injury in the same way that many flowers react to sunshine or rain or darkness. They are affected by these changes in their environment, and 'behave' accordingly, but we do not suppose that they *experience* anything. This is because we do not suppose that they have any kind of consciousness: in Plato's language, they have no minds[58] which the disturbances in the body can penetrate to. But I think our normal view is that worms do have a consciousness of a kind, and can properly be said to *feel* some things.

Nothing, then, can count as having experiences, as we use the word 'experience',[59] unless it can also be said to be conscious of those experiences. Admittedly, when we are concerned with a subject which clearly is, in general, conscious of its experiences, we may sometimes speak of it as having experiences and perceptions of which it is not conscious. For example, when an advertisement is flashed upon the cinema screen so quickly that I am quite unaware of it, it may nevertheless be said that I must in some sense have seen it, for otherwise we could not explain why I start to show an interest in the product advertised. Or again it may be said that I must have been feeling the mosquito bite, for otherwise we could not explain why I continued to scratch it as I did, even though my attention was so riveted by the drama unfolding before me that I could honestly say, afterwards, that I was not aware of it at the time. But this kind of case must be the exception and cannot be the rule. It would be ridiculous to claim that plants are constantly perceiving or experiencing their environment, though they are never conscious of doing so. 'Perception' and 'experience' are evidently the wrong words to use in this case.

But to be conscious of something is not yet to make any judgement about it—not even to bring it under some scheme of classification—as the case of the earthworm reveals. Much the same may be said of very young children. When an infant cries because it is hungry, it is natural to suppose that it is conscious of its hunger, and is not simply reacting in the way that a plant reacts to lack of moisture. So we can say that it *feels* hungry. But of course it cannot say this, and presumably it cannot characterize its experiences (to itself) in anyway at all. For it has not yet learnt to label or classify things as being of one kind rather than another. We, of course, have mastered this skill so long ago that we cannot really imagine what it

---

[58] I ignore the fact that in Greek a plant *can* be said to have ψυχή, because it does have life, if not mind.

[59] Plato's word, πάθημα, is less specialized, and it *could* be used of the changes brought about in a plant by its environment. So he can quite reasonably distinguish, as at 179c, between the occurrence of these changes and the perception (αἴσθησις) of them, i.e. the consciousness of them, without admitting that perception includes judgement.

is like to be without it. It seems to us that our experiences come to us already labelled, sorted, and pigeon-holed, and perhaps that is the right thing to say in our case. (Perhaps, that is, the experiences that penetrate to our consciousness are already furnished with an interpretation by the time they get there.) That is why we find it difficult to form any clear conception of a creature that genuinely is conscious of experiences but yet makes no judgements at all, not even judgements that classify the experiences that it has. Nevertheless it ought to be admitted that such a creature is possible. For, despite what Kant has to say on our topic in his *Critique*, it seems to me that Plato is right to say that to have experiences is one thing and to make judgements about them is another.

But it is not at all obvious that he is right when he goes on to claim that *perception* is just the having of experiences, and does not include any judgement. It has been argued on the other side that perception is essentially a matter of forming beliefs about one's environment—beliefs that are caused in some appropriate fashion by the way that the environment impinges upon us, but do not *have* to be mediated by any experiences of which we are conscious.[60] Both of these positions may well seem rather extreme. To leave experience out of the account altogether strikes most of us as simply changing the subject, for we wish to distinguish between cases where I can say that my reason for believing that *P* is that I can perceive that *P*, and other cases where I cannot say this. On the other hand the Platonic position is that it is never proper to say that I perceive that *P*, for the judgement that *P* must always go beyond what perception can provide. But while we may agree that judgement goes beyond the mere having of experiences, there is no obvious reason to agree that it exceeds the resources of perception. On the contrary, one might reply that learning to perceive just is learning to make judgements about—or, more usually, on the basis of—one's experiences. There will be plenty of room for dispute about just which judgements do qualify as judgements *of perception*, but the fact that we do not find it very easy to draw the boundaries of this class is not a very good reason for taking Plato's line and insisting that the class is empty.

As for the reason that Plato himself provides, this depends upon a theory about the mental prerequisites to judgement which we should not accept. But I postpone a discussion of this topic—the

[60] See e.g. Armstrong, *A Materialist Theory of the Mind* (1968), ch. 10.

theory that one must be 'in touch with' the various terms of one's judgement before one can frame the judgement at all—until we have seen, in the second part of the dialogue, some of the problems which it can create.

IV

INTERIM REVIEW

1. RETROSPECT ON PART A

From the perspective of the *Timaeus* (chapter I, section 2(iv)), if knowledge is distinct from belief-or-perception, then there must be forms to be what knowledge is of; but if there is no such distinction then knowledge, if it exists at all, will simply have to be identified with belief-or-perception. Hence Ross (1953, p. 103) and Cornford (1935, *passim*) suppose that the main point of the first part of the *Theaetetus* is to explore the hypothesis that knowledge is just perception, as the only possibility that is left if there are no forms. The final conclusion, that knowledge cannot be identified with perception, then shows that this is not after all a possibility, from which we may infer that there are forms. The inference is supposed to be: if knowledge and perception are distinct, then they must also have distinct objects, so the objects of knowledge will have to be imperceptible. But it is impossible to believe that *this* is the intended moral of the *Theaetetus'* discussion of perception.

The *Theaetetus* does indeed argue that no perception can be knowledge, but it shows no tendency to infer from this that there cannot be knowledge *about* perceptible things. On the contrary, it evidently presumes that there can be. Right at the beginning Theaetetus suggests that the arts of the shoemaker and other craftsmen are forms of knowledge, and Socrates seems perfectly happy to accept these as examples (146d–e). In fact he himself makes use of the idea that it is the expert who has knowledge, in his argument against Protagoras, giving as examples the man who is proficient at the art of warfare, or medicine, or navigation (170a). There is no hint here that knowledge is confined to the forms, whereas there is a very strong suggestion that these experts know what will happen in the future (177c–179c). But the crucial point is that in the final argument of Part A we are told that knowledge is not perception but is to be found in our reasoning *about* those very things that we perceive (186c–d). This, I have argued, must mean that the judgements which we ordinarily call judgements *of perception* very often will be examples of knowledge, though in Plato's view they are not in fact examples of perception. If we may anticipate some points from the second part of the dialogue, we may add that the discussion of the wax tablet will simply assume that some things, e.g. a person, can be both known and perceived (191b–194b); and the example of knowing a person apparently continues to be accepted as a perfectly good case of knowledge all through the second part (201c, 209a–210a).[1] Moreover, the argument that is given to distinguish knowledge from mere true belief very clearly implies that an eyewitness to a crime may *know* who committed it (201b).

The *Theaetetus*, then, accepts the premiss that perception and knowledge are distinct, and in a way it accepts the point that they have different objects (since what is known is true and what is perceived is not). But it (very properly) refuses to infer that there is no knowledge *about* perceptible things. Indeed, it directly denies the claim that the *Timaeus* makes in support of this inference. The two dialogues share the premiss that knowledge must be of what is, but the *Timaeus* then adds that the verb 'is' (in its present tense) should only be used of what is permanent and unchanging. By contrast the *Theaetetus*, in its final argument about perception, simply treats it as uncontentious that we do say, of a sound heard or a colour seen, that each of them *is*. It therefore makes no scruple about allowing being to impermanent things, and is in direct conflict with the *Timaeus* on this point.

If we ask what ground the *Theaetetus* has for its more liberal attitude to being, the answer must presumably lie in its rejection of the Heraclitean theory of flux. Once we make explicit the evident truth that a thing may be changing in some respects while it yet remains stable in others, it is at once clear that the view that perceptible things are *always* changing in *all* respects is just silly. Though perceptible things do no doubt change in some ways, still they also exhibit a fair stability in other ways, and this is quite enough to allow them to be described. Plato perhaps took this to show that 'things turn out to be both changing and at rest, and it is

---

[1] Since this appears to be a case of *connaître* rather than *savoir* it does, of course, raise a question about how the two parts of the dialogue are related. I discuss this further in my final chapter.

no more correct to say that everything changes than to say that everything is at rest' (181e5–7). From this he may have inferred that there is no special significance in the fact that perceptible things do change, and in particular that this fact is not a good reason for avoiding the use of the verb 'to be' (in its present tense) when speaking of them. So it is natural to suppose that, because in the *Theaetetus* he has thought more closely about what the flux doctrine actually implies, he now feels entitled to disagree with what he had said in the *Timaeus* on whether perceptible things can properly be said to be. But in any case the two dialogues certainly do disagree, and that seems to be why they contain quite different views on what objects we can know about.

On this question of being it is fairly clear that it is the view of the *Theaetetus* that prevails in other late dialogues. Thus at *Sophist* 248e–249d Plato protests against 'the friends of the forms' that it will not do to exclude all changing things from being, and we must allow that being includes both changing and unchanging things. Again in the *Philebus* it is twice emphasized that the things that come to be do indeed come into *being* (26d8, 27b8–9), and the same point is also made at *Laws* x. 894a6–8.[2] The *Philebus*, at any rate, proceeds to draw the appropriate consequence for knowledge. Although it continues to claim that knowledge of unchanging forms is the 'purest' kind of knowledge (55d–59d), still it does not deny the title of 'knowledge' to other kinds, and indeed it argues that they too should be included in the good life (61e–62d). However the position of the *Sophist* on this latter topic is less clear. At 249b–d it argues that if there is no change anywhere then there is no knowledge, for only minds can know, and minds are changing things. But it goes on to argue that if there is change everywhere then there is equally no knowledge, since only what is stable can be known. This is *consistent* with the view that perceptible things— and, indeed, minds—do have enough stability to be known, but that point is certainly not made explicitly. And when the passage is taken in context it seems more probable that the thought is that only the unchanging forms can be known. But we may perhaps explain this by noting that what Plato is talking of here is the kind of knowledge that philosophers value (249c7–10). Anyway, the point is something of an aside, and I think it would be wrong to put too much weight upon it. The central topic of the *Sophist* is being, and

---

[2] Compare also *Parmenides* 163d1–3, and perhaps *Philebus* 54c4.

not knowledge, and on being—as we have seen—it agrees with the *Theaetetus* and not the *Timaeus*.

There is another way in which the *Theaetetus* contradicts a presupposition of the *Timaeus*, and that is in its insistence on distinguishing perception from belief (or judgement, δόξα). The *Timaeus*, like the *Republic*, runs these two together, sometimes contrasting knowledge with belief, and sometimes contrasting it with perception, as if it is making the same contrast in either case. But the *Theaetetus* firmly distinguishes them. Its first part argues that perception is not even the right *kind* of thing to compare or contrast with knowledge, since it cannot reach truth whereas knowledge must. But belief is at least the right kind of thing, for it can reach truth. Whether, in the end, knowledge can be said to *be* belief of a special kind is the topic that the second part of the dialogue promises to investigate,[3] but it has already become clear that it was a mistake to write as though belief and perception were the same thing. This too is a mistake that is avoided in other late dialogues. The topic comes up in the *Philebus*, where (as I have noted, p. 117) a perception is again thought of simply as a disturbance (πάθημα) that reaches through the body to the (conscious) mind (33d–34a), and it is added that this may be retained or recalled by the memory (34a–b). But this is contrasted with a belief concerning what one perceives, which is likened to a proposition (*logos*), either true or false, written in the book of the mind. This piece of writing may be accompanied by a picture, but the proposition and the picture are distinguished from one another (38e–39e). Thus the idea that perceptions are not true or false in themselves, though the accompanying beliefs are, is carefully maintained.[4]

In the light of these considerations, I find it impossible to believe that the *Timaeus* was written after the *Theaetetus*. On every point of disagreement that we have mentioned, other late dialogues side with the *Theaetetus* and against the *Timaeus*, with only one possible exception, and that a rather uncertain one (i.e. the *Sophist* on

---

[3] One hesitates to say that this promise is fulfilled.

[4] Ryle (1966, p. 251) supposes that the *Philebus* *defines* belief as the conjunction of perception and memory at 38b–c and 39a. But this cannot be right, both for the reasons that I have just given and because the *Philebus* at once goes on to talk of beliefs about the future, which indeed are the beliefs that it is mainly concerned with (39e ff.). (This disposes of Ryle's sole reason for dating the *Philebus* earlier than the *Theaetetus*. Other reasons have been offered by Waterfield (1980), but I do not find them at all convincing.)

knowledge and stability). But perhaps it is more telling to note that on virtually every point of disagreement it is obvious that the *Theaetetus* is right and the *Timaeus* is wrong. It *is* silly to suppose that the perceptible world is affected by such radical change that one should not use the verb 'to be' when describing it, and it *is* silly to conclude, simply on this ground, that nothing about it can be known. While one may, of course, continue to value a priori knowledge (of the forms?) more highly than empirical knowledge, it carries no conviction at all to urge that I cannot strictly be said to *know* even that something now looks white to me, just because I am not always in that state. Again, it is evidently a mistake to suppose that belief and perception are more or less the same thing. Whether or not perception can reach truth—and that may be debated—it is clearly not the case that the truths (and falsehoods) that can be believed all concern what one is perceiving. The refutation of Protagoras has made this point clearly enough, and it will be made again, in a yet more telling way, during the discussion of false belief in the second part (195e–196c). If the *Timaeus* does repeat these errors, after the *Theaetetus* has clearly exposed them as such, and presumably after the *Sophist*, *Philebus*, and *Laws* x have confirmed the viewpoint of the *Theaetetus*, then there is surely no convincing account of why Plato's thought should have developed in the way that it did. So I conclude that that cannot be the right chronology, and the *Timaeus* must precede the *Theaetetus*.

It may seem tempting to add another disagreement between the *Timaeus* and the *Theaetetus* in this way: the *Timaeus*—one might suggest—requires, whereas the *Theaetetus* refutes, that elaborate theory of becoming which the *Theaetetus* develops in its pursuit of the claim that nothing (in the perceptible world) 'is one thing just by itself'. But both these suggestions would, I think, be mistaken. In fact the *Timaeus* does not endorse this theory, and does not need to, while the *Theaetetus* does not clearly refute it in any important way.

It is true that the two dialogues do broadly agree with one another in their view of the physical mechanisms underlying perception, and it is also true that the *Timaeus* will not allow anything perceptible to be called 'this', or be said to be. But there is not very much more that they have in common, and there is no reason to say that the *Timaeus* is committed to the wilder aspects of the theory of the *Theaetetus*. For example, it has no reason to claim that a thing can only be white or sweet or hot when it is being perceived and to the thing that is perceiving it. It might perhaps be committed to saying that what we regard as a physical object, e.g. a stone, is really a collection of images of forms, images that inhere in an unchanging space. But it evidently need not accept the suggestion that these 'images of forms' are perceptions, which occur *between* places but not *at* any place. On the contrary, these aspects of the theory, so reminiscent of Berkeley's doctrine that to be is to perceive or be perceived, are surely dictated by the quite special concern of the *Theaetetus* to elaborate a theory which will conform to the claim that perception is infallible. And the *Timaeus* certainly does not make that claim.

Nor would it be right to say that the *Theaetetus* clearly refutes this theory. With good reason, the theory is corrected on the point that it has tacitly denied the existence of minds (ψυχαί), for it is really minds which perceive and not such things as eyes, ears, and tongues.[5] With equal good sense the theory's more extravagant claims about the universality of qualitative change have been rejected, but we observed at the time that these claims were never really needed. In consequence, the theory is corrected again by the observation that what we perceive can be said to be, as well as to become. But it would seem that the theory can essentially survive these corrections. After all, the theory is very similar to the theory of 'neutral monism' held by Hume and (at one time) by Russell, and their versions were free of these errors. One can therefore have a great deal of sympathy with those commentators who have claimed that the theory is not refuted in any important way.[6] All the same, there is no reason to suppose that Plato himself believed this theory to be (essentially) correct.

Cornford argues that there is (p. 49), on the ground that Plato must give what he conceives to be the *correct* account of perception if he is to argue validly that perception is not knowledge. It clearly would not do to give what he believed to be an incorrect account of perception and then to show that on *that* account perception is not knowledge. But this pays too little attention to the way that Plato's final argument is actually constructed. It clearly does not argue that

[5] Consequently it is not after all correct to say that a thing which perceives on one occasion may be perceived on another.

[6] e.g. Cornford (1935, p. 49, crediting the point to Jackson 1885), Owen (1953, p. 324), Crombie (1963, pp. 15, 25–6), McDowell (1973, esp. pp. 145, 184), White (1976, p. 161), Sayre (1983, pp. 216–18).

perception fails to reach being because perceptible objects only become, but do not be (if I may talk that way). On the contrary, it begins by claiming that these objects do have being. The controversial premiss on which it does rely is that the objects that can be perceived can be perceived by only one sense. That premiss could indeed be represented as a consequence of the elaborate theory developed earlier, but it by no means commits Plato to the whole theory,[7] and anyway I have argued that Plato's own justification for it was quite different. The view that, strictly speaking, I perceive only my own experiences does not by itself imply any theory about the nature of those objects (e.g. stones) or qualities (e.g. whiteness) that we ordinarily talk of perceiving, and it has appealed to many philosophers who have been anxious to allow for a distinction between what is (or becomes) and what appears. We may well suppose that Plato was himself in this position.

A rather different argument for the view that Plato himself endorses this theory of becoming is given by Sayre (1983, pp. 216–18), who claims that the theory contains many details that would be superfluous if its only aim were to support the thesis that perception is infallible. In his view, all that is required for this purpose is 'that objects of perceiving be generated pairwise with unique acts of perceiving (to ensure infallibility), and that those objects change so rapidly as to rule out fixed description (to preclude such objects from admitting existence)'. Among the details that he regards as irrelevant for this purpose are the claim that everything in the perceptible world is change and nothing else, the distinction between slow and fast motions, and the doctrine that such things as men and stones are collections (of slow motions, on his interpretation, p. 63 above). He therefore concludes that Plato's motive for putting in these extra claims, not required by the main structure of his argument, must be that he thinks they are correct. Part of this argument I in a sense agree with. There is no motive for introducing the 'slow motions', on Sayre's interpretation of what they are, or for calling men and stones collections of them. But just for that reason I have argued that Sayre's interpretation of them is improbable (pp. 68–70). And if we adopt the usual interpretation, by which the 'slow motions' are identified with collections of fast motions, then Sayre's argument collapses. As we have seen, a concern for the infallibility of perception certainly can motivate the claims that only

---

[7] As Crombie seems to suppose (p. 25).

changes exist, and that such things as men and stones are collections of fast motions (pp. 51–4).

We are left, then, simply with the point that this theory of the nature of the perceptible world is not in any serious way refuted. It is introduced to support the claim that perception is infallible, and that claim is certainly rejected, but the theory that supports it is merely corrected in various ways, and it appears that it could survive those corrections. This does not tell us whether Plato himself did or did not believe the theory (in its corrected version). Nevertheless, it seems to me obvious that he did not. In fact one of his 'corrections', namely the introduction of minds, cuts more deeply than we have so far admitted.

The theory that we are now envisaging claims that minds are collections of perceivings. But when Socrates does 'correct' the theory by introducing minds, his point is that we have to account somehow for the *unity* of consciousness. As he says, 'it would surely be strange if we had several senses sitting in us, as if in a wooden horse, and it wasn't the case that all those things converged on some one kind of thing, a mind or whatever one ought to call it: something with which we perceive all the perceived things by means of the senses, as if by means of instruments' (184d1–5). His point, as he continues to stress in his next sentence, is that there is some *one* thing which has *all* the various perceptions. He appears to break off before offering an argument for this point, but, as McDowell suggests (p. 189), an argument can certainly be extracted from his ensuing remarks. If it is the mind that makes judgements about its perceptions, and in particular comparisons between them, then they must all be perceptions of one and the same mind. Now the mere introduction of judgement, as something distinct from perception, already shows us that there must be something more to a mind than a mere collection of perceptions. But as we reflect further on this point it appears that it will not do simply to reform the theory by saying that a mind is a collection, not only of perceptions, but also of judgements, and no doubt other things too (e.g. emotions). Mere collections do not seem to provide for the kind of unity that Socrates is pointing to. He wants some *one* thing of which we can say that it *is conscious of* its various perceptions, it *makes* judgements and comparisons concerning them, it goes in for such *activities* as reasoning and calculating, and so on. But it is difficult to say how this unity is accounted for if the 'one thing' in question is taken to be merely the collection of all the things which, as we say, 'it' does.

Now this point about the unity of consciousness is a tricky one, and I would not claim that the line of thought just sketched is conclusive. But I would be very surprised if Plato was happy with the view that minds are mere collections. Certainly, he cannot have thought that they were collections of nothing but *perceptions*. No one who had clearly distinguished perceptions from judgements could think this. And anyway it would be quite incompatible with a view which we know that Plato never abandoned, namely that the mind (or soul, ψυχή) is immortal, and continues to exist even when the body is no longer supplying it with perceptions. So if he did hold any theory along the lines that we are considering, then it must have been a theory more like Berkeley's than like Hume's. The things that perceive cannot just be collections of their perceivings, but perhaps the things that we ordinarily take to be perceived, e.g. stones, are merely collections of our perceptions of them?

I do not know of any conclusive reason for saying that Plato did not hold such a view, at the time when he wrote the *Theaetetus*, but again I think it very unlikely that he did. On this view one would have to hold that our own bodies count as things that are perceived, and therefore as collections of perceptions. But in that case it would be distinctly misleading to say that a perception is an experience (or simply a disturbance, πάθημα) that reaches *through the body to the mind*. No sense can be attached to the idea that my experience 'travels through' a collection of experiences to get to me, especially as many of the experiences in the collection will presumably be experiences that reach *other* minds than mine. More generally, the point is that in the final stages of his argument about perception, where he is certainly arguing *in propria persona*, Plato evidently treats the distinction between body and mind in a perfectly straightforward and realistic way (as, indeed, he does everywhere else). But if he really believed that there was no more to bodies than our perceptions of them, so that bodies are in a way mind-dependent, then one would surely expect that at this crucial point in his argument he would express himself more carefully. It thus seems to me better to suppose that he never did really believe this at all.

I suggest, then, that it is not at all likely that Plato was ever himself drawn to the view that the world we live in consists of nothing but perceptions. Certainly, he cannot have held the

Humean version of this theory, which applies it to minds as well as bodies, and I think it very improbable that he held the Berkeleian version, which applies it just to bodies. He *may* possibly have held that the world we live in—excluding our own minds—could be characterized as change and nothing else, though I am sure he would wish to add something about the space that that change occurs in, as in the *Timaeus*. (He also wishes to add, in our dialogue, that this does not mean that everything is *always* changing in *all* respects.) But the point of the theory elaborated in the *Theaetetus* is that these changes, of which the world consists, are all *perceptions*, for that is what is needed to support the claim that perception is infallible. And there is no reason at all to suppose that Plato believed that.

He develops the theory mainly to draw out the implications of the claim that perception is infallible, which he—no doubt rightly—sees as the heart of Protagoras' doctrine that man is the measure of all things. This is a doctrine with which he sharply disagrees, and a large portion of the first part of the dialogue is devoted to its refutation. He is also able (by some sleight of hand) to couple the theory with the flux doctrine normally associated with Heraclitus, for he also has things to say about this doctrine. In effect what he has to say is that in earlier writings, especially the *Timaeus*, he had exaggerated it, and it will not support the conclusions that he had based upon it. In particular, he no longer wishes to say that there can be no knowledge of the perceptible world. But still, he goes on, perception by itself cannot yield this knowledge, for knowledge always involves judgement, which perception does not. This is the most important point that he wishes to make about knowledge and perception, and his argument here is meant to be independent of the (false) theory he began by elaborating. For he would wish to maintain this argument even against an opponent who did *not* begin by claiming that perception is infallible. That is, even if the judgements that we tend to credit to perception are not always true, and hence even if the theory we began by elaborating loses its rationale altogether, still Plato would wish to say that the perception is one thing and the judgement is another. And for that reason perception by itself is *never* knowledge.

This brings us to the second part of the dialogue. If to know is never just to perceive, because to perceive is not yet to judge, can we say that to know is to judge in some special way, e.g. truly?

2. TRANSITION TO PART B

In my discussion so far I have (for the most part) accepted McDowell's view that what Plato means to contrast with perception is *judgement*. But the Greek word in question (δόξα, δοξάζειν) is more naturally taken to mean *belief*, rather than *judgement*, and indeed belief is the more appropriate notion to compare and contrast with knowledge.[8]

The main distinction between belief and judgement is that a judgement is usually thought of as something that takes place at a particular time, whereas a belief is a more or less permanent state of a man. Thus if we say of someone that he judged that the world was round, we would normally be taken to be referring to some particular time when he made that judgement, whereas if we had said simply that he believed that the world was round that would have no such implication: no doubt there was a longish period during which he believed this. Belief, then, is essentially a dispositional notion, and this shows itself (in English) by the fact that we do not have an episodic present tense 'he is believing' to contrast with the habitual present tense 'he believes'. But we do have such a contrast between 'he is judging' (i.e. now) and 'he judges' (i.e. habitually). In this respect knowledge is similar to belief and not to judgement. Knowledge too is a dispositional rather than an episodic notion, and again we have no episodic present tense 'he is knowing' to contrast with 'he knows'. (Of course, this is not to deny that there are episodes of *coming* to know and *coming* to believe, but these are not episodes of knowing and believing.)

Another distinction between belief and judgement is that to call something a judgement is usually to imply that it is consciously formed, and formed on the basis of evidence: one weighs the considerations on one side, and on the other, and eventually one comes to a decision, which is one's judgement. But there is no oddity in the suggestion that a good many beliefs were never consciously formed in this way: rather, one just finds oneself believing this or that, without ever having been through any process of working it out. In this too knowledge is, I think, similar to belief rather than judgement. Admittedly philosophers have often claimed that nothing could count as knowledge unless one has evidence for it, but this is a controversial claim,[9] and it surely is not built into the notion of knowledge. Certainly there is no reason to suppose that if I now know that *P* then there must have been a time when I consciously formed the judgement that *P*.

Knowledge, then, seems more naturally compared with belief than with judgement. On the other hand, McDowell certainly has a reason for preferring his translation 'judgement', for when Plato describes how he himself understands the notion, at 189e–190a (quoted above, p. 124), what he is actually describing does seem to be judgement rather than belief. It would be possible to claim (as several have) that what he is *trying* to describe is belief, only he has not got the description quite right. But it is surely much better to say that the rather fine distinctions that I have been drawing introduce more precision than one would expect to find in Plato's text. His word δόξα covers both belief and judgement indiscriminately, and I shall therefore feel free to paraphrase what he says sometimes with 'belief', sometimes with McDowell's 'judgement', and sometimes simply with 'thought'. It will not matter at all to the argument. Such distinctions as there may be between 'to believe that *P*', 'to judge that *P*', and 'to think that *P*' are entirely irrelevant to what Plato has to say about the suggestion that knowledge is belief, or judgement, or thought, of some special kind.

The broad structure of the second part of the dialogue is this. We begin with the suggestion that knowledge is to be found in the region of what the mind does 'by itself', and that that is belief (187a). But clearly knowledge and belief cannot just be identified, since what is believed may be false, while what is known has to be true. At best, then, knowledge is true belief (187b). This leads into the first main section of the discussion, where it is asked how there can be any belief which is *not* true (187c–200d). Returning to the main thread at 200d, it is very briefly argued that knowledge must after all be something more than mere true belief, and the suggestion is raised that knowledge is true belief with an 'account' (λόγος) added to it. The examination of this suggestion then runs to the end of the dialogue (201c–210a). But in the end it is concluded that there is no way of understanding an 'account' which would make the

---

[9] And apparently an untenable one (pp. 238–9 below).

suggestion correct, and no further suggestions are forthcoming. So the dialogue ends without an answer to the question with which it began.

PART B

KNOWLEDGE AND BELIEF

V

FALSE BELIEF

The problem of how it is possible for anyone to believe falsely is introduced at 187d as an old and familiar puzzle: Socrates tells us that it has often bothered him on other occasions. In fact it has already been mentioned earlier in this dialogue, as one of the defences that Protagoras might rely upon (167a6–b1), and Plato's readers have indeed met it before.[1] But whereas on previous occasions Plato has been content to dismiss it as a mere sophistry, in our dialogue the topic receives an extended treatment. Although a good portion of Part A has already been devoted to arguing against the Protagorean claim that all beliefs are true, still we now set about investigating 'in a different way' (187d7–8) some puzzles seeming to show that no belief can in fact be false. (The point, of course, is that they are different puzzles, not that the same Protagorean argument is now to be treated once more, but in a different fashion.)

The discussion naturally divides into five sections. The first presents a problem for false belief which is actually not the old familiar puzzle at all, but an entirely new one (187e–188c). But unfortunately the presentation is so brief that it is difficult to see, at this stage, just what the new puzzle is. The second then presents the familiar puzzle, but in a somewhat unexpected way, as if it were a kind of *alternative* to the first puzzle (188d–189b). The third section, on 'other-judging' (ἀλλοδοξία), begins as a solution to the second and familiar puzzle—though only a partial solution, it would seem —but Socrates then argues that it too runs into a difficulty (189c– 191a). It is clear that this difficulty is at least strongly related to the new puzzle that we began with, but the precise interpretation of the text is here controversial. The fourth section then gives us the most elaborate attempt at a solution to the new puzzle, introducing the idea that the mind contains a wax tablet as its memory, and this does appear to get somewhere with the problem, but not—it seems—far

---

[1] *Euthydemus* 284b–287c, *Cratylus* 429d, and one might be tempted to add *Republic* v. 478b–c, where Plato rashly tries to use the puzzle to his own advantage.

enough (191b–195c). Finally we have a further attempt at a solution, with the mind viewed now as containing an aviary, but this again proves to be unsuccessful (197b–200c). So in the end Plato's new problem about belief is not resolved.

I shall first run through the five sections in order, noting a few points in passing, but mainly trying to settle difficulties of interpretation. The major task here is to see just what Plato's new problem is. I then add a discussion of why it is a problem for him, and of how this ostensible 'digression' on false belief relates to our main topic 'What is knowledge?'. Socrates apparently hints at 187e1–2 that it will have some contribution to make.

1. FIRST PUZZLE: KNOWING WHAT ONE IS THINKING OF (187e–188c)

Socrates opens with the claim that, when one has any belief, one must either know or not know the things that one's belief is about. It seems to be assumed that, at any rate in the case of a false belief, there will always be two such things, and the example we are offered is the false belief that Socrates is Theaetetus, with Socrates and Theaetetus counted as the two things that the belief is about. Then the argument is simply that one cannot have the belief at all unless one knows Socrates and knows Theaetetus, but if one does know them both then one could not make such a mistake.

It is not at all clear *why* we are supposed to agree that, if one knows both the items concerned, then the mistake would be impossible. A simple explanation of the argument, which has appealed to some commentators,[2] is that the notion of knowing a thing is being used ambiguously, first for knowing *something* about the thing, and then for knowing *everything* about it. For it is rather plausible to say that I cannot have any belief about Socrates unless I know *something* about him, and if we confuse this with knowing *everything* about him then it will seem that I cannot make mistakes about him at all. A variant on this explanation starts from the observation that Plato's example here is an identity-judgement, and supposes that Plato means to confine his attention to judgements of

---

[2] e.g. Fine (1979*a*, p. 72). Cf. Crombie (1963, p. 111).

this kind.[3] Then the explanation is that Plato equates knowing Socrates with knowing who Socrates is, and takes this to be a matter of knowing everything about his *identity*, i.e. of knowing the truth-values of all identity-statements concerning him.[4] But all that we can say at this stage is that our text does not suggest any explanation along these lines. The trouble is that it does not seem to suggest any explanation at all. It simply claims that if I do know both Socrates and Theaetetus then I cannot believe that Socrates is Theaetetus, and leaves it at that.

As the discussion proceeds we shall find that more light is shed on just what Plato's new puzzle is, but for the moment it seems best to leave the question open. We should also leave open the question of whether Plato means to be restricting his attention to identity-statements, for certainly he does not say so. But it is perhaps worth recalling at this stage a more modern problem about identity-statements, which appears to be somewhat similar.[5] The principle known as Leibniz's Law (p. 73) tells us that if *a* and *b* are the same thing then whatever is true of *a* must also be true of *b*. Now, whatever *a* may be, it will always be a trivial and uninteresting truth that *a* is *a*. But then can we not infer, by Leibniz's Law, that if *a* is *b* then it must equally be a trivial and uninteresting truth that *a* is *b*? (The inference treats 'it is a trivial and uninteresting truth that *a* is . . .' as something that is true of *a*, and so ought to be true of *b* too, if *a* is *b*.) To modify the example slightly, since everyone who knows *a* believes that *a* is *a*, ought it not to follow that if *a* is *b* then everyone who knows *a* believes that *a* is *b*? Here, then, we have a little argument that seems to show, paradoxically, that every true identity-statement must be believed. Plato's problem (if indeed it is a problem about identity-statements) seems to be the converse of this, for he argues rather that no false identity-statement can be believed. His grounds have not yet become clear, but perhaps it is not unreasonable to conjecture that the two puzzles are related?[6] But we must read on to find out.

---

[3] *This* supposition is very popular, e.g. Cornford (1935, p. 113), Ackrill (1966, p. 385), Sayre (1969, p. 106), Lewis (1973, p. 124), McDowell (1973, p. 195), White (1976, p. 164), and many others.

[4] McDowell (pp. 196–7).

[5] The *loci classici* are Frege's 'On Sense and Reference' and Russell's 'On Denoting'.

[6] Lewis (1973, pp. 130–3) relies on the similarity between the two puzzles, but gets into some trouble over the difference between them. See further note 27 below.

Before we do, it is worth noting one more point. Plato's puzzle—whatever it is—makes use of the verb 'to know' with a direct object (French *connaître*). But if the moral of the first part of the dialogue was supposed to be that knowledge differs from perception, because perception takes a direct object whereas knowledge is always knowledge *that* something-or-other (French *savoir*), then the second part of the dialogue opens by ignoring the result of the first part. We may also put the point this way. This second part began with the idea that knowledge is similar to belief, rather than perception, since belief is at least capable of reaching truth, and knowledge always reaches truth. Now the verb 'to believe' (or 'to judge' or 'to think') does not take a direct object construction,[7] so it is right to say that what is believed is always either true or false, and of course what is truly believed must be true. That is the point of the suggestion that knowledge might just be true belief, for it also seems right to say that what is known must be true. But as soon as this suggestion is introduced we at once become involved in a 'digression' which makes use of the notion of knowing Socrates. And Socrates is not a truth. Is not this very odd?

In fact, there is something even odder. I said a moment ago that the verb 'to believe' does not take a direct object construction, and I would maintain that that is equally true of the Greek verb in question (δοξάζειν).[8] But Plato here writes as if it does. He uses the verb with a direct object construction in this passage at 188a7–8, and often hereafter. McDowell translates this use as 'to have a thing in one's judgement', and in my summary above I spoke of the things that a belief is *about*. But Plato's own idiom is distinctly unusual. We can, perhaps, approach something of its flavour with the verb 'to think': it is as if he had said 'When one is thinking that Socrates is Theaetetus, one must be thinking Socrates and one must be thinking Theaetetus'. One can see—at least roughly—what such a sentence must mean, but it is a very odd form of expression. Are we supposed to notice that something rather strange is going on? But I shall leave this question hanging until we have worked through to the end of the comparison between knowledge and belief.

---

[7] Of course we can speak (in English) of believing a person, in the sense of believing what he says. I ignore this.

[8] Again there is an irrelevant use. One can be said (in Greek) to δοξάζειν a person, where this means that one thinks *well* of him.

2. SECOND PUZZLE: BELIEVING WHAT IS NOT
(188d–189b)

It is a standard Greek idiom that to believe falsely is to believe what is not. (*We* naturally fill in '. . . what is not *the case*', or something similar.) The old and familiar problem of false belief is the one based on this idiom, and it is this version of the problem that is given very full treatment later in the *Sophist*, but here it gets only a short hearing. Nevertheless it should be noted that we are here given two distinct versions of the puzzle, simultaneously presented. On one version, to believe falsely is simply to believe[9] what is not 'just by itself'; on the other version, it is to believe what is not 'about one of the things which are' (188d9–10, 189b1–2). Plato offers the same argument in either case, but in fact they need separate consideration.

Let us take first the simpler version, which is the really familiar form of this puzzle, according to which to believe falsely is simply to believe what is not (the case). Then the argument is just that there is no such thing as what is not (the case); it is a mere nonentity. But just as you cannot perceive a nonentity, so equally you cannot believe one either, for it simply is not there to be believed, or perceived, or anything else.

We may find it natural to reply to this argument by distinguishing on the one hand propositions and on the other hand facts, situations, states of affairs, and so on. Then we shall say that the things that are believed are propositions, not facts or states of affairs. Admittedly, there are no such things as 'false facts', but we shall insist that there are such things as false propositions, and so a false belief is not directed at a non-existent. Now I do not quarrel with this way of approaching the problem, but it should be noted that we can state the problem in slightly different terms, which apparently resist this solution. We can do this in English by speaking of

---

[9] McDowell wishes to exclude my first version from consideration and for that reason translates δοξάζειν throughout this section as 'to have in one's judgements' rather than simply 'to judge' (or 'believe'). His reasons are that the initial statement at 188d3 mentions only the second version, and that the solution offered at 189c1–3 applies only to the second version. But (*a*) I do not believe Plato could have expected his audience to interpret δοξάζειν in that unusual sense, when the usual sense gives a perfectly satisfactory reading; (*b*) McDowell's own account of the distinction which I say introduces two versions (p. 199) seems to me quite unconvincing; and (*c*) it is of course my first version that *is* the *familiar* version of this puzzle. How could Plato think it reasonable not even to mention it?

believing *in* something, rather than believing something. For suppose I believe that Socrates and Theaetetus are actually the same person (despite what Plato says). Then we can also describe the situation by saying that I believe *in* the identity of Socrates and Theaetetus. But since Socrates is not in fact the same person as Theaetetus, there is not actually such a thing as the identity of Socrates and Theaetetus: this alleged case of identity does not exist. So, the argument goes on, I seem to be believing in a non-existent thing. But non-existent things simply are not 'things' at all, and there is *no thing* that I believe in, which apparently implies that I believe in nothing. But, surely, a belief in nothing is not a belief at all?

When the argument is put in this way, it seems to me that there is only one reply, which is to insist that it *is* possible to believe in non-existent things. Perhaps it is right to say that non-existent things cannot be seen, touched, or in any other way perceived. (Of course the point may be disputed—consider Macbeth and his dagger—but let us let that pass.) But we began this part of the dialogue by remarking that perception and belief were not the same, and this is just one of their differences. It arises because the kinds of things that are believed in (in the relevant sense[10]) are not simple physical objects (or sense-data) but a special kind of *complex* thing, to be named by 'nominalizing' a whole sentence. (The idea is that what we describe as a belief *that P* can often be redescribed as a belief *in* something, by turning the whole sentence '*P*' into a complex noun-phrase. Thus to believe *that* snow is white is to believe *in* the whiteness of snow; to believe *that* God's in his heaven and all's right with the world is to believe *in* the heavenly location of God and the rightness of all that pertains to the world; and so on. Admittedly, when we are faced with more complicated sentences, the contortions required to create the appropriate noun-phrase can be quite daunting, but with simple sentences there is usually no problem.) Anyway, the point is that it is 'complex things' of this kind that are believed in, and they can be believed in whether or not they exist.

It is clear that Plato never gives this answer to our paradox, either

[10] Of course one can *also* speak of believing in a person (in the sense of believing that he is honest, reliable, trustworthy, etc.), or of believing in a thing of any kind— e.g. God, democracy—in the sense of believing that it does exist, or ought to exist, or is of fundamental importance, or something of the sort. But that is not the usage we are here concerned with.

in this dialogue or later in the *Sophist*.[11] Although the present version of the paradox, in terms of sheer non-existence, is apparently stated again in the *Sophist* (e.g. at 237a–239c), still if Plato has a way of disarming it there, it is not the way I have suggested. Indeed, one's first impression[12] of the *Sophist* is that it has nothing to say about this version of the paradox, and instead considers only my second version. But whether or not that is the right thing to say about the *Sophist*, it evidently is the right thing to say about the *Theaetetus*. Let us come, then, to the second version.

If I believe something false about an object *x*, then we can equally say that I believe about *x* what is not (the case) about *x*. But now it is no longer plausible to take not being as equivalent to not existing. No doubt what I believe about *x* is something that is not (the case) *about x*, but it obviously does not follow from this that it is not (the case) *at all*, and so is a mere nonentity. (That is, something that is not (the case) about *x* may yet be (the case) about other things.) To guard against this fallacy, then, we must be careful to keep in the phrase 'about *x*' all through the argument, and it may be noted that when we do this the parallel with perception is a little surprising. It is claimed that we cannot perceive about *x* something that is not (the case) about *x*, and this is already doubtful if perception is still being identified with appearance (p. 42). But even if it is not, still there seems to be an implication that we *can* perceive about *x* something that *is* (the case) about *x*, which is apparently an admission that perception can 'attain being'. So again it seems that the conclusion of the first part of the dialogue is being ignored. But let us set this aside to consider the argument that is actually offered about belief.

The argument is simply this. Suppose I believe about *x* what is not (the case) about *x*. Nevertheless, I do believe something about *x*, which is to say that I believe some one thing about *x*, and hence a thing that is about *x*. That apparently shows that whatever I believe about *x* must in fact be a thing that is (the case) about *x*. To see what is wrong with this argument, we have only to try restoring the bracketed expression '(the case)' all the way through. No doubt, I believe something about *x*, but this cannot be glossed as 'I believe something the case about *x*'. Rather, we must say that I believe

---

[11] He may at one stage have *considered* it. The line of thought developed at *Parmenides* 160b–e, though not directly on our problem, would be quite congenial to this way of resolving it.

[12] For a second impression, see p. 195 below.

something *to be* the case about *x*, or more clearly that there is something such that I believe that it is (the case) about *x*. So the only conclusion that follows is that I believe a thing that is *to be* the case about *x*, or more clearly that there is a thing that is (full stop), such that I believe that it is (the case) about *x*. But we can agree to this, and quite consistently add that this thing that is (full stop), which I believe to be (the case) about *x*, is not actually (the case) about *x*. To put the point succinctly, the 'being' that can be argued to apply to what I believe about *x* is only 'being (full stop)' and not 'being (the case) *about x*'. So this version of the paradox, unlike the first version, is straightforwardly fallacious: it simply trades on a confusion between a thing that is (full stop), and a thing that is (the case) about *x*.

It would be over-charitable to say that Plato gives us a clear diagnosis of this confusion, but nevertheless he does put his finger on the important point. For his next suggestion is that one may believe one thing about *x*, even when it is really something else that is (the case) about *x*, if one somehow mistakes the one for the other. But he is careful to point out that *both* what one believes about *x and* what is the case about *x* may still be things that are.[13] Only one of them is (the case) *about x*, but both may be things that are (full stop).[14] This is fairly clearly an anticipation of the solution later put, with more elaboration, in the *Sophist* (261c–263e). But in our dialogue it is not the end of the matter, because in the next section this solution is made to lead back to the original puzzle over whether one *knows* the things one is thinking of. (That puzzle is never mentioned in the *Sophist*.)

Before we move on, it is worth noting a strange feature of Plato's discussion so far. Socrates begins with a puzzle about whether, when one has a false belief, one knows the items that the belief is about. Without resolving this, he suggests that we *instead* adopt the view that a false belief is a matter of believing what is not, and goes on to develop a puzzle for this view. But the second puzzle is not an *alternative* to the first: we would not escape the first simply by resolving the second, and we would not escape the second simply by

[13] This comment assumes what I take to be the orthodox interpretation of 189b12–c4. I shall recommend a slightly different interpretation below (pp. 172–3), but it will not affect the present point.

[14] Does this mean that both predicates are (the case) about something-or-other? If so, we shall have a problem about how it is possible to believe that *x* is a unicorn, since it is not (the case) about anything that it is a unicorn.

resolving the first. Why does Plato seem to suggest that we would? I have no answer to this question, except to observe that in our dialogue the point is of no importance. For it is clear that our dialogue is mainly concerned with the first puzzle, and although we are offered a solution of (one version of) the second puzzle, it is soon made clear that the first puzzle is still outstanding, and that puzzle is the point of interest henceforth. So Plato does not really suppose that, if we can solve one puzzle about false belief, then we are entitled to disregard any others, although his presentation rather suggests this. But is he perhaps inclined to think that, if we can solve one version of the puzzle about believing what is not, then we may disregard the other? I regard that as implausible, but it is really a question for the interpretation of the *Sophist*, and I shall say no more about it here.[15]

3. RETURN TO THE FIRST PUZZLE: 'OTHER-JUDGING' (189c–191a)[16]

The idea that a false belief arises through mistakenly exchanging one thing for another, though both are 'things which are', is at once illustrated by Theaetetus in this way: it happens 'whenever someone has in his judgement ugly instead of beautiful, or beautiful instead of ugly' (189c6). This appears to be a perfectly straight-forward suggestion: when considering some object *x* one may think that *x* is ugly when the truth of the matter is that *x* is beautiful, and in that case one has mistakenly exchanged being ugly for being beautiful. But if this is how Theaetetus takes it, it appears that he did not listen closely enough to Socrates' own way of putting the suggestion, which was that false judgement occurs 'when someone makes an interchange in his thinking and *affirms that* one of the things which are is another of the things which are' (189c1–2).[17] Presumably Theaetetus is not supposing that when I say 'ugly' where I should have said 'beautiful' I am *affirming that* being beautiful is being ugly. Yet it appears that Socrates does stick to his

[15] For my brief (and unargued) view of the *Sophist* on this issue, see p. 195.

[16] The word 'other-judging' (ἀλλοδοξία) is coined by Plato specially for this occasion.

[17] Although the sentence is slightly odd, I think that McDowell's translation is fair. The Greek is: ὅταν τίς τι τῶν ὄντων ἄλλο αὖ τῶν ὄντων ἀνταλλαξάμενος τῇ διανοίᾳ φῇ εἶναι.

own description of the situation, and it is this description that he then argues to be absurd.

In detail, it goes like this. Socrates first restates the thesis to be discussed as the thesis that 'it's possible to put something in one's thoughts as being something else, not the thing it is' (189d7–8). Here the phrase 'as being something else' must be taken as describing how one is thinking of the thing in question: for example, one is thinking of the beautiful as ugly. At this point it seems that Theaetetus should have objected that when I say 'ugly' where I should have said 'beautiful' I am not thinking of the beautiful at all: in this situation, being beautiful is not something that I do 'put into my thoughts'. Curiously, Socrates seems deliberately to offer him the opportunity of making just this objection, for he goes on 'Now when someone's thought does that, isn't it necessary that it should be thinking either both the things or one of them?' (189e1–2). We hope that Theaetetus will reply 'Yes, *one* of them: the man is thinking of ugliness but not of beauty'. But this is not how he does reply. Instead he at once concedes that both are being thought of, and the option of saying that only one of the exchanged terms occurs in the thought is never seriously considered. (It is mentioned again, only to be at once dismissed as impossible, at 190d7–10.) Consequently Socrates has no difficulty in demonstrating the absurdity of the situation. Thinking, he maintains, is a matter of saying things to oneself, so one who thinks that one thing is another is saying to himself that the one is the other. But this is not something we ever do. No one ever does say to himself that the beautiful is ugly, that the odd is even, that the ox is a horse, or that 2 is 1.

Ackrill's interpretation of this discussion (1966, pp. 388–9) acquits Socrates of any fallacy by supposing that the whole passage is only concerned with judgements that explicitly identify two predicate-terms which are in fact distinct. On his account of the matter, in the first statement of the problem we were considering only identity-statements whose terms are ordinary names, such as 'Socrates' and 'Theaetetus', and Plato genuinely (but mistakenly) thinks that one cannot believe any such statement if it is false. Similarly, in the present passage we are again considering only a special kind of statement, viz. identity-statements whose terms refer to properties, such as being ugly and being beautiful, and again Plato genuinely thinks that no statement of this kind can be believed if it is false. (Somewhat rashly, Ackrill suggests that on this occasion Plato is right, but presumably one can wrongly believe that being beautiful is the same as being brightly coloured.[18]) So, as Ackrill sees the situation (p. 395), two rather special cases where Plato genuinely thinks that we cannot make a mistake are mentioned first, as a preliminary to the discussion of the wax tablet, which will explain how in other cases we can after all make mistakes. (Cornford takes a somewhat similar line.)

On Ackrill's account, Plato does not see the results that he has reached so far as at all paradoxical, but takes them to be perfectly correct. But this is highly implausible. Even if we grant, for the sake of argument, that in the first statement of his puzzle Plato is limiting his attention to identity-statements, still to make his interpretation at all plausible Ackrill has to add a further restriction, namely that the terms of these identity-statements must always be proper names in the ordinary sense (pp. 386–7). But there is nothing in the text that suggests this, and there is something in the text that denies it. When Socrates is introducing the wax tablet at 191a–b, he points out that we obviously can believe that the man in the distance is Socrates, when he is not, *and* he treats this as something that was not permitted by his first statement of the puzzle (191a8). But 'the man in the distance' is not a proper name, and an argument which is taken to show that this false belief is impossible is certainly paradoxical. Moreover, the present passage on other-judging is surely meant to be paradoxical too. For it begins with the idea that *all* false belief can be described as 'other-judging' (189b12–c2), and it proceeds to an illustration which at least seems to cover false beliefs that some object is ugly (189c5–7). But these are not false beliefs of the special type that Ackrill thinks are here being discussed. Similarly, when Socrates concludes that after all it will not do to define false belief as 'other-judging' (190e1–2), he is presuming that the definition would seem plausible at a first glance. But on Ackrill's account of the very special type of belief that 'other-judging' is, no one in his senses would wish to say that all false belief is of this kind.

Consequently it has seemed more appealing to modify Ackrill's account along these lines. We shall say that it is initially plausible to regard all false belief as 'other-judging', taking this to be having one predicate in one's thoughts where one should have had another.

[18] *Phaedo* 100d. (I take the example from Fine (1979*a*, p. 74). Of course one might also add the possibility of believing that being a group of 7+5 things is the same as being a group of 11 things (195e–196b).)

Then Socrates' argument should be taken as having two stages: first he argues that one cannot be in this position without also judging that the one predicate-term is the other, and then he applies the argument he began with to show that this latter is impossible. In other words, a false belief is not itself a belief of the special Ackrillian kind, identifying two distinct predicate-terms, but Socrates' claim is that it always *involves* such a belief. (This is the interpretation adopted by Lewis (1973, pp. 135–43) and by McDowell (1973, pp. 203–4).) In that case, the crucial point will be to see *how* Socrates argues that saying 'ugly' where one should have said 'beautiful' does involve the belief that to be ugly is the same as to be beautiful, for it certainly does not seem to. But when one looks closely at the passage to find such an argument, it simply is not there. On the face of it, Socrates just assumes this, right from the start, and there is no explanation of why we should be expected to accept it. But this is very unsatisfying. It is time, then, to turn to a different interpretation.

The interpretations so far have supposed that our passage is *somehow* concerned with judgements that identify two distinct predicate-terms. But Plato's language does not compel this interpretation, for the general formula that he uses, viz. 'thinking that one thing is another', need not be intended to focus on identity-judgements at all.[19] Moreover, we have been given a strong hint that the judgements now under consideration are subject–predicate judgements, for example the judgement that Theaetetus is ugly. (This is a false judgement, as 185e tells us.) With the previous interpretation, the problem has been to see how this judgement can reasonably be said to 'involve' in some way the thought of being beautiful, for it certainly does not seem to. But there is surely an alternative suggestion, which is that it does not involve the thought of *being beautiful*, but rather the thought of *a beautiful thing*. That is, on Plato's principles one evidently cannot think that Theaetetus is ugly without thinking of Theaetetus. By hypothesis, Theaetetus is a beautiful thing. Hence, in having this thought, one *is* thinking of a beautiful thing. Of course, one is not thinking of it *as* beautiful, but rather as ugly. So the situation is that one is thinking of one thing, a beautiful thing, *as* another, i.e. as ugly (—or, if preferred, as an ugly thing). There is no reason why the formula 'thinking of one thing as another' should not be intended to cover this kind of case, and if it

<hr>

[19] The point is noticed by Cornford (1935), p. 113.

does then it certainly covers a wide range of false judgements, and not just those of the special Ackrillian kind.[20]

On this account, the opening characterization of 'other-judging' at 189b12–c2 needs reinterpreting. 'Other-judging' is said to be 'affirming that one of the things which are is another of the things which are', and we now understand this as, e.g. affirming that a beautiful thing is ugly. The point that both the items concerned are 'things which are' is now taken as a point about both the subject-term (a beautiful thing) and the predicate-term (being ugly). Now 'other-judging' is said to come about 'by an interchange in one's thinking', and we previously took it that the items interchanged were the same two items as the two which are said to be 'things which are', but that now seems improbable. It is very odd to think of this judgement as arising through an interchange of subject-term and predicate-term, and much more reasonable to hang on to the view that the interchange is between the two predicates 'ugly' and 'beautiful'. Theaetetus' next remark strongly confirms this. So the point will be that as a *result* of interchanging the two predicates one ends up thinking of the subject as something other than what it is, and it is this latter which is the 'other-judgement'. The interchange itself is now no longer regarded as a thought or judgement at all, and Socrates is therefore acquitted from the fallacy with which we charged him.

What, then, does Socrates find puzzling about 'other-judgement', as we are now construing it? Well, the argument can be put, very neatly and simply, like this. Suppose that

(i) I think that Theaetetus is ugly.

Nevertheless the fact is that

(ii) Theaetetus is a beautiful thing.

Then apparently we must infer

(iii) I think that a beautiful thing is ugly.

But, Socrates protests, one cannot think that. For to think something is to say it to oneself, and nobody could say to himself 'a beautiful thing is ugly'. Once we turn our attention to subject-term

---

[20] Williams, who offers this interpretation of the argument, claims that the formula can be so manipulated that it will cover *all* false judgements without any exception (1972, p. 299). But I would rather say that, as often, Plato is simply concentrating on simple cases, and has given no thought to Williams's complexities.

and predicate-term, rather than to two predicate-terms, the argument emerges as a very pretty fallacy that does threaten to undermine false belief entirely.[21]

The reason why the argument is a fallacy is, of course, that the crucial sentence (iii) is ambiguous. Under one interpretation it is perfectly fair to conclude that I am thinking that a beautiful thing is ugly, i.e. where this is taken to be equivalent to 'There is a beautiful thing such that I am thinking that *it* is ugly'. So understood, the sentence reports what kind of thing I am thinking of, but does not say *how* I am thinking of it; in particular, it does not imply that I am thinking of the thing *as* a beautiful thing. In the jargon, this is called a *de re* construction, or equivalently we may say that the phrase 'a beautiful thing' is to be taken 'transparently' and not 'opaquely', or 'extensionally' and not 'intensionally'. The point is that the phrase is *not* to be taken as giving part of the content of my belief, but simply as indicating which object—or which kind of object—the belief is about. But the same sentence can also be differently interpreted, as stating that I am saying to myself 'A beautiful thing is ugly'. Whether this means that I am saying to myself that there is *some* beautiful thing that is ugly, or that *any* beautiful thing is ugly, does not matter here. The point is that the sentence is now being interpreted as giving the whole content of my thought. In the jargon, this is a *de dicto* construction, or equivalently the phrase 'a beautiful thing' is now being taken 'opaquely' or 'intensionally'. That simply means that it is now a part of what I am saying to myself. The diagnosis, then, is that under the second interpretation the crucial sentence does state an absurdity but does not follow from the premisses, whereas under the first interpretation it does follow from the premisses but does not state an absurdity. So the fallacy consists in giving it first one interpretation and then another.

It should be noted that, in drawing this distinction, we are not

---

[21] If this interpretation is right, then McDowell's translation must be corrected, for it simply assumes that we have two predicate-terms under consideration throughout. Thus McDowell represents the absurd statements which one never does believe as stating that beautiful is ugly, that odd is even, that ox is horse, and so on. But the Greek has a definite article throughout (e.g. τὸ καλὸν αἰσχρόν) and so is literally rendered '*the* beautiful is ugly', '*the* ox is (a) horse', and so on. That sentence can certainly play the ambiguous role that my reconstruction assigns to 'a beautiful thing is ugly'. (In the *de re* interpretation, I am thinking, of *the* beautiful thing in question, that it is ugly; in the *de dicto* interpretation, either I am thinking that *whatever* is beautiful is ugly, or—perhaps better—we understand a demonstrative, and I am thinking that *that* beautiful thing is ugly.)

denying Socrates' premiss that thinking is always a matter of saying things to oneself. One might reasonably take this premiss as implying that any thought can be reported in a *de dicto* construction, simply by giving, in the report, the same words as the thinker is saying to himself. That is not at issue here. In the sense in which it is perfectly true to say that I am thinking that a beautiful thing is ugly, this reports a thought of mine using a *de re* construction and not a *de dicto* one. But presumably the same thought can be reported in a *de dicto* way, simply by saying 'I think that Theaetetus is ugly'. The premiss that whatever can be thought can be said, and that thinking it is a matter of saying it to oneself, may appear rather doubtful when one examines it more closely.[22] But for the purposes of the present argument we may happily accept it. What we should not accept is the more deeply buried premiss that *any* way of reporting my thoughts will be a report of what I am saying to myself, for a *de re* report does not do this.

Now it may be objected: surely this fallacy is much too obvious? Why should Plato think it worthwhile to present a puzzle about belief that is based on it, when the diagnosis is so simple? Besides, it may be added, the present passage on 'other-judging' is surely meant to be a way of reinstating the puzzle we first began with, but that first puzzle does not seem to be anything to do with a confusion between *de re* and *de dicto* ways of reporting a belief. I postpone the second part of this objection until we have seen the puzzle in action again, at the end of the discussion of the wax tablet (pp. 183–5). But in reply to the first part it is worth pointing out here that the diagnosis is not really so simple. The point that has to be recognized is that to obtain an account of what I am thinking it is not good enough just to say which objects I am thinking of, for it will also make a difference *how* I am thinking of them, or *as being* what (e.g. as Theaetetus, or as a beautiful thing). As we may also say—but still without any notable precision[23]—the same object may figure in my thoughts under various different *aspects*, and it will generally make a difference under which aspect I am thinking of it. For indeed I may be thinking of the same thing under two different aspects at the

[22] I touch upon this at p. 234 below.
[23] I shall not attempt to formulate the point more precisely, and I do not intend to mark any disagreement with McDowell's way of putting it, which is that one may have various different 'lines' on to the same thing (pp. 216–17). Nor am I disagreeing with Frege's way of putting it, which is that the same thing may be presented to one in different 'modes of presentation' ('On Sense and Reference', p. 57).

same time, without recognizing that it is the same thing that I am thinking of under each aspect. This is not really an obvious point, though it is a point one must see if one is to see clearly why the fallacy is a fallacy. In the next section of his discussion Plato shows that he has at least half seen it, though not—it seems—as clearly as one might hope.

Before I move on to this, I add one further note on the present passage. The first statement of our puzzle introduced the idea that a thinker must *know* the things his thought is about, or the things that 'occur in' his thoughts. In the example of that passage the things in question were ordinary perceptible objects, and the thought in question was a judgement of identity. By contrast the present passage speaks rather of *thinking* (of) the things that occur in the thought (διανοεῖσθαι, 189e1–2; δοξάζειν, 190c6, d4–7), or more vaguely still of *having a grasp* of them (ἐφάπτεσθαι, 190c6, d9). The requirement of knowledge is no longer insisted on. Also, the present passage certainly applies this requirement to the predicates of one's thoughts, and—if my reconstruction is right—it is a subject–predicate judgement that we are supposed to be considering, e.g. 'Theaetetus is ugly'. It is insisted that one cannot have such a thought without thinking of both terms, but the problem that in fact arises concerns one's thought of the subject. For the point is that our subject *is* beautiful, though it is not thought of *as* beautiful, and that is a distinction which the argument professes not to find intelligible.

4. FIRST SOLUTION: THE WAX TABLET (191a–196c)

Socrates begins his first serious attempt at a solution by casting doubt upon the opening thesis that if you know something you do not also not know it (191a–c). At least, he and Theaetetus agree that it obviously is possible to be in the situation of thinking that Socrates is the man in the distance, when in fact one does know Socrates but does not know the man in the distance, and he thinks that this looks rather like a case of both knowing and not knowing the same thing. I presume his point is that the man in the distance is, in an ordinary sense, someone you do not know, and yet in another sense he must be someone you do know, for at least you 'know' him sufficiently well to have a thought about him. But it cannot be the best way of describing the situation to say that you both do and do not know this man, and in order to find a better description Socrates turns to consider how knowledge is acquired. This introduces the idea of the wax tablet in our minds, where images are stored.

The wax tablet records what we remember. In the first place, it contains copies of various perceptions, and if I have a sufficiently clear copy of a perception of some object, then I am said to remember that object and to know it.[24] (This is obviously a little over-simple, but let us not fuss about that.) There are also other imprints on the wax, representing our knowledge of general terms such as 'man' and 'horse', and in particular of the numbers, and these, we are told, do not result from perception (195d–196a). But these only enter the argument at a later stage, and we begin by focusing on the imprints which are caused by previous perceptions. Then the idea is that when I perceive something I 'recognize' it by fitting the present perception into an already existing imprint on the wax, caused by a previous perception, and it is here that Socrates thinks that error may arise. For we may incautiously fit a perception into the *wrong* imprint, and this will give rise to the false belief that the object perceived is the same object as the one remembered. What is happening is a 'mismatch' of perception and memory.

The general point behind this theory is that it brings vividly to our attention the fact that there are two quite different ways in which one may have sufficient contact with a thing for it to figure in one's thoughts, viz. by remembering it or by perceiving it. In a way this point has already been made earlier in the dialogue (in the argument with Protagoras, 163d–166b), but Socrates is surely right to suppose that it is a highly relevant point in the present context. For it is intuitively clear that a thing thought of in one of these ways may or may not be identical with a thing thought of in the other way, without my being in a position to tell this. So we have made room for at least some false beliefs. In fact quite a number of false beliefs seem to be catered for by this model, for evidently we can also apply it to false beliefs arising from mismatching a perception of an object with an imprint that represents one's understanding of a general term such as 'man' or 'horse'. (Theaetetus actually does apply the model this way at 195e5–7, to explain how one can make a mistake about the number of a group of perceived objects.) So although it is

---

[24] Socrates henceforth reserves the notion of *knowing* an object for the case when one remembers it.

true that throughout the main discussion Socrates' language strongly suggests that what he is concerned to explain is always a mistaken identity-judgement, this is in fact quite incidental, for the model will stretch much further. Indeed it is possible that Socrates did not intend to be taken as speaking only of identity-judgements. If earlier at 189d–190d he can talk of thinking that one thing is another when he has in mind such examples as thinking that a beautiful thing is ugly, then perhaps here at 192c–d he can talk of thinking that things one knows are other things that one perceives while wishing to include such examples as thinking that being ugly (which one knows) is the case with that object over there (which one perceives). But I leave that merely as a speculation. Let us come back to the model in more detail.

I said a moment ago that on this model it is 'intuitively clear' how some mistakes come to be made, and I do not think that in fact we can say very much more than that. As Robinson noted (1969, p. 64), we are not in fact given any clear account of exactly how a false belief now becomes possible, or how this model evades the previous argument to show that false belief must be impossible. Ackrill has offered an explanation (1966, pp. 392–3), relying on the premiss that it is specifically identity-judgements that Plato finds puzzling. On his account, the model of the wax tablet provides a solution by showing that the judgement that the man in the distance is Socrates is not really an *identity*-judgement at all. Rather, it turns out upon analysis to be a judgement about two quite clearly different objects, one the image presented by perception, and the other the impression on the wax which my memory preserves. When I make the mistake in question, I do not think that the image *is* the impression, which really would be an incomprehensible identity-mistake, but rather, I think that the image and the impression stand in a certain *relation* to one another, namely the relation of being of—or perhaps caused by—the same man. On this account, then, the terms of the judgement—i.e. what it is *about*—are not after all Socrates and the man in the distance, but the two items in my mind that represent them to me. That is why the judgement is not really an identity-judgement, and that is why it is possible to get it wrong.

Now it is obvious that this explanation goes beyond anything that is explicitly stated in the text, and so must be regarded as a conjecture. If this is indeed the 'solution' that Plato has in mind, he certainly has not troubled to spell it out to us in detail, or even to give us any very clear hint of it. For one thing, he never really suggests that we *think about* the image and the impression themselves. When I make a mistake, it is because 'I attach the seeing of one thing to the imprint which belongs to another, like people who put their shoes on the wrong feet' (193c4–6). This is a matter of *doing* something wrong, rather than *thinking* something wrong. 'Or alternatively my going wrong is because the same sort of thing happens to me as happens to sight in mirrors, when it flows in such a way as to transpose left and right' (193c7–d1). On this latter account, the error is not even due to something that I do, but simply to something that *happens* to me. It certainly does not sound as if this 'misfitting' of a perception to an imprint is *itself* a false judgement; rather, it *gives rise to* a false judgement, but the false judgement it gives rise to is never described as a judgement *about* the perception and the imprint. It is characterized always as a judgement that one thing, that one knows, is another thing, that one perceives, where the thing that one perceives may or may not also be a thing that one knows. But we cannot make sense of this if we suppose that the thing that one knows is an *imprint* on the wax, and the thing that one perceives is an *image* given by perception, for on that way of construing it a thing that one knows could not also be a thing that one perceives: no imprint *is* a perceptual image. I conclude that such hints as may be drawn from our text are not at all favourable to the explanation that Ackrill suggests. When we add to this the consideration that there is no very good reason for accepting his leading premiss, i.e. the premiss that it is only false judgements of identity that are under suspicion, I think we can justifiably be sceptical of his account.

But this is not because there is some other and more attractive account which fits the text very much better. Certainly there is another, and—in my view—more attractive, account. Instead of supposing that the perception and the imprint on the wax are playing the role of two clearly distinct objects that the judgement is about, we may instead say that they represent two different aspects which may or may not be aspects of the same object. What the judgement is *about* is the object or objects that present these aspects (which *is* how our text represents the matter), but in order to give a full account of what the judgement is we must somehow indicate the aspects involved. For a judgement in which an object figures under one aspect is not the same judgement as one in which the same object figures but under a different aspect. Evidently this is a moral that *could* be drawn from the model of the wax tablet, and it is a moral that would be very relevant to the paradox of the preceding section (at least, on my interpretation of that paradox). But again, it is not yet evident that it is the moral that Plato did draw, or that he was trying to draw. One might say that it is *implicit* in his discussion that the judgement that the man in the distance is Socrates is not the *same* judgement as the judgement that Theaetetus is Socrates, even when Theaetetus is the man in the distance. So one might reasonably go on to infer that the judgement that Theaetetus is ugly is not the same judgement as the judgement that that handsome man over there is ugly, even when that handsome man over there is Theaetetus. But all this is left implicit, and at the moment this explanation appears no less conjectural than Ackrill's. But the conjecture does receive some further support when we turn to the refutation of the wax tablet, which I now do.

The trouble with the wax tablet, as Socrates has presented it, is that it is far too narrow. It is designed to allow for mismatch to occur when one of the items concerned is a perception and the other is a memory, but that is all. In fact Socrates explicitly rules out the idea that one perception may be mismatched with another, or one memory with another. This is the point he is making at length in his long catalogue of what mistakes are and are not possible at 192a–194b, and it is the point that he reiterates at 195c7–d2 when preparing to expose the weakness of the theory. But this means that the theory cannot account for false beliefs that have nothing to do with perception, and it is clear that there can be false beliefs of this kind. Socrates takes an example from arithmetic. Clearly it is possible to make a slip in one's calculations, and so come to think that the sum of 7 and 5 is 11, but there is nothing in the model of the wax tablet, as so far presented, that could explain this mistake.

Now the obvious remedy seems to be to try to expand the model of the wax tablet so that it can explain a wider range of errors. For example it evidently is possible to mismatch a perception with a perception, e.g. when I think that the clock that I can see is the same clock as the clock that I can hear, though actually it is not. Equally it is possible to mismatch a memory with a memory, and such a mismatch may lead me to believe that Socrates and Theaetetus are the same person. (Suppose that Socrates and Theaetetus look alike, and that I have been introduced to one on one occasion and to the other on another. We can easily imagine circumstances that would lead me to suspect that it was actually the same person that I was introduced to, under different names, on the two occasions.) There seems, then, to be ample room to expand the ideas behind the wax tablet, in order to give a more comprehensive account of errors that are connected with perception. Perhaps, if we did this, it would also allow us to explain what one might call 'purely intellectual' errors? Why does Plato not attempt this?

Well, it may be, as Ackrill suggests (1966, pp. 393–4), that he was prevented from seeing this possibility by an adventitious feature of his model. He thinks of a correct matching of perception and imprint as a matter of fitting a seal into 'its own' imprint (193b10–c4), as one might fit a foot into its own footprint. Correspondingly, an incorrect matching will be fitting a foot into a footprint rather like its own, but not its own. But it makes no sense to talk of fitting a foot into a foot, or a footprint into a footprint, and thus 'mismatches' of perception with perception, or memory with memory, are automatically ruled out by the model. This may indeed be the complete explanation of why Plato never tries to expand his model, even to cater for other errors that arise in connection with perception. But I wonder whether there might not also be a deeper reason, namely that he still could not see how it would account for 'purely intellectual' errors, even if it could be made to cover a wide variety of errors about the perceptible world.

In order to use this model to account for the mistake of thinking that $7+5$ is 11, one would have to suppose that there is an impression on the wax corresponding to '$7+5$', that it is *not the same* impression as the impression corresponding to '12', and hence that it is possible to 'mismatch' it with the impression corresponding to '11'. But then we ask: how did this impression get there, and how is it different from the impression of 12? Now Plato deliberately does not tell us how the impressions of the numbers themselves come to be on the wax. He does say emphatically that they are *not* due to perception (195d–196a), but he gives no positive account of how they do arise.[25] But if we may conjecture the explanation he would give, still within the terms of the wax tablet, it seems that it would

---

[25] Should we perhaps think of them as 'conceptions (ἔννοιαι) which we ourselves conceive' (191d5–7)? But it is difficult to believe that Plato would ever have looked favourably on the suggestion that we ourselves *invent* the numbers.

have to be that it is the numbers themselves that have left these impressions on the wax, in their own likeness. And on this account the problem does appear insuperable. For how can the impression made by 12 be a different impression from that made by the fifth number after 7?

We may put the point generally like this. It is an entirely familiar idea that different perceptions may yet be perceptions of the same object. Supposing that impressions are copies of perceptions, there is then no difficulty in seeing how there may be different impressions which are yet impressions of the same object. The general principle involved here is something like this: an impression arises through some kind of causal contact with an object, namely the object it is an impression of, and we can get different impressions of the same object as a result of different occasions on which we have been in causal contact with it. But how can we apply this principle when the causal contact is no longer a perception? What are the supposed different causal episodes, which are each a contact with the *same* number, but sufficiently different from one another to give rise to *different* impressions of it? Given Plato's premiss, that our knowledge of the numbers is *not* due to perception, it seems perfectly correct to conclude that different 'impressions' of the same number would be inexplicable, and there is therefore no way of using the ideas behind the wax tablet to explain arithmetical error.

As a matter of fact it would not help us very much to abandon Plato's premiss, and to allow that our knowledge of the numbers may be somehow based upon perception. For it is altogether too implausible to suppose that *all* the many different ways of describing the same number correspond to different ways of *perceiving* it. And it may be noted that the same remark applies also to all the many different ways of describing the same perceptible object; some of them may correspond to different ways of perceiving it, but surely not all. (My false belief that the person waiting for me in the next room is Socrates need not arise from any *perception*—or memory—of the person waiting for me in the next room, which I have mismatched to my memory of Socrates.) So we must conclude that the model of the wax tablet, which does focus upon perception, will not in the end do as a final answer to Plato's problem. It provides some useful and relevant ideas, but it is—as Plato himself saw—too narrow. But the reason why we can draw this conclusion with some confidence is that it has now, at last, become quite clear what Plato's problem actually is.

No one in his senses would worry about how it is possible to believe that 7+5 is 11 unless he also had an argument which appeared to show that this was not possible. Our text makes it quite clear what that argument is, namely a fallacious application of Leibniz's Law. Since 7+5 is actually 12, it seems that to believe that 7+5 is 11 must be the same as to believe that 12 is 11, but surely no one could believe that (196a–b)? Now this is almost exactly the same fallacy as what I earlier called a failure to distinguish between *de re* and *de dicto* reports of beliefs, for in fact these applications of Leibniz's Law only are fallacious when we presume that the beliefs are being reported in a *de dicto* fashion, as giving what one 'says to oneself'. When someone believes that the number which is the sum of 7 and 5 is 11, it is not illegitimate to report him as believing that 12 is 11, so long as it is clear that this is to be taken as a *de re* report. That is, so long as one means by it that, concerning a number which is actually 12, he believes that *it* is 11, with no implication as to how he is thinking of the number in question. But of course it is equally possible, and perhaps more natural, to take the statement 'He believes that 12 is 11' as a *de dicto* report, meaning that he says to himself '12 is 11', and when it is taken in this way it does not follow from the premiss that he says to himself '7+5 is 11'. It should be noted that it is not at all important to this fallacy that the statement believed should itself be an identity-statement. Thus suppose someone believes that 91 is a prime number. Then since 91 is actually 7×13, we can say that he believes that the product of 7 and 13 is a prime number, and this is a perfectly correct report on the situation if it is taken *de re*, but not if it is taken *de dicto*. For no one could seriously say to himself 'the product of 7 and 13 is a prime number' unless he had temporarily forgotten what was meant by 'prime'. I think, then, that we may characterize Plato's problem about belief as essentially this problem: how can it be reasonable to make a distinction between *de re* and *de dicto* reports of belief? Or equivalently, how can it be reasonable to deny that Leibniz's Law applies to the descriptions of belief? There are some who *still* find this something of a problem.[26]

We are now in a position to return to the way that Plato first set

[26] See e.g. Kripke's article 'A Puzzle about Belief' (1976).

out his problem in 187e–188c. When first discussing this passage I observed (p. 163) that a fallacious application of Leibniz's Law can easily seem to lead to the conclusion that we cannot disbelieve any true identity-statement, but that it is not quite so easy to see why it should also seem to imply that we cannot believe any false one. However a little ingenuity will readily supply an argument that seems to do the trick. Suppose that *a* and *b* are actually different things, so that one of the things that is actually true of *b* is that it is not *a*. Another thing that is true of *b* is, of course, that it is *b*. And *b* is the only thing of which both these are true. That is, *b* is *the thing that is not a but b*. By Leibniz's Law it apparently follows that if I falsely believe that *a* is *b* then I thereby believe that *a* is the thing that is not *a* but *b*. But no one could say to himself '*a* is the thing that is not *a* but *b*', and hence no one could believe that *a* is *b*, unless this belief is actually true.[27]

Now you may say: that is a very pretty little fallacy, but what has it got to do with Plato's text? If Plato had wished to perpetrate such a fallacy, in order to introduce his problem, why does he not do so more explicitly? But I reply that if you look at the text it is exactly what he does do. He asks, concerning someone who has a false belief,

> Is he thinking that things he knows are not those things but other things he knows? (188b3–4).

To apply this to someone who knows both Socrates and Theaetetus, the question is

> Can he be thinking that Socrates is not Socrates but Theaetetus?

The reply is that this is impossible, but earlier we could not see *why* it was supposed to be impossible. The answer is now clear: it *is* impossible if the question is taken *de dicto*. No one could ever say to himself 'Socrates is not Socrates but Theaetetus'. But why should it be supposed that one who believes that Socrates is Theaetetus should *also* be believing that Socrates is not Socrates? Well, the only

---

[27] This argument, using $b = \imath x (x \neq a \ \& \ x = b)$, is obviously reminiscent of what has become known as 'the Frege argument'. (See e.g. Quine's *Word and Object* (1960), pp. 148–9, for an application of this argument to *de re* and *de dicto* beliefs.) It is *much* simpler than the very complex argument constructed from the same premiss by Lewis (1973, pp. 130–3). Lewis's version brings in many extra premisses, some of them very implausible, for example the premiss that if I do not *know* that *a* and *b* are the same then I must *know that* I do not know this.

answer seems to be, as I have just suggested, that Theaetetus *is* one who is not Socrates, and hence to believe that Socrates is Theaetetus must be to believe that Socrates is one who is not Socrates, which is perfectly all right when taken *de re* but wholly wrong when taken *de dicto*. The argument is thus almost exactly the same as that which I set out, a little more formally, in the last paragraph.

It is difficult to say how much clarity on this topic it is reasonable to attribute to Plato. As he presents the discussion, Socrates is portrayed as continually falling into the fallacy I have described when he is trying to say what is problematic about false belief, and one must admit that he never shows any reluctance about accepting the particular result that one cannot believe that Socrates is Theaetetus. This may of course be because Plato himself *accepts* the fallacious arguments involved as valid arguments, and although it is obvious that problems then arise, as he points out, it is possible that Plato himself is quite at a loss as to how they have arisen. But it seems more reasonable to suppose that he does have *some* idea of what is causing the problem, just because the model of the wax tablet really is a good start on a diagnosis. The true answer to the problem, I have claimed, is to see that, when describing a belief, we must not only say what object the belief is about, but also how that object is being thought of, or under what aspect it figures in the belief. It is when this point is overlooked that the fallacious applications of Leibniz's Law can seem so compelling, and in the limited range of cases to which the wax tablet applies it does bring out exactly the point required. Thus, since the first attempt at a solution that Plato offers really is quite a good attempt at a solution, it is very tempting to suppose that he had a pretty adequate grasp of what was causing the problem. But the first solution, as we have seen, will not cover all the cases. One therefore hopes that in his second solution Plato will try to produce some suitable generalization of what was right about the first solution. Unfortunately this is not exactly what happens, as we shall see.

5. SECOND SOLUTION: THE AVIARY (196c–200c)

Such success as the wax tablet had could certainly be said to be due to the fact that, in a way, it allows us both to know and not know the same thing. That is, I may know a thing in one way (as an object perceived) without knowing it in another (as an object remembered). So it is very reasonable for Plato to pick out this point as the crucial one in his conclusion (196c7–8), and it is understandable that his next suggestion involves another way in which we might admit the possibility of knowing and not knowing the same thing. The idea is that I may *possess* knowledge of the thing, which is a disposition, without having that knowledge 'in hand'—i.e. actively before the mind—which is an occurrence. Of course this is a perfectly fair distinction in itself (except that the relevant occurrence is not actually called 'knowing', p. 156), but it is not really very helpful with the present problem.

The general idea is that we already possess knowledge of various objects, including the numbers, and these 'knowledges'[28] are like birds flying about in our aviary. When we wish to bring one of them to mind, we go down to the aviary to catch it. But it can happen that we get hold of the wrong one by mistake, and that will then give rise to a false belief. Now one can see a way in which this picture *might*, apparently, be used to extend the ideas of the wax tablet. Suppose I am asked the question 'what is 7+5?' I then have 'the occurrent thought, 7+5', which is actively before my mind, and is similar to a perception. So I go down to my aviary looking for the (already known) number that 'matches' that thought, and I may catch 11 instead of 12, and think that 11 is the number that matches it. But this is not at all the way that Socrates himself develops the image. He does not say that I go down trying to catch the number that matches '7+5', but that I go down *trying to catch 12*: the term '7+5' has simply dropped out of the account (199b2–5). This leaves him with no defence against the objection: if what you were looking for was 12, and you actually caught 11, how could you fail to recognize that what you had caught was not the number you were looking for? Indeed, Socrates actually says that in this position one thinks that 11 is 12 (199b3–4[29]), even though it has earlier been agreed that no one ever does have such a thought (190b–c).

We cannot set this down as a momentary slip on Socrates' part, for it is implicit in the whole account of arithmetic that he gives

---

[28] Plato's Greek contains a very odd use of 'knowledge' in the plural. McDowell very reasonably translates 'pieces of knowledge'.

[29] Cornford (1935), who sees (half of) the problem, wilfully mistranslates. He renders 'mistakes 11 for 12' instead of 'thinks that 11 is 12'.

when leading up to his solution (198a–199b). The art of arithmetic he wishes us to think of as 'a hunt for pieces of knowledge of everything odd and even', i.e. for knowledges of all the numbers (198a7–8). This is a somewhat odd description, but we find that he means it seriously. One who practises this art, he says, does already possess knowledges of all the numbers (198a10–b1, b8–10), and yet he may 'sometimes do some counting: either numbers themselves, to himself, or something else, some external thing that has a number' (c1–2). Counting, he goes on, we will regard as 'investigating how large some number is' (c5), and so he concludes that our man is 'investigating something he knows as if he didn't know it' (c7–8). That is, he is hunting for a piece of knowledge which he already possesses, and this is possible because what he is trying to do is to bring the knowledge before his mind again, which is not the same as possessing it.

One has only to think for a moment to see that this is really an absurd account of the matter, and the source of the trouble is quite clear. When our arithmetician is counting 'numbers themselves', he is presumably doing a calculation rather than simply rehearsing the number series to himself. Thus he sets himself to 'investigate how large some number is' when, for example, he asks himself what $7+5$ is. In what sense is this 'investigating something he knows'? The suppressed premiss must be that since $7+5$ *is* 12, to investigate how large $7+5$ is is the same thing as to investigate how large 12 is, and he already knows how large 12 is. Similarly with counting external objects. When the number of matches in the box *is* 52, Socrates takes it that to ask 'What is the number of matches in the box?' just is to ask 'What is 52?', and then he brings in the distinction between possessing knowledge and having it in mind in order to explain how the *latter* question is a sensible question to ask. The case is similar again with the man who can read, who knows all the letters already, and so is regarded as setting out to investigate something he knows when he sets out to read something (198e). McDowell rightly comments (p. 222) that this account of reading is 'not very plausible as a description of the ordinary reading of words', and suggests that we might think of the reading of an oculist's test card. But the account is no more plausible in that case either. To set oneself to find out which letters are on the card is not at all the same as to engage in the nonsensical attempt to discover which letters are 'L', 'M', and 'N', even when 'L', 'M', and 'N' *are* the letters on the card.

What has happened appears to be this. The wax tablet, as we saw, gave us *some* defence against the fallacious argument that if '*x*' and '*y*' refer to the same object then to think that *x* is thus and so must be the same as to think that *y* is thus and so (where, in each case, the construction is construed as a *de dicto* construction). It did this where the different expressions '*x*' and '*y*' represented different ways of thinking of the object in question (viz. by perceiving it and by remembering it). But it gave us no defence against the fallacy when perception was not involved, and hence no way of blocking the argument that to think that $7+5=11$ must be the same as to think that $12=11$. Now we naturally expect that the next attempt at a solution will try to provide some way of blocking that fallacious argument, but actually this is not what happens. Instead, Socrates *accepts* the fallacious argument, as my last paragraph shows, and therefore *accepts* that we can think that $12=11$, and his solution is designed to show how *this* thought is after all a possible thought to have.

The solution he offers is entirely specious, though at first sight it may seem to be all right. His idea is that we go down to our aviary trying to catch the bird that is 12, we do indeed get hold of a bird, but it is the wrong one. Then what we are imagined to think to ourselves is '*this bird* is 12', though—unknown to us—it is actually 11. Is it not just as easy to think that a bird is 12, when it is actually 11, as it is to think that a bird is a pigeon, when it is actually a dove (199b5)? But this account derives what plausibility it has from our tendency to forget that the aviary is a metaphor, and to take the picture too literally. There are not actually any birds in our heads, and we do not have thoughts about them which we express (to ourselves) using such phrases as 'this bird'. When we remember that the bird merely represents our knowledge of 11, and that to 'get hold of' the bird is to bring that knowledge explicitly before the mind, then it is clear that the thought which is expressed in the metaphor by using 'this bird' is expressed in fact by using '11'. So there is actually no explanation at all here of how the thought '11 is 12' could ever occur. Or we could bring out the absurdity in a different way by insisting on putting *every* feature of the situation *in* terms of the metaphor. I go down to my aviary 'to try to catch 12'. Since I understand what I am looking for, my knowledge of 12 *is* before my mind at the time, which is to say that I already have the bird that is 12 in my hand. Nevertheless, I go down to the aviary to try to catch this bird that is already in my hand, I do catch a different bird, and I think that that *is* the one I'm already holding! Clearly, Socrates should never have undertaken the task of explaining how we can think that 11 is 12, for he was right earlier when he said that we could not.

Incidentally, it is worth remarking that my earlier suggestion about how the aviary might be applied will not, in the end, prove to be any more satisfactory. The point is that we cannot separate the 'occurrent thought' of 7+5 from all knowledge that is already possessed, for this thought is understood, and on the model we are considering any arithmetical thought is understood by bringing before the mind some piece of knowledge that is already possessed. What, then, is the knowledge that is brought to mind when we think of 7+5? We shall wish to say that it is knowledge of 7+5, and that this is *not* the same as knowledge of 12, but how can we maintain this distinction? I am not suggesting that it cannot be done, but only that the distinction between knowledge possessed and knowledge in mind will not help us to do it. As Ackrill observed (1966, p. 402), 'the distinction between the dispositional and the actualised way of knowing is unhelpful, for one who understands what he is saying must be actualising his knowledge of the items referred to'.

The aviary, then, does not help us with our problem. Indeed, if my reconstruction is right, then the problem to which it is actually addressed is a wholly unreal problem, and nothing would count as its solution. Nevertheless, as several commentators have noted,[30] its refutation is peculiarly weak. Socrates complains that on this account knowledge of a thing is causing ignorance of it (199d), presumably on the ground that it is my possession of the knowledge of 11 that allows me to fail to recognize it for what it is (namely 11, and not 12). But one might reply: well, why not? After all, we said earlier that it is only because I know Socrates that I am in a position to hold the mistaken belief that the man in the distance is Socrates, and there seems to be nothing wrong with that. On closer reflection the two cases are not really parallel, as we have seen, but they certainly do bear a superficial resemblance, and what Socrates actually says by way of refutation would fit both cases equally.

[30] e.g. A. E. Taylor (1926, pp. 345–6), Cornford (1935, pp. 136–8), Robinson (1969, pp. 65–6).

Should we perhaps conclude that in *Plato's* eyes it is the refutation that is at fault, and not the theory allegedly refuted?

The temptation to this view arises because the theory of the aviary is reminiscent of Plato's own theory of Recollection (chapter I, section 2(i)). In fact McDowell suggests that we are meant to see an allusion to that theory at 198c8–9, where, having explained the odd situation of the arithmetician who is investigating what he knows as if he didn't know it, Socrates adds 'I dare say you sometimes hear puzzles on those lines'. This he takes to be an allusion to the paradox of inquiry at *Meno* 80d, which is precisely what leads Plato to introduce his theory of Recollection for the first time.[31] Consequently McDowell supposes that the criticism of the aviary is an implicit criticism of the theory of Recollection, remarking that the two theories are structurally parallel (1973, pp. 221–3). But in view of the fact that the explicit criticism is in fact very weak, is it not more tempting to suppose that Plato is trying to indicate to us that his own theory of Recollection *does* contain the solution to the present problem?

Now certainly there are differences between the aviary as presented here and the theory of Recollection. For one thing, our passage speaks of the aviary as empty at birth (197e), and imagines that it becomes stocked with various knowledges by teaching, which is a matter of one man 'passing on' the knowledge to another (198b). By contrast, the theory of Recollection claims that we enter this life with an aviary already fully stocked, i.e. with a latent knowledge of all the forms, and that we can only turn this latent knowledge into explicit knowledge by a priori reflection. It denies that this can be done by 'teaching', except in so far as the teacher may, by his questioning, stimulate the pupil's own recall of the knowledge already within him. It may at first seem, as McDowell claims, that these differences do not affect the argument, but in fact they do. The crucial difference is that in the *Theaetetus* there is normally no difficulty about catching a bird that is already in one's aviary; admittedly we began by saying that one could sometimes slip up, and get the wrong bird by mistake, but normally the knowledge that one possesses can be brought to mind readily enough. But this is not so in the theory of Recollection, where the 'birds' would

---

[31] It seems to me better to take the passage as alluding to *Euthydemus* 276d–277c. The solution that Socrates gives there (277e–278a) is rather similar to what he says here.

represent latent knowledge, that most people never do bring to mind at all. This means that the latter theory is in fact in a stronger position when it comes to the explanation of error.

In both theories, the birds in the aviary are supposed to represent our understanding of language, but the point of the Recollection theory is to explain how there can be two different levels of understanding. The ordinary everyday understanding of such words as 'justice' or 'equality' is due to the fact that we do have a recollection of the relevant forms, while the fact that we lack a proper 'philosophic' understanding, and so cannot 'give an account', shows that the recollection is only a dim one and not a clear one. Thus someone might understand the thesis that justice is equality, because he does dimly recollect the forms in question, though he might at the same time fail to see that it is false, because his recollection is not clear. In terms of the aviary, he cannot actually catch the birds in question. Equally, he could understand the thesis that justice is an inner harmony of the soul without yet knowing whether it was true, for the same reason. But in this case, since the thesis is in fact true (*Republic* iv. 441–4), with any luck a 'click' of memory will supervene, and he will see that it must be true. There are no doubt many ways in which this theory is inadequate, but it would not appear to be open to the criticism that it makes error impossible.

All the same, it is very difficult to believe that Plato could have thought that this theory holds the key to the problem of how one can believe that 7+5 is 11. Certainly, if he genuinely supposed that to believe this is to believe (*de dicto*) that 12 is 11, and that this really is a possibility because our recollection of the forms 12 and 11 is so dim, then he was very foolish indeed. For he also has to explain why no one will say to himself '12 is 11', and everyone will claim to know that 12 is not 11, with as much certainty about this—i.e. as much of a 'click' of memory?—as about any a priori truth. So the theory of Recollection can only help if one *begins* by distinguishing an understanding of '7+5' from an understanding of '12', and once this distinction is achieved there is really no more work to do. But the theory of Recollection does not itself help us to draw this distinction, and in fact it seems only to make the distinction more difficult, as my remarks on p. 182 above indicate.

I conclude that the theory of Recollection does not help us with our problem, and that it is not at all likely that Plato thought that it did. I also add, *contra* McDowell, that it is a mistake to suppose 'that the criticism of the aviary can be taken as implicit criticism of the use of the Theory of Recollection to solve the puzzle of *Meno* 80d1–e5' (1973, p. 223). In fact the explicit criticism of the aviary is quite inconclusive even against the aviary itself. It is yet more question-begging if considered as directed at the theory of Recollection. But the truth is that the aviary is of no use with the present problem, which is a rather more 'modern' problem than that of *Meno* 80d–e, and the likelihood is that Plato realized this, even if he did not see how to say very clearly why it was of no use.[32]

When the original version of the aviary is abandoned at 199d, Theaetetus offers a revision. On the original version, the aviary contained only bits of knowledge, and these were clearly conceived as each a knowledge of some *object* (e.g. the numbers). Theaetetus suggests that perhaps we should have included bits of 'unknowledge' as well. Such a bit of 'unknowledge' obviously cannot be a *lack* of knowledge of an object, and it is difficult to see how it might be construed as a *misconception* of an object. (What would be the ground for saying that '7+5' is a misconception of 11, rather than a perfectly correct conception of 12?) So the natural suggestion is that these bits of 'unknowledge' are simply false beliefs, conceived as flying around in our aviary because they are things we have acquired, and now possess, and can (normally) call to mind when we wish to.

To this Socrates brings an objection, the point of which seems to be that it is no advance on the original theory. The original theory led us to say that we could catch the bird 11, fail to recognize it for what it was (namely 11), and so be led into error. This, we had to admit, seemed implausible. The revised theory seems to be that we can catch the bird '7+5=11', fail to recognize it for what it is (namely a falsehood), and so again be led into error. And this, Socrates says, is equally implausible: the problem of how one can fail to recognize a possessed item for what it is has simply been put back a stage, but not resolved. (Alternatively, if it is 'misconceptions of objects' we are concerned with, the complaint is that it has not been explained how we can fail to recognize a misconception for

---

[32] The claim that knowledge of a thing cannot cause ignorance of it would appear to be a special case of the *Phaedo*'s (mistaken) principle that nothing can cause its own opposite (*Phaedo* 101a–b).

what it is, namely a *mis*conception.) Actually, this seems to be the wrong criticism to bring. No doubt it would be implausible to suppose that one could catch the belief that 7+5=11 and not recognize it as that very belief, but it seems all right to say that one could catch it without recognizing that it was false. However, as a solution to the problem before us, it evidently will not do, since it simply assumes that we can acquire false beliefs in the first place, to put into our aviary. (The same point may be made about 'misconceptions', for even if a misconception is not itself a false belief still it must presumably be construed as somehow containing such a belief within itself. That is why it is a *mis*conception.)

I think, then, that the objection that is actually raised against the revised aviary is not cogent, just as the objection that is explicitly raised against the original aviary is inconclusive. But the truth is that neither version of the theory is in fact of any help with the present problem, and Plato is quite right to dismiss them. I do not imagine that he was writing with his tongue in his cheek in either case. It is much more likely that he realized that the distinction between possessing knowledge and having it in mind will not in fact do anything to block the fallacious inferences based on Leibniz's Law, even though his objections do not seem to be directed quite to the point that they should be directed to. And since he has no more suggestions to make, the original problem thus remains unsolved.

6. DISCUSSION

I shall begin with a speculation on how Plato may have reached his new puzzle about belief.

At the end of the first part of the dialogue Plato has claimed that perception cannot reach truth, whereas knowledge must reach truth. This naturally leads us to consider the relationship between knowledge and belief, for at least belief resembles knowledge in this: it too can reach truth. But, unlike knowledge, it does not have to: belief can also suffer from falsehood. Presumably, if perception cannot reach truth then equally it cannot suffer from falsehood. So one contrast between perception and belief is that belief can be either true or false, while perception cannot be. But it appears that this point about belief can also be put in a slightly different way by saying that the objects of belief may either exist or not exist, and this gives us another contrast with perception, for it is plausible to say that the objects of perception must always exist: you cannot perceive what is not there, though apparently you can believe it. But is not this, on reflection, really rather strange?

It does seem puzzling that a belief can be directed at a non-existent object. It is even more puzzling to someone who, like Plato in the *Cratylus*, sees no essential difference between sentences and names, and is ready to assign truth and falsehood to both alike.[33] For if a false sentence states what does not exist, it then seems that a false name should name what does not exist, and it will be difficult to see how such a name could ever have been introduced into the language. One cannot, surely, point to a non-existent thing in order to assign a name to it. It seems to me quite likely, then, that reflection on the old and familiar problem of false belief led Plato to see that names and sentences should not be assimilated, and a fairly obvious difference between them is that names are simple expressions whereas sentences are always complex. To put this in terms of belief, the object of a belief will always be a complex object, and here is another contrast with perception, which is always directed at simple objects. Moreover, it appears to provide a useful start on the problem of non-existence. For although the object of a false belief will not exist, still it will not be, as it were, *entirely* non-existent. Even if the complex as a whole does not exist, still the simpler entities that make up this complex will exist perfectly well.[34]

The object of a belief, then, will be a complex thing, put together from several *terms*. I do not imagine that Plato was, at this stage, nearly as clear about the nature of these terms, and the way in which they are put together, as he was later in the *Sophist*.[35] It is not unreasonable to conjecture that he thought of the terms as linked to

[33] *Cratylus* 385b–c, 431a–b, 432e.

[34] Note that I am not *recommending* this line of thought that I am attributing to Plato. In a developed language any complete sentence will show some semantic complexity, but that is not the reason why a sentence can be false. There could still be false sentences even in a very primitive language which just had one (unstructured) word for each sentence.

[35] At 197d we are told of the birds in the aviary that 'some fly in flocks, apart from the others, some in groups of a few, and some alone, flying about just anywhere among them all'. Is 'being' one of those that flies about just anywhere? (And do sameness and difference, perhaps, behave in the same fashion?) But there is no way of knowing just what distinctions Plato was adverting to in this enigmatic aside.

one another by 'being', as the argument at the end of the first part of the dialogue seems to require, but we cannot be sure of this. I also do not imagine that he has as yet seen how to give a complete answer to the riddle of non-existence. He believes that *some* of the mystery can be dispelled by pointing out that the terms of a belief-complex will exist, but this still does not really explain how the complex as a whole may fail to exist and yet be believed. In so far as the later *Sophist* does offer a solution to this riddle, it is I think by pressing hard on the distinction between naming and stating: to say something true or false is not to *name* anything. But, it suggests, one is only tempted to think of a false statement as 'saying what is not' if one does think of it as attempting to name something.[36] I would guess that at the time of writing the *Theaetetus* Plato would not have been so clear about the difference between naming and stating, and that he thought rather in terms of simple items as opposed to complex items: perception is directed at simple items, while belief is directed at complex items, and that explains many of the differences between them.

Now I have been setting out a possible train of thought that might have led Plato to hold that it is essential to a belief that it should be complex. Whether or not this speculation is on the right lines, it is clear that Plato did come to hold this. It is evidently a presupposition of the whole discussion of false belief that any belief has several terms. But this now seems to raise a problem.

We said that knowledge, like belief, must be directed to complexes if it is to attain truth. But it also seems right to say that anyone who can grasp a belief must stand in some appropriate cognitive relation to the terms in it, since one understands the whole by understanding its parts. But what is this relation? Is it not natural to say that it is a matter of *knowing* the items concerned? If so, then knowledge is after all directed at simples, as well as at complexes, and the conclusion of the first part of the dialogue appears to be undermined. Now on closer reflection it is not necessary to insist upon *knowledge* of the terms involved, at least in the ordinary sense. For I may surely believe things about the man in the distance without, in the ordinary sense, knowing that man. In this case, it is

---

[36] I cannot defend this (controversial) view of the *Sophist* here. But it may be noted that, if I am right, then the *Sophist* has not after all got to the bottom of the problem. No doubt a sentence does not name anything, but it can often be 'nominalized' (as on p. 166) to form an expression which apparently does name something, and something that does not exist if the sentence is false.

enough that I am 'in touch' with him by perception. But do we have any alternative to the notion of knowledge when it is imperceptible items that concern us? Certainly, no obvious alternative comes to mind, and in fact when the discussion turns to imperceptible items (in the aviary) Socrates speaks always in terms of knowledge, and never suggests that this may not be the right word. Have we, then, found here a kind of knowledge which, like perception, is directed to simples and does not reach truth? To be clear about this, we must see what exactly this so-called knowledge amounts to. (For simplicity I shall continue to use the word 'knowledge' to cover our grasp of perceptible objects, as well as imperceptible ones.)

But at this point Plato runs into a puzzle which he cannot fully resolve. It arises because one naturally assumes that to say that a man knows some item is to say that he stands in a certain relation to it, a simple two-termed relation between the thinker and the object his thought concerns. So it seems evidently right to say that either he knows that object or he does not, and he cannot both know it and not know it. But while there is, of course, strictly nothing wrong with this, still it is apt to be very misleading, for it tends to make us overlook the fact that an object can be known in one way but not in another, or known *as* one thing but not *as* another, or known under one *aspect* but not under another. And if we do overlook this, the result is disastrous, because we then have no defence against logical fallacies which lead, from acceptable premises, to quite obviously absurd conclusions. When I say that we have 'no defence' against these fallacies, I mean, not that we cannot recognize them as fallacies—for we obviously can—but that we cannot say clearly *why* they are fallacies, and *what* exactly is wrong with them. I think we may fairly say that Plato's new problem about belief is the problem of saying just what is wrong with such arguments.

I imagine that Plato thought of the fallacies in question as affecting virtually all false beliefs. Perhaps the simplest cases are those that arise with identity-statements, and many of Plato's illustrations are of this kind. But I do not imagine that he means to confine his discussion to such statements, and in fact the passage on 'other-judging' (as I interpret it) concerns subject–predicate statements which are not identity-statements. Indeed I doubt whether it would have occurred to Plato that identity-statements using the verb 'is' are in any way special, or even that they constitute a particular kind of statement.[37] It is just that they happen to be extremely convenient for illustrating the fallacies in question. In fact any statement in which some particular object is referred to will be open to a simple abuse of Leibniz's Law, which will generate a fallacy (when the statement reports a belief), whether it is true or false. But there is no indication that Plato has realized that his puzzle affects true beliefs just as much as false ones.

Because the solution to this problem is to recognize that a thing may be known under one aspect but not under another, and hence that it may 'figure in one's thought' under one aspect but not under another, it is quite fair to say that what needs to be done is to make it clear how, in a sense, one can both know and not know the same thing. Since Plato seems to be aware that it is this feature of his wax tablet that accounts for its partial success, he must be credited with making some progress with the problem, even though the *precise* way that the wax tablet achieves its success seems not to have been closely analysed. If it had been, one would expect the model to have been presented in a less constricting form, so that it allowed for more false beliefs than it does, and—more importantly—one would expect greater clarity on exactly how this model undermines the paradoxical inferences that set the problem. Since we do not get either of these, it is reasonable to infer that Plato has not seen clearly enough either how the problem arises or how it should be met. His instincts are, as it were, in the right place, but they are still unarticulated instincts and not yet a clear understanding. At any rate, he (correctly) observes that the wax tablet will not provide a complete solution to the problem, but then offers an alternative suggestion which is no use whatever. It would appear that he cannot see how to block the fallacious inferences where imperceptible objects are concerned, and so tries to provide a solution which *accepts* those inferences. But this is a hopeless endeavour, and he must—I think—have realized this, even though his account of why it will not do is not specially convincing. So, in the end, the problem is not resolved, and there is no reason to think that Plato thought he had another solution up his sleeve.

At this point it is relevant to notice a different line of interpretation, according to which Plato did not see these problems over false

---

[37] I have argued in my 'Plato on "is not"' (1984) that even in the *Sophist*, where it is vital to Plato's purpose to distinguish between the 'is' of identity and the 'is' of predication, he fails to do so.

belief as affecting his *own* position at all.[38] Fine (1979*a*) gives a simple version of this view, for she holds that the difficulties all stem from the premiss that knowledge is the same as true belief, and of course Plato does not accept this premiss. But I do not understand why she supposes that, if you do think that knowledge is just true belief, then you will also be bound to say that if one knows anything about an object then one must know everything about it, which is her explanation of the fallacy involved (pp. 72, 77).[39] A more guarded view of this kind is to be found in Gosling (1973, pp. 137–9), who supposes that the problems with false belief that Plato uncovers are problems for his 'opponents', but not for him. As to who these supposed 'opponents' are, Gosling suggests that they are reformed Protagoreans, who have been led by the argument at the end of the first part of the dialogue to admit that knowledge involves judgement, but who still wish to confine this to perceptual judgement. That is, they still *think* of knowledge as a matter of perceiving things, though they now admit that judgement is involved too. When the discussion turns to imperceptible things, such as the numbers, they therefore hang on to the idea of perception, except that it is now perception with the 'eye of the mind', and not that of the body. 'There is nothing to suggest that the knowledge we have is not thought to be images of whatever we know, as Protagoras would presumably hold, and the strongly visual suggestion of the passage makes it all too likely' (p. 139). Gosling's view is that *this* view of knowledge does indeed give rise to the problems with falsehood that Plato points out, but that there is no reason to suppose that it is Plato's own view. It is the view of his 'opponents'.

I do not find this a very plausible account. If we are indeed considering what a 'reformed Protagorean' would think, it is surely unfair of Plato to build in the assumption that our knowledge of the numbers is not due to perception. That is one of *Plato's* assumptions, but surely not a natural assumption for his 'opponents'. And if we do think of our knowledge of the numbers as based on perception, and as consisting of images, then it is obvious how to distinguish our knowledge of $7+5$ from our knowledge of 12. The first will be an image of two groups of objects, one containing 7

---

[38] I shall not discuss Cornford's interpretation (1935), which has been adequately refuted by Robinson (1969).

[39] Her own explanation involves a gross misunderstanding of Russell's concept of 'knowledge by acquaintance', but even so it makes little sense to me.

objects and the other containing 5 objects, while the second is simply an image of a single group of 12 objects. On this conception, it is not at all puzzling that one might make the mistake of matching one's image for 7+5 with one's image for 11, for three clearly distinct images are involved. I conclude that if Plato is here arguing against some 'empiricist opponents', then he has been very foolish in his choice of example, since the opponents will easily see a way of meeting it. (No doubt there would be other examples—e.g. involving larger numbers—where this 'empiricist' reply would be less plausible.) But the truth is that the assumption that our knowledge of the numbers themselves is not due to perception is Plato's *own* assumption, and that this assumption plays a crucial role in the development of his problem, since it is this that prevents us from suitably extending the ideas behind the wax tablet. Without a starting-point in perception, we can no longer give any account of how two different 'images' of the same number might arise. I see no ground, then, for supposing that Plato thought that his new problem about belief applies only to rival theories, and does not affect his own. And it is a problem that he does not see how to resolve.

What, then, is the relevance of this 'digression' to our main topic, the question 'What is knowledge?'? Well, one thing that it certainly does is to turn our attention away from the notion of knowing *that*, which has been the focus of Part A, and towards the notion of knowing an *object*. I shall argue that, with one small exception to be mentioned in a moment, it is the notion of knowing an object that is under consideration henceforth. Another thing that it does is to bring to our attention a special kind of knowledge of objects—if indeed 'knowledge' is the right word—which is the relation that a thinker must have to any object if that object is to 'occur in' his thoughts, and we have uncovered an awkward problem about this kind of knowledge. As a matter of fact, where the objects in question are perceptible objects, it seems that 'knowledge' is not the right word, and Plato may perhaps have thought that the ideas behind the wax tablet could be made to resolve the problem. But where the objects are imperceptible it appears that 'knowledge' is the right word—at any rate, no alternative has been suggested—and the problem seems specially acute. So when Socrates concludes the digression by saying that it will be impossible to understand false belief until we have first acquired an adequate grasp of what knowledge is (200d1–2), should we take it that it is specifically *this* kind of knowledge that he proposes to investigate further?

If so, then certainly the very next page of the dialogue is a mistake on his part.

7. TRANSITION: KNOWLEDGE AS REQUIRING AN ACCOUNT (200e–201c)

Part B has opened with the suggestion that knowledge is the same as true belief, and now that the digression on false belief is over this suggestion is repeated (200e). It is at once rather quickly refuted, and replaced by the next suggestion that knowledge is true belief with the addition of an 'account' (λόγος). It is this latter suggestion that is then discussed for the remainder of the dialogue.

Now the view that knowledge is just true belief is certainly most naturally taken as a view about knowing *that*, and the refutation we are given does indeed take it in that way. It is argued that a jury may form a true belief about who committed the crime, being persuaded by the advocate, but that this does not count as knowledge. Evidently the knowledge in question, which the jury lack, is knowledge *that* so-and-so did the deed, and the point being made seems to be very straightforward. But when the passage is looked at more closely, a distinct oddity emerges.

At first it appears that the jury do not count as having knowledge because they have been *persuaded* (by the advocate's skill with words), and have not been *taught* (201a7–b3). This is a contrast between knowledge and true belief that we have met at *Timaeus* 51e (quoted above, p. 26). But almost immediately we are given a different reason, namely that the jury do not know because they did not actually witness the crime. (They have a true belief 'about things which it's possible to know only if one has seen them, and not otherwise', 201b7–8.) Now it appears that it is not teaching that is needed but perception. This need not be taken as conflicting with the conclusion of the first part of the dialogue, since it is quite consistent to hold that in such matters perception is a necessary, but not a sufficient, condition of knowledge. Nevertheless the point is distinctly unexpected in its present context, as we can see if we ask how Theaetetus should have reacted to it. Clearly, he should have admitted that knowledge is not just true belief, and he should have gone on to try the suggestion that it is true belief *based on perception*. But what he does try is the quite different suggestion that knowledge is true belief *with an account*. Why should we not say that this suggestion is already refuted? No matter what further 'account' we give to the jury, they still will not have witnessed the crime, and still will not know.

On any view of this passage, Plato is writing carelessly here (as also in the very similar passage at *Meno* 97a–b). One might suggest that it was so very obvious to him that knowledge is not just true belief that he simply put down the first argument that came into his head,[40] without stopping to think about how it affected his overall plan for the dialogue. But it is tempting to add a little more by way of explanation, on these lines. Perhaps it is right to say that there are some things that can only be known by a witness, but evidently that cannot apply to all knowledge. And what Plato is now *interested* in is a different kind of knowledge, where perception is not very relevant. It is this different kind of knowledge that he thinks may plausibly be said to require 'an account', and since that is where his interest now lies he hastens to move on to it, without noticing that his transitional passage fails to motivate the new suggestion.

Let us, then, move on with him. What kind of knowledge is it that he does have in mind in the next section of the dialogue?

---

[40] Perhaps *Meno* 97a–b was in his head. At any rate, Theaetetus' remark at 200e4–6 is reminiscent of *Meno* 97c–98c, as McDowell notes (1973, p. 227).

VI

TRUE BELIEF WITH AN ACCOUNT

1. THE THEORY OF SOCRATES' DREAM (201c–202d)

Theaetetus introduces the idea that knowledge is true belief with an account as something that he has heard from someone else, but does not remember very well. Indeed he apparently quotes this person as introducing a word to mean 'knowable' in the course of expounding his theory (201c8–d3).[1] Socrates admits that he too has heard something of the kind (201d5), but at once introduces the idea that both of them have 'dreamt' the theory (201d8, 202c5). He then recounts his own version of this dream, introducing it as something he 'seemed to hear some people say' (201d8–e1), though the vague phrase 'some people' is soon specialized once more to 'the person who said these things' (202e7). It is a plausible hypothesis that the theory is introduced in this way because Plato genuinely is quoting someone else's theory, but one that was put forward some time after the dramatic date of our dialogue. That is why Socrates and Theaetetus cannot admit to knowing its proper author, and have to call it a 'dream'.[2] However, as we have no independent information about this theory that is at all reliable,[3] this hint does not help us to interpret it, which is a pity, for the interpretation of the theory is contested.

The crucial problem is to decide what is meant here by the Greek

---

[1] The word is ἐπιστητόν, and this appears to be its first known occurrence. It is not found elsewhere in Plato (though Aristotle uses it readily enough), and in fact Plato does not use the word again here, either in expounding or in discussing the theory, but employs the more familiar word γνωστόν instead.

[2] The view that Socrates says he may have 'dreamed' at *Philebus* 20b appears to be that put forward at *Republic* vi. 505b–c (but the dream metaphor is used differently at *Charmides* 173a, *Republic* iv. 443b, and *Cratylus* 439c). (Burnyeat (1970, pp. 103–8) disputes this explanation of our 'dream' in the *Theaetetus*.)

[3] On the basis of an obscure passage in Aristotle's *Metaphysics* (H3, 1043b23–32) it has been suggested that the author is Antisthenes. This attribution is sceptically discussed by Hicken (1958, pp. 133–9), and forcefully rejected by Burnyeat (1970, pp. 108–17).

word '*logos*', which is neutrally translated 'account'. The word has a wide range of more specialized meanings. In one sense, a *logos* can be a reason, argument, or justification, and one might well begin by expecting that to be the sense that is relevant here. After all, the view that knowledge is *justified* true belief does seem to be one that is well worth discussing, and it is essentially this view that the *Meno* once endorsed (p. 16). But very few interpreters have in fact supposed that that is the right way to understand '*logos*' in this passage,[4] since it is clear that our theory aims to contrast a *logos* with a *name*. In fact it claims that a simple element has a name but does not have a *logos*, whereas a complex that is put together from several simple elements does have a *logos*, that *logos* being a weaving together of the names of the simple elements concerned. In view of this, it is pretty clear that of all the many senses that '*logos*' can bear there are just two that are serious candidates here. According to one interpretation, a *logos* is here a *statement*, and the point is that statements are combinations of names. According to the other, a *logos* is here a *description* of a thing, and more particularly a *definition* or *analysis* of it, and the point is that only complex things can be defined. '*Logos*' certainly can mean 'statement', and it certainly can mean 'definition', and though it can mean lots of other things too, no other meaning gives us such a plausible contrast with names.

Now if '*logos*' is here ambiguous between 'statement' and 'definition', then there will be a related ambiguity in the cognate verb '*legein*', which can usually be translated 'to say', but which is also analytically tied to the noun '*logos*'. At any rate, it is quite clear that in our passage to *legein* is to *legein* by means of a *logos*. So if a *logos* is here a statement, then to *legein* will here be to state, which is an entirely usual meaning for the verb. But if a *logos* is here a definition, then to *legein* will be to define, and although that is not a very usual usage of the verb it does seem to be a possible one. The point is correctly acknowledged in McDowell's translation, which renders '*logos*' as 'account' and '*legein*' as 'to express in an account'.[5] But to bring out the ambiguity more clearly, it may be

[4] An exception is Morrow (1970), who takes a *logos* to be a mathematical proof (and an *element* to be a mathematical axiom).
[5] McDowell rightly extends this rendering to ἐρεῖ (a2), ῥηθῆναι (b1), and ῥητὰς (b7), which are clearly functioning here as parts of the verb λέγειν. For example at 202b6–7 we are evidently intended to understand ἄλογον (not having a *logos*) as contrasted with ῥητὸν (having a *logos*). My rendering will do the same.

useful if I provide a semi-translation of the passage, in which '*logos*' and '*legein*' are simply left untranslated (and '*legein*' is treated as if it were an English verb). The crucial passage (201d8–202b7) then reads like this:

> I too seemed to hear some people say that the primary elements (if I may so call them), of which we and everything else are composed, have no *logos*. Each of them, just by itself, can only be named, and one cannot say anything else in addition,[6] either that it is or that it is not. For that would be to attach being or not being to it, but nothing should be attached if one is to *legein* it, itself, alone. Thus neither 'it' nor 'itself' nor 'each' nor 'alone' nor 'this' should be attached, nor many other such things. For they run around and get attached to everything, being themselves different from what they are attached to, whereas if it were possible to *legein* the thing, and if it had a *logos* peculiar to itself, one would have to *legein* it apart from everything else. But in fact it is not possible to *legein* any of the primary things with a *logos*; there is nothing else one can do to it except name it, for a name is all it has. But as for what is put together from these primary things, when the names are woven together as the things themselves are, then they become a *logos*. For a weaving together of names is just what a *logos* is. Thus the elements have no *logos* and are unknowable, but perceptible; whereas the complexes are knowable and *legein*-able and believable by true belief.

Let us first consider the view that a *logos* is a statement, and hence that to *legein* something is to state it.[7] On this view, the point that our theory is making is very much the point that I was myself attributing to Plato on pp. 193–5 above. A simple element is the kind of thing that can be perceived, but it is not the kind of thing that can be known or believed, since what is known or believed must always be complex. In fact, it must be the kind of thing that is expressed in language by a whole statement, for only a whole statement is capable of being true. A name by itself does not state anything, and has no truth-value. We do not get a statement, with a truth-value, until we have several names, suitably 'woven together'. It will be apparent, from what I have already said earlier, that I think it entirely plausible to suppose that Plato should have been, at this stage, very interested in a theory along these lines.

---

[6] Burnyeat (1970, p. 119), objects to this rendering of προσειπεῖν, but I do not find his reasons convincing.

[7] This interpretation is mainly due to Ryle, in (unpublished) lectures, and in his 1939 article (pp. 136–40). Among its adherents may be counted Meyerhoff (1958, pp. 135–7), Runciman (1962, pp. 42–5), Crombie (1963, pp. 114–17), and McDowell (1973, pp. 231–50).

In that case, of course, the interesting thing is that he goes on to *reject* the theory. On Ryle's way of developing this interpretation, what lies behind the rejection of the theory is a dissatisfaction with the metaphorical talk of *weaving*. Just what is implied by the claim that a statement is a weaving together of names? On the first alternative, nothing very much is implied, and we are to regard the statement as a mere aggregation of names. It consists just of several names put side by side, as in a list. But it is obvious that a statement is not merely a list, and to name several things one after another, as in reciting a list, is not yet to have stated anything at all. So we had better take the other alternative, and see some genuine significance in this 'weaving together': it must somehow combine the names into a genuine unity, and not leave them a mere plurality. But how exactly is that to be understood, and how can we avoid the objection that nothing has been explained? For we began with the idea that a name could not state anything because it was just a simple expression, not analysable into several parts, but now we seem to be saying that a weaving together of names is something that is equally simple and equally unanalysable. This appears to be something of a dilemma, and Ryle's suggestion is that at the time of writing the *Theaetetus* Plato could not see how to resolve it. But later in the *Sophist* (261c–263d) he reaches the true solution: a statement is made by putting together two expressions of *different* categories, for one of them is a name but the other is not a name but a predicate. The *Theaetetus* therefore shows Plato *en route* between the very unsatisfactory position of the *Cratylus*, which takes a sentence to *be* a name, and the much better position of the *Sophist*, which gives the true relation between names and sentences.

Now it will be obvious that this sketch of how our theory is refuted is rather a long way from the text.[8] It is quite an attractive picture of the way Plato might have been thinking, but the refutation that he actually gives us makes no mention of names, sentences, and what it is to state something. Instead, it invokes the notion of knowing, and

---

[8] It is also a fair distance from what Ryle himself says of the refutation, at least in his 1939 article (p. 138). There he supposes that the second alternative introduces the idea that there is something more to a statement than the names that compose it, namely their arrangement. But this is then construed as the view that a statement *mentions* an arrangement, alongside the various other things that it mentions. So after all a statement is still not distinguished from a list, and the second alternative collapses back into the first. (Evidently, this is even further from the text than what I said.)

argues that it cannot be right to say that a complex is knowable while its simple elements are not. So I am myself inclined to think that this general line of interpretation is better developed in accordance with my suggestions earlier (pp. 195–6). Plato has argued that knowledge, unlike perception, is always of complexes, but now he finds a difficulty, because knowledge of a complex does seem to presuppose some kind of knowledge of its simpler components. But on either of these versions of the refutation we can still say that the point of the theory that is refuted is that it claims that what can be known must always be something that can be *stated*, and what can be stated must be complex. To put the point in our terminology, what can be known, and what can be (truly) stated, is a *fact* and not an *object*. Objects are named but not stated, whereas facts are stated but not named.

However, tempting as it may be to suppose that this is the claim made by the theory of Socrates' dream, still a little reflection will show that this interpretation is untenable. The objections to it are overwhelming. I shall mention three, in increasing order of importance.

(i) The theory opens with the claim that 'we and everything else' are composed of the elements in question (201e1–2), so presumably *we* are suitable complexes. But clearly a person is an object and not a fact: persons can be named but *not* stated. The same applies to the illustration of the theory that follows, where a syllable is taken to be a suitable kind of complex (203a); again, a syllable is *not* the kind of thing that is stated.[9] No doubt one can make various statements *about* syllables, or persons, but that will not satisfy our theory. For the theory very clearly implies that if a thing has a *logos* (in the relevant sense) then that *logos* is peculiar to it (202a5–8). But there is surely no reason to say that statements about persons, or syllables, are peculiar to the things they are about. This could only be said if we were confining attention to a very special kind of statement about the thing in question, e.g. to one that *defines* it.

(ii) When the discussion of Socrates' dream has been concluded, Socrates explicitly asks how we are to understand the notion of a *logos*, and three suggestions are made. The second of these is the

---

[9] This objection is made by White (1976, p. 194), and seems to be conceded by McDowell (1973, p. 232, p. 240).

suggestion that to be able to give a *logos* is 'to be able, when one is asked what anything is, to provide an answer in terms of its elements' (206e6–207a1). We are offered the illustration that to give a *logos* of a wagon is to enumerate all the parts of a wagon, and the suggestion is summed up in this way: 'it's impossible to *legein* anything in a knowing way, until (in addition to one's true belief) one can go through the thing element by element'. And at this point Socrates adds 'as we also said somewhere earlier' (207b6–8). This must be a reference back to the theory of the dream, for there is nowhere else in the dialogue that it could reasonably be taken as referring to. The implication is clear. In the dream theory too to be able to give a *logos* was to be able to enumerate the elements of whatever thing was in question. Moreover, this is exactly what does happen when the dream theory is illustrated at 203a–b: we give a *logos* of the syllable 'SO' by enumerating its elements as 'S' and 'O'. But of course this is a much more specialized use of '*logos*' than that in which to produce a *logos* is just to produce a statement. It is specifically definitions or analyses that are in question, and not just any kind of statement.[10]

(iii) The theory of Socrates' dream was introduced in order to give some substance to the suggestion that knowledge was to be distinguished from true belief by adding the extra condition that one who knows must be able to give a *logos* (in addition to his true belief). On the interpretation that we are considering, the extra condition to be added is that one who knows must be able to *state* what he knows. The passage translated above (p. 204) continues (202b8–c5):

When someone gets hold of the true belief of something without a *logos*, his mind is speaking the truth about it, but does not know it. Someone who cannot give and receive a *logos* of the thing lacks knowledge of it. But if he gets hold of a *logos* as well, then it is possible for all that to happen and for him to be in a perfect position with regard to knowledge.

But if '*logos*' means 'statement' this is simply absurd. It is obviously stupid to suppose that my ability to state what I truly believe is enough to show that I know it, and in fact it is exactly this point that

[10] White also makes this objection (1976, p. 194). It may be replied: if the sense of '*logos*' at 206e–208b is the *same* as its sense in the dream, then Socrates is discussing the same theory twice. But why should he wish to do that? I discuss this later (pp. 219–21), but meanwhile I simply repeat that it is Socrates himself who says that it is the same theory.

is made about the *first* of the three subsequent suggestions for the meaning of '*logos*' (206d–e).[11] But presumably the theory of the dream is not as stupid as this. It must, then, mean something more than simply the ability to produce a statement when it talks of the ability to give a *logos*, and it is by now pretty evident what it does mean: one produces a *logos* when one gives a *definition* or *analysis* of whatever thing is in question.[12]

One consequence may be noted at once. The topic under discussion is not knowledge of truths (or facts) in general, but knowledge of *things*, and the idea is that knowledge of a thing requires the ability to give an account *of that thing*. So one might reasonably say that we begin with the question of what it is to know a thing (*connaître*), and that this is immediately equated with the question of what it is to know what that thing is, which is a special case of *savoir*. But it is only a very special case. Knowing what a thing is is presumably a matter of knowing some truth about the thing, viz. that it is so-and-so, but it is not knowledge of truths in general that we are concerned with, but only knowledge of rather special truths, namely those that say what some thing *is* (in a somewhat technical sense of that expression). The theory of the dream then specifies exactly what knowledge is to count as the knowledge of what a thing is: it is the ability to spell out the elementary constituents of the thing in question. When one has this ability one counts as knowing the thing, but without it one can at best have a true belief of the thing.

Many features of the exposition of this theory now fall into place at once. The somewhat surprising claim that one cannot say, of an element, that it is or that it is not, is now seen to mean that such a statement—though no doubt one can make it—does not *define* or *analyse* the element. An appropriate definition must be peculiar to the item defined: it cannot simply 'attach to it' something that can equally be 'attached' to lots of other things too. Again, such words as 'it', 'itself', 'alone' *can* no doubt be used of elements; it is just that they are of no use when what one is trying to do is to provide a definition of the element, something which fits that element and fits nothing else. All commentators have noted that (with one excep-

---

[11] Note that at 206d2 a *logos*, in the sense of a statement, is said to consist of names and other expressions (ὀνόματα καὶ ῥήματα), but in the dream a *logos* is taken to consist of names (ὀνόματα) and nothing else (202b4–5).

[12] This last objection is noted by Fine (1979*b*, p. 374).

tion[13]) the words which we are told cannot be applied to elements actually are applied to elements in the preceding sentences. This makes it appear that Plato is trying to indicate that the theory refutes itself: it says that one cannot do something which it itself has to do in order to make its point. But the subsequent discussion contains no hint of any such self-refutation, so presumably it is not actually being counted as an objection to the theory, and on the present interpretation that is easy to explain. The passage merely brings out, in a striking way, that to speak of a thing is not the same as to define it: such words as 'it, itself, alone' may well be used to speak of a thing, but they do not provide a definition of it. For a definition should fit the thing defined and nothing else, and these words evidently do not fulfil this role.

Admittedly there are some other oddities in the exposition of this theory which it is not quite so easy to explain away. The exposition apparently assumes that it is particular physical things that we are trying to define or analyse, by enumerating their simple parts, and that is why it is reasonable to say both that the parts in question will be perceptible and that they will be peculiar to the things analysed. For example, the wheel which is a part of this particular wagon will not also be a part of any other wagon. But, when Socrates comes to illustrate the theory, he is evidently not thinking of giving an account of some *particular* wagon, but of giving an account of what, in general, a wagon is. So an answer such as 'A wagon consists of wheels, axle, body, rails, ·yoke' (207a6) does not mention items *peculiar* to the thing defined. Hand-carts and chariots have wheels too. Similarly with the illustration used in immediate connection with the dream theory, namely the syllable 'SO'. It is not being supposed that we are discussing some particular *token* of the syllable, whose parts are a particular *token* of the letter 'S' and a particular *token* of the letter 'O', which are parts of that token of 'SO' and parts of no other syllable-token. Rather, it is the syllable as a *type* that is under discussion, in the sense in which it is the *same* syllable that occurs both in 'Socrates' and in 'soccer' (if I may Anglicize the example). (Compare 208a.) Hence the elementary parts of the syllable are the letters 'S' and 'O' considered as letter-*types*, and of course these letters are by no means peculiar to that syllable, but occur as elementary parts of many other syllables too.

---

[13] The exception is the word 'this'. A variant reading proposes the word 'the' instead (both here and at 205c8), but it would still remain an exception.

No doubt it is reasonable to say, on more or less any view of what an analysis is, that an analysis should *as a whole* fit the thing that is to be analysed and nothing else. But this may be achieved even though the analysis does mention, within itself, items which 'run around and get attached to' other things too.

Presumably, then, this aspect of the theory of the dream is not something that we are intended to take very seriously: when it is a universal that is being defined—as it is, in Socrates' illustrations—the 'elementary parts' that are mentioned in its definition will again be universals, and will not be peculiar to the thing being defined. I suspect that another aspect of the theory that we are not meant to take very seriously is the claim that all the simple elements we are concerned with will be perceptible. (No doubt particular wheels are perceptible, but is 'a wheel', taken generally, a perceptible thing? Compare 195d6–10.) I suspect, then, that these features of the theory may be included only because the original author (whoever he was) included them, and that he included them just because he was assuming that it was individual, particular, perceptible things that one could be said to know. But clearly these features are inessential, and the theory could perfectly well be applied to other kinds of things that one may be said to know. For the *main* point of the theory very clearly is that one counts as knowing a thing (of any kind) only if one can give an 'account' of it, and that to give an 'account', in the relevant sense, is to give an analysis which resolves the thing into its simpler components. Clearly this general theory could be applied to knowing things of the most diverse kinds (including, e.g., Platonic forms).

But however exactly this theory is to be applied, it is bound to have a consequence that appears very odd indeed: the simple elementary components into which all other things are ultimately analysed (or in terms of which they are defined) will not themselves have any analysis (or definition). Hence, according to the theory in question, they cannot be known. But if the elementary constituents are *unknown*, how could it help to explain other things in terms of their elementary constituents? Thus, suppose I want to know what X is, and I am told that X is some suitable combination of Y and Z, where Y and Z are elementary. (It may be that X is some chemical combination of Y and Z—as e.g. water is a particular combination of hydrogen and oxygen—or it may be that X is of the genus Y with the differentia Z—as e.g. man is an animal which is rational—or it may be some other way that Y and Z 'combine' to yield X.) By hypothesis, Y and Z are elementary, and therefore unknown. So it would seem to follow that the combination YZ, however exactly it is construed, must equally be unknown. Hence the information that X is YZ simply tells me that X is the same as some unknown. But how could that suffice to make X known?

Generalizing, it appears that if we do wish to say that analysing a complex thing into its constituents is a way of coming to know it, then we cannot *also* say that this is the *only* way of coming to know a thing, for if we do it must follow that the elementary constituents cannot be known. This is exactly the consequence that our theory draws, and it is this consequence that Socrates fastens upon as untenable (202d8–c1). As I have just indicated, there seems to be good reason to suppose that it genuinely is untenable. So let us now turn to the arguments that Socrates offers in order to demonstrate this point.

2. THE REFUTATION OF SOCRATES' DREAM (202e–206c)

Two separate arguments are offered in refutation of the theory. The first, 202e–205e, one might reasonably call a theoretical argument. It does not rely on any specific examples of elements and complexes, and would be equally applicable to many different ways of filling out the details of the theory. But to confirm his result Socrates then adds another and more empirical argument (206a–b), which does rely on specific examples of elements and complexes. Finally he claims that yet other disproofs of the theory would be available (206c1–2). Let us take the first argument first.

Socrates claims that the author of the dream theory must have had letters and syllables in mind as an illustration (παράδειγμα) of his theory,[14] and he proposes to use this illustration himself (202e). So we begin by agreeing that a syllable ('SO') does have an 'account', which one gives by specifying its letters (as 'S' and 'O'), while a letter does not (203a–b). In the first argument nothing will hang on this agreement, and it may perfectly well be understood as simply an agreement 'for the sake of argument'. It merely allows us

---

[14] Presumably this is because the words στοιχεῖον and συλλαβή, used for the elements and complexes of the theory, were quite frequently applied to letters and syllables in ordinary Greek.

to work with a familiar example. Then Socrates poses the dilemma 'Are we to say that a syllable is both its letters—or all of them, if there are more than two—or that it is some one form (μίαν τινὰ ἰδέαν) that comes into being when they are put together?' (203c4– 6). He proceeds to argue that in either case the syllable will be no more and no less knowable than its letters, but unfortunately neither branch of his argument is at all satisfactory.

Against the first horn of the dilemma he appears to offer a straightforward fallacy of division. If the syllable just is both the letters, he claims, then to know the syllable is to know both the letters, which is to know each of the letters (203c8–d10). But this argument appears to be no better than the obvious fallacy: if the syllable just is both the letters, then to divide the syllable into two letters is just the same as to divide both the letters into two letters, which is to divide each of the letters into two letters. Clearly this is absurd. But one might perhaps try to rescue the argument from this objection by taking the hypothesis that the syllable is the two letters in a somewhat extreme way. Perhaps the hypothesis is meant to be that the syllable is, as it were, a *plural item*: it simply is not *one* thing at all. It is improper, then, to call it *a* syllable, or *a* composite thing, or *an* aggregate, or *a* collection, and so on, for all of these expressions treat it as if it were one thing.[15] Then the argument is that if the syllable is a plural item we should not say that it *is* known (which treats it as singular) but that 'it' *are* known, i.e. that the letters which 'it' is are known. But then there appears to be no fallacy in moving from the plural 'the letters are known' to the singular 'each letter is known'. However, it is obvious that the cost of rescuing Socrates' argument in this way is to throw all the weight of the refutation on the second horn of the dilemma. Of course the syllable is not a plural item, but is one thing put together from its two letters.

Socrates' argument against the second horn of the dilemma is startling, for its main claim is that anything that has parts must be the same as all its parts (and hence must be a plural item?). Granting this claim, it is of course easy to reach the desired result about the syllable. The hypothesis is that the syllable is not the same as all its letters (204a1–3), but it is agreed that if the syllable has parts at all those parts must be its letters (205b8–13), so it now follows that the

---

[15] This suggestion arises from some remarks in the *Parmenides*, which I shall discuss shortly.

syllable has no parts (205c1–2). But the reason why the dream theory claimed that elements could not be known was precisely that they had no parts, so the theory is now committed to saying that the syllable cannot be known either (205c4–d5). Socrates can therefore sum up his argument in this way. On the first hypothesis, that the syllable is its letters, we find that if, as the theory claims, the syllable can be known, then so can its letters. And on the second hypothesis, that the syllable is not its letters, we find that if, as the theory claims, its letters cannot be known, then neither can the syllable. Either way, the theory cannot maintain its claim that the syllable can be known but its letters cannot (205d7–e8). This all looks very neat indeed. But now let us go back to the crucial claim that anything that has parts must be the same as all its parts. How does Socrates purport to establish this?

The argument opens with Theaetetus maintaining quite generally that any whole is some one thing, and not the same as all its parts (204a7–10). However, he is willing to admit that a whole may not be the same as what we may call a sum[16] (204a11–b9). Socrates then proceeds to argue that a sum certainly is the same as all its parts (204b10–e6). His argument here is not particularly compelling: in essence it seems to be that the number of things in a collection is both the sum of those things and all of those things.[17] But anyway one might admit this claim and still preserve Theaetetus' distinction between a whole and a sum. The position will be that both wholes and sums have parts, but a sum is the same as all its parts while a whole is not (204e3–13).[18] However, Theaetetus is induced to abandon his distinction when faced with the claim that a whole and a sum can each be characterized in the same way, as 'that from which nothing is missing' (205a1–7), and this gives Socrates his conclusion. It is agreed that a part can only be a part of a whole or a sum, and now we have found that there is no distinction to be drawn between wholes and sums, and we have earlier said that a sum is the

---

[16] More literally 'an all'. The Greek word in question, τὸ πᾶν, is the word 'all' in the singular, which Socrates is going on to equate with the word 'all' in the plural, τὰ πάντα.

[17] Note, in passing, that the number 6 seems to be treated as itself a collection, presumably of ones (204c).

[18] The reasoning goes off the rails a bit here. Socrates has claimed that whatever has parts is composed of parts (e3), and seems prematurely to assume that only sums are composed of parts, hence inferring that if wholes and sums are different then wholes are not composed of parts (e8–9). But the correct position is reached at e11–13.

same as all its parts. It follows that whatever has parts is the same as all its parts.

It is rather difficult to believe that Plato was convinced of the soundness of this reasoning. It is even more difficult to believe this if we suppose that he had already written the second part of the *Parmenides*, which does seem to reveal that something must be wrong. That dialogue affirms the premiss that a whole can be characterized as that from which no part is missing (137c7–8). It does not contain anything answering to our argument, to show that this premiss implies that a whole just is all its parts, but it does at one point make the assumption that a whole just is all its parts. However it then proceeds to use this assumption to generate a contradiction (145b–e). On the one hand it is argued that each part is contained in the whole, and hence all the parts are contained in the whole, and hence the whole (which is all its parts) is contained in itself (145b6–c7).[19] On the other hand it is argued that if the whole were contained in all its parts then it would have to be contained in each of its parts, which is impossible. Hence the whole is not, after all, contained in itself (i.e. in all its parts) (145c7–e1). (Note that the first of these arguments assumes that what holds of each of the parts will hold of all of them, and the second assumes that what holds of all of the parts will hold of each of them.) Later on, at 157c5–e1, it is argued that a whole must be some *one* thing (μία τις ἰδέα) composed of many parts but not the same as them. The argument boils down to this: if a whole were all its parts then any part of the whole would be a part of all its parts, and hence a part of each of its parts, which is absurd. (So again it is assumed, but with a different example, that what holds of all the parts will hold of each of them.)

Now of course one can never tell, with any argument in the second part of the *Parmenides*, what Plato himself thought of it. It is not clear, for example, whether he has noticed that there is something funny about the assumption that when dealing with a 'plural item', such as 'all the parts', one can move freely from 'all' to 'each' and back again. Consequently it is not clear whether he thinks that the argument to show that a whole is not a plural item is a good argument, and perhaps he really does wish to maintain the claim of the *Theaetetus* that a whole *is* a plural item. But at least he

[19] It is *also* claimed elsewhere, and on other grounds, that nothing can contain itself (e.g. 138b1–4, 150e5–151a2).

must have been aware that there are problems in this area, and that there is something puzzling about the relationship between a whole and (all) its parts. One feels, then, that if the second part of the *Parmenides* was written before this section of the *Theaetetus* then Plato must at least have realized that this argument that he brings against the theory of Socrates' dream is highly suspicious. There is, however, no strong reason to suppose that the second part of the *Parmenides* was written earlier, and it is a possibility that it records a later stage in his thought. Perhaps, when he was writing the *Theaetetus*, he had not yet noticed the problems which this way of thinking gives rise to. Did he perhaps really think that he had firmly established the result that a whole just *is* all its parts?

But the problem is that, even if we set the *Parmenides* aside, still the argument in the *Theaetetus* is so very obviously a bad one. Quite apart from the oddity of the suggestion that wholes are essentially plural items, one very simple and natural objection is this. We may plausibly regard the 'sum' of the two letters 'S' and 'O' as the collection (or set) which has just those two letters as members. On this account, the sum of 'S' and 'O' is precisely the same thing as the sum of 'O' and 'S', since collections (or sets) are the same if and only if they have the same members. But of course the syllable 'SO' is not the same syllable as the syllable 'OS', so a syllable is not a mere sum or aggregate of its letters. It may perhaps be regarded as the *ordered* set consisting of the two letters 'S' and 'O' taken in that order, but evidently the order of its letters is essential to the identity of the syllable. We might say that a syllable is indeed a whole, but it is a *structured* whole, and not a mere sum or aggregate of its parts. To apply this point to the argument that Socrates actually presents, we must therefore maintain (with Theaetetus) that sums and (structured) wholes are different, which of course is very straightforward. Perhaps a sum can be characterized as 'that from which nothing is missing', meaning by this that the sum exists so long as all its parts are present.[20] But a (structured) whole cannot be characterized in the same way, since it will exist only so long as all its parts are *both* present *and* in the right arrangement. When the parts are

---

[20] I intend the word 'present' to suggest some measure of togetherness. Thus one may regard a crowd as a 'sum' of people, but to destroy the crowd all one has to do is to scatter the people; there is no need to liquidate them. (But anyway the distinction I am drawing is only a rough and ready one.)

rearranged, nothing is 'missing', but nevertheless the whole is destroyed. (To put this a little more accurately: no *part* is missing. The arrangement is missing, but an arrangement of parts is not itself a part, and we will get into hopeless difficulties if we suppose that it is.[21]) Structured wholes (such as syllables) are therefore quite different from mere sums or aggregates, and the argument to show that they are not is thoroughly unconvincing.

It has been suggested by Fine (pp. 382–4)[22] that we can rescue Plato's argument in this way. He is entitled to use, against the theory of the dream, the assumption that a complex thing just *is* all its elements, because that is an assumption which the dream theory makes itself. It claims that to know a thing is just to be able to enumerate its simple elements, and it says nothing at all about the order and arrangement of those elements. So according to the theory itself there is nothing more to a complex thing than the elements of which it is composed, for if there were then simply being able to list those elements would not be an adequate test of whether one knew the complex.

Now I do not deny that one *could* construct an objection to the dream theory along these lines, but (*a*) it would not be a very upsetting objection, and (*b*) it is anyway not what Plato does. To take the second point first, it is obvious that in the crucial stretch of argument from 204a to 205a Socrates is giving his *own* reasons for the claim that whatever has parts just is all its parts. He never once refers to the dream theory during this stretch of argument, and nowhere suggests that the argument was unnecessary since its conclusion would anyway have to be granted by his opponent. Fine's suggestion, then, gives a possible way of reconstructing Plato's argument, but it will not do as an account of what the argument actually is. Moreover, it would not seem to be a very damaging criticism of the dream theory in any case. For suppose our dream theorist is presented with the objection that in order to give an adequate analysis of a syllable one must specify not only the letters that it contains but also the order of their occurrence. He could surely *accept* this objection, and admit that his previous account of what an analysis was needs revision: the requisite order

[21] Compare Aristotle's discussion at *Metaphysics* Z17, 1041b11–33.
[22] References to Fine throughout this chapter are to Fine (1979*b*). For the view in question, compare McDowell (1973), p. 244 (and perhaps Cornford (1935), p. 151).

and arrangement of elements must be specified, as well as the elements themselves. But this still allows him to maintain his main point, that only complexes have an analysis, and hence only complexes can be known. Fine thinks that he could not so readily accept this revision of his theory because he has insisted that the elements that are mentioned in the analysis of a complex must be *peculiar* to that complex, whereas principles of order and arrangement will not be peculiar in this way (pp. 383–4). But I have already observed that this feature of the dream theory is not in fact taken seriously anywhere in the discussion. The letter 'S' is not peculiar to the syllable 'SO', and wheels are not peculiar to wagons. Nor should it be taken seriously: the genuine problem which the dream theory sets does not in any way depend upon it.

Furthermore, suppose for the sake of argument that Plato genuinely does think that he is entitled to ignore complications about structured wholes, since the dream theory implicitly denies them. It is, then, only mere sums or aggregate wholes that need to be considered. Is his argument then satisfactory? On my account of it, his argument is that sums or aggregate wholes are plural items, and that when we are dealing with a plural item what holds of all will hold of each. I take it that no one will wish to defend this as a good argument, for even an aggregate whole is something singular and not plural. And if we insist on this, then it appears to be straightforwardly a fallacy to argue that if the whole is known then so is each of its parts. But Fine wishes to defend this argument by importing a premiss from the dream and employing a general principle about knowledge which she calls the principle that 'knowledge must be based on knowledge' (p. 381). As she construes the argument, the dream claims that to know the whole 'SO' one must decompose it into its elementary parts 'S' and 'O', and Socrates replies that this will not yield knowledge of 'SO' unless we already know 'S' and know 'O'. So his argument is not a formal fallacy, though admittedly it invokes a principle about knowledge that the dream theorist would not accept.

Now again it is pretty clear that this is not a fair account of what the argument at 203c7–d10 actually is, as Fine supposes. The argument that is actually stated does not make any use of the dream theory's account of what it is to know a syllable, but does profess to be using the hypothesis that the syllable just is all its letters, whereas

Fine's reconstruction ignores that hypothesis altogether.[23] If Fine's reconstruction were correct, then there would be no need to go on to consider the alternative hypothesis that a syllable is not all its letters but some one thing that is made from them. For, without relying on either hypothesis, Plato has already shown that a premiss from the dream theory, combined with (what he takes to be) a correct principle about knowledge, leads to results which are inconsistent with the dream theory.

But there is also a further point worth making about Fine's reconstruction of this argument. She supposes that a special principle about *knowledge* (to which Plato subscribed) will avoid the charge that 203c7–d10 contains a straightforward fallacy of division. So the fallacy is not licensed generally, but only in the special case of *knowledge*. However Socrates does employ it in another instance too. When he is summing up his argument at 205d7–10, he claims that if the syllable just is all its letters then not only will it and they be equally knowable but also it and they will equally have an account. How is he entitled to that? On my version of the argument it is simple: if all the letters have an account then each of the letters has an account. But on Fine's version we need the supplementary principle that 'accounts must be based on accounts', so that if 'SO' has an account (viz. that it is 'S' and 'O') then 'S' and 'O' must equally have accounts. But while she does indeed maintain that this is what Plato himself believes—a view I shall discuss later (section 4(ii))—I suspect that even she would hesitate to view it as a *premiss* to be used against the theory of the dream.

I conclude that the argument that Plato himself gives against the theory of the dream simply must be viewed as a wholly unsatisfactory argument, and that Fine's attempt to rescue it does not succeed. Did Plato himself think that the argument was satisfactory? Or did he perhaps mean us, the audience, to infer that there was nothing wrong with the theory of the dream after all? But the answer to this last question must be 'no'. Plato is evidently convinced that it cannot be right to say that complexes are knowable while their simple elements are not. This emerges clearly enough when we go

[23] In fact Fine appears not to have seen the basic fallacy involved. Supposing that $X = Y + Z$, she admits that it is not obviously legitimate to equate knowing what X is with knowing what $Y + Z$ is. (This is an application of Leibniz's Law that one might well wish to resist.) But apparently she does not see that it is even less clearly legitimate to equate knowing what $Y + Z$ *is* with knowing what (each of) Y and Z *are*.

on to consider his subsidiary, and more empirical, argument against the theory of the dream.

In this second argument (206a–b) Socrates assumes that letters and syllables do indeed count as elements and complexes in the sense required by the theory, and he simply points out that it *is* possible to know letters, since that knowledge is exactly what we acquire when we learn to spell. He adds that the same is true of the notes of music, which all would agree to be the 'elements' of music. And he concludes that, at least in the cases of elements and complexes that we are familiar with, 'the class of elements admits of knowledge that is far clearer, and more important for the perfect grasp of every branch of learning, than the complex' (206b7–9).

The first thing to notice about this argument is what Socrates has in mind when he claims that we can and do 'know letters'. What he says about this is 'When you were learning, you spent your time doing nothing but trying to tell the letters apart (διαγιγνώσκειν), each one just by itself, both when it was a matter of seeing them and when it was a matter of hearing them, in order that you wouldn't be confused by their being put into arrangements, whether spoken or written' (206a5–8). When you have mastered this skill, then apparently you count as 'knowing the letters'.[24] Knowing a thing, then, is here being construed as having the ability to recognize it, in the various contexts in which it occurs, and to discriminate it from other similar things. This is quite a different view of what it is to know a thing from that propounded by the dream theory, and we may note two points. First, on this view of knowledge it is evidently possible to know a complex without yet knowing its elements (for we learn to recognize and distinguish spoken words long before we learn how to spell them). Second, there is no suggestion that one who has this kind of knowledge will thereby be in a position to 'give an account' of the things he knows. A person who can spell will no doubt be able to answer the question 'What is the letter "S"?' by pointing to and producing examples, but that is surely not 'giving an account' in any reasonable sense. So if this is a good objection to the theory of the dream, it is also an objection to the whole idea that knowledge involves the ability to give an account. Why, then, does our dialogue not yet reject this idea, but spend another four pages discussing various versions of it?

[24] Compare *Republic* iii. 402a7–b3.

One suggestion, which I do think has its attractions, introduces a hypothesis about how the dialogue was composed. It is that when Plato first planned the dialogue he did not intend to include the dream theory at all. Originally the dialogue would have ended with the last four pages as its only discussion of the view that knowledge involves the ability to give an account, and the dream theory is a later addition. This hypothesis would explain two distinct oddities in the construction of this last part of the dialogue as we have it. One is that the question of what sense we are to give to the word 'account', which one would expect to be the *first* question to be raised as soon as accounts are mentioned, is not in fact raised (at 206c) until *after* one view of what an account is has been very thoroughly discussed and (apparently) dismissed. The other is that although this theory is refuted, it is not in fact dismissed, but soon appears again as the second of the three proposed senses for 'account' at 206e–208b. Admittedly the initial statement of the dream at 201d–202c contains many more details than the bare suggestion at 206e–207c that an account is an enumeration of elementary parts, but the extra details in the dream theory have played no role in its discussion. So far as the actual discussions are concerned, it is exactly the same theory that is being discussed at the two places, though certainly the objections raised against it are quite different. So it is perfectly sensible to include both discussions, but very odd to separate them as our text does.

The hypothesis is, then, that after Plato had planned, and perhaps written, his closing pages, he determined to add the dream passage. But he did not wish to put it where it apparently belongs, namely under the second of the three senses of 'account', because that would disturb the balance of his nicely worked out ending. So he put it where it now is, accepting the odd consequences that result, and merely adding the brief acknowledgement at 207b6 that it is the same theory that is discussed in the two places. If this hypothesis is correct, then of course it also allows us to explain why the dialogue continues to discuss 'accounts' even after 206a–b has shown them to be irrelevant. But notice that it is a consequence of this explanation that it must be possible to make adequate sense of the last few pages of the dialogue on their own, and without the discussion of the dream theory preceding them.[25]

[25] It is possible to do this on the interpretations of Fine and White (discussed below). But it is not possible on the interpretation that I shall eventually advocate.

But there are also at least two other explanations that we can suggest. On one view,[26] Plato *has* noticed the implication that 'accounts' have already been shown to be irrelevant, and is going to bring it to our attention, though he is not ready to do so quite yet because there is something else he wishes to say first. On the other view,[27] he has simply failed to notice the implication. I noted earlier that at 201b–c Plato gives an example to show that knowledge is not just true belief, which—if he is right—*also* shows that knowledge is not true belief with an account. But apparently he cannot have noticed this implication, and I suggested that the reason for this oversight was that he was not really interested in that kind of knowledge. His attention was focused on a different kind of knowledge, for which it did seem plausible to say that it required the ability to give an account. Should we perhaps say the same about 206a–b? The idea will be that what Plato is actually interested in is *neither* the kind of knowledge that a witness has of who pocketed the silver teaspoon *nor* the kind of knowledge of letters that we all acquire when we learn how to spell. So although our knowledge of letters and syllables may provide a convenient way of illustrating the problems that Plato is really concerned with, still it is of no interest to him in itself, and that is why he overlooks the implications of his empirical argument against the dream. But a consequence of this suggestion must be that the empirical argument does not give his real reasons for being dissatisfied with the dream; it is a mere afterthought, of no real importance to him. In that case, what *is* his reason for rejecting the dream? Does he really trust in his more theoretical argument, which seems so very unconvincing to us? Or is there something else at work?

Well, it seems overwhelmingly probable that there is something else at work, namely the principle that 'knowledge must be based upon knowledge'. If the ultimately simple notions, in terms of which others are defined, are themselves *unknown*, how could the definitions confer knowledge? As the *Republic* says, 'Where the starting-point is not known, and the conclusion and the intervening steps are woven together from what is not known, how could such agreement ever become knowledge?' (533c3–5).[28] It appears to be

---

[26] This is the view I shall endorse.

[27] This view might appeal to Fine, as a revision that her interpretation requires, if my criticism on p. 249 below is conceded.

[28] The *Republic* is talking here of knowledge of truths (in mathematics) rather than knowledge of things. But the point seems to apply in either case.

very plausible to claim that anything that is to count as a basis or starting-point for knowledge must itself be known, for otherwise what is built from it will be without any secure foundation. But that is exactly what the dream theory denies. This is evidently such a very good reason for being dissatisfied with the theory that it is difficult to believe that it was not Plato's reason. But at the same time one has to admit that the arguments that he actually brings against the dream simply do not mention this point. It is really rather surprising.

I shall return later (in section 4) to the question of what moral we are supposed to draw from this discussion of the dream that Socrates and Theaetetus shared. It will be convenient to look first at the rest of the investigation of 'accounts'.

3. THREE WAYS OF TAKING 'AN ACCOUNT' (206c–210a)

Socrates introduces the final stage of the discussion by suggesting that there are just three ways in which one might take the notion of an account (206c). The first need not detain us, since this suggestion is that to produce an account is simply to express one's thought in speech, which Socrates thinks that everyone can do 'more or less quickly'.[29] Anyway, it is clearly inadequate to distinguish knowledge from true belief, and is swiftly dismissed (206d–e). The second, as we noted, returns to the same view of an account as was employed in the dream theory: to know what a thing is is therefore to be able to go through all its elements. (And there is an added suggestion that to have a true belief as to what a thing is is to be able to pick out some of its parts, but not the elementary ones, 207a5–c4.) Against this theory Socrates now produces a completely different objection, but one that continues to use words, syllables, and letters as examples (207d–208b).

The objection is that one may correctly enumerate the elements of a thing, e.g. the letters of which a word or syllable is composed, while still lacking knowledge, and hence that the condition proposed is not sufficient for knowledge. (By contrast, the moral of the discussion of the dream *may* be that the condition is not necessary for knowledge, since elements which have no account can also be

---

[29] For the assumption that whatever can be thought can be said, cf. p. 175 above and p. 234 below.

known.) The point that Socrates has in mind does not seem to be that one might get the spelling of a word right purely by *chance*.[30] If that were his point we could obviously meet it simply by adding the condition that one consistently get the word right. Rather, the objection seems to be that one might get the word right, but without any proper understanding of what one is doing. (The suggestion that Plato frequently thinks of knowing as understanding is, I think, common ground among all interpreters.) Thus consider a child, learning to spell, who has learned how to spell 'Theaetetus' in the sense that he consistently gets *that* word right. But suppose also that when he is asked to spell 'Theodorus' he gets its first syllable wrong. This, Socrates claims, will show that he does not know the first syllable of the two names. Indeed, the child may be in the same situation with regard to every syllable in 'Theaetetus'. In that case he has a true belief concerning 'Theaetetus', and he has an 'account' of it in the sense in question, but he does not have knowledge.

Now it seems reasonable to say that there is a presumption here about spelling which would certainly not be satisfied by the English language, namely that the spelling of a word follows by general principles from its pronunciation. Granting this presumption, the nub of the objection is that the child we are considering has not yet got a proper grasp of the principles involved, and this is shown by the fact that he still gets some words wrong even though he gets others right. But the precise way in which Socrates develops his point is not very satisfactory, for his argument comes to this. The child we are considering *can* spell 'Theaetetus', for he (consistently) gets that word right, but he *cannot* spell its opening syllable, for he sometimes gets that wrong (namely, when it occurs in other words). It would follow, according to the theory under consideration, that the child knows the whole word, but does not know its opening syllable, and may not know any of its syllables. This consequence Socrates treats as absurd. But is it? It would appear that he is simply assuming that knowledge of the whole word must be based upon knowledge of its syllables, but it is not obvious why we should accept that assumption.[31] Moreover, if we do wish to accept it—

[30] I agree here with White (1976, p. 178), McDowell (1973, p. 254), and Fine (1979*b*, pp. 387–8), against Cornford (1935, pp. 157–8), Sayre (1969, p. 135), and Morrow (1970, pp. 309–10).

[31] Certainly, if to know a thing is *just* to be able to recognize it, and distinguish it from others (as on p. 219) then the assumption must be rejected.

perhaps on the ground that the child is being taught to spell whole words by first breaking them up into syllables—then there appears to be a simple way of modifying the interpretation of 'an account' which will do the trick. Let us say that to be able to give an account of a thing is to be able to enumerate not only its elements but also the elements of all of its non-elementary parts. To conform with a presumption that Socrates is evidently making, we add that this assumes the ability to *recognize* the non-elementary parts—i.e. the syllables—wherever they occur. With this revision, Socrates' objection appears to collapse.

One can imagine him continuing his argument in some such way as this. Suppose we began teaching our child to spell by first teaching him the whole word 'Theaetetus'. (It is his own name, perhaps.) Building on this, we then concentrate on the syllables in this word, and the child is taught to recognize them wherever they occur, and to write them correctly. So he now satisfies the revised condition for knowing the word 'Theaetetus'. But what we have done so far has not necessarily led him to see that the two[32] letters in the syllable 'THE' correspond to two sounds which may each occur in combination with other sounds. So although our child is well-trained with the syllables 'THE' and 'US', there is as yet no ground for supposing that he can deal with 'THU' or 'THUS' or 'SE' or 'SETH', and so on. And Socrates is very likely to suppose that until he can do this he does not really count as *knowing* the word 'Theaetetus', for he does not really understand what is going on when one spells it out into its elements. In general, then, the ability to get things right is never an adequate guarantee of knowledge, because one can acquire that ability without any understanding of the principles involved. This is a general moral which can quite reasonably be drawn from Plato's example, though one can hardly say that our text does explicitly draw it.

But perhaps Plato does not have anything quite so general in mind, and his own thought may be more closely concentrated on the particular account of knowledge under discussion. In that case, it is tempting to look at the matter in this way. Suppose that he has noticed, and is endorsing, the implications of his empirical objection to the dream theory. He is then accepting that one counts as knowing a particular letter when and only when one can recognize that letter, and discriminate it from others, in all the various

---

[32] 'TH' is one letter in Greek.

contexts in which it occurs. By this criterion, the example is an example of a child who does not yet know the particular letter 'TH', since he is not aware that it occurs in the word 'Theodorus'. Consequently, the point being made here can be seen as building directly upon the discussion of the dream theory. There Plato had argued that it must be possible to know the simple elements of which a (knowable) complex is composed, and here he goes on to claim that unless one does know the elements in question, an ability to spell out the complex into its elements will not yield knowledge of it. The argument is set out, for dialectical purposes, as an argument about one who does not know the syllable 'THE' rather than one who does not know the letter 'TH'. This is perhaps because we have already discussed, and rejected, what the theory claims about the possibility of knowing an individual letter, and it appears that we can make the required point without explicitly reopening that issue. For the theory is also committed to the premiss that the child does not know the syllable 'THE', since he cannot spell it into its two letters. But it is obvious that the reason why he cannot do this is that he cannot always recognize the syllable, wherever it occurs, and that this in turn is because he cannot always recognize its opening letter. So it is the fact that the child does not *know* the letter 'TH' that lies at the heart of the example, even if this is not explicitly mentioned.

It is evident that these last two paragraphs have been somewhat speculative. I now set aside such speculations in order to return to the text.

The final suggestion as to what it is to be able to give an account is, we are told, 'what most people would say', namely 'being able to state some mark (σημεῖον) by which the thing one is asked for differs from everything else' (208c7–8). An example would be being able to say of the sun that it is the brightest of the heavenly bodies (208d1–3). Although Socrates does not mention the point, it is clear that being able to enumerate the elements of a thing was intended to be *one* way of stating a distinguishing mark for it, for it was assumed that nothing else would have exactly the same elements (in the same arrangement, as we ought to add). So the present suggestion can be viewed as a generalization of the previous one. But the difficulty that Socrates finds with it is quite different from anything that we have had before.

His argument (209a–210a) rests upon the premiss that it is

supposed to be possible to have a true belief of something—for example Theaetetus—without yet knowing it, i.e. being in possession of a suitable account. But, he claims, anyone who can think of Theaetetus at all must already have some mark that distinguishes him from all others, for otherwise it would not be Theaetetus he was thinking of. So to require a distinguishing mark *in addition to* true belief is not actually to require anything extra at all. And if we try to avoid this difficulty by saying that what is required is not just a true belief of how the thing in question differs from all others, but *knowledge* of this difference, then the account has collapsed into circularity. For, quite generally, one cannot explain knowledge as the addition to true belief of the *knowledge* of anything at all, whether a distinguishing mark or anything else.

There are many things wrong with this argument. Let us begin with Socrates' claim that in order to be able to think about Theaetetus at all I must be in possession of a distinguishing mark for him. Arguing for this, he first says that if all that I believe of Theaetetus is that he is a man, with nose, eyes, mouth, and so on, then my thought is no more of him than of any other man (209b2–8). Next he adds that if my thought is of one who has a snub nose and prominent eyes, still there are many people of that kind (209b10–c2). Each of these are cases where what I have in my thought is 'something common', and so my thought is not a thought of a particular thing at all (209a10–11; cf. 208d7–9). Finally he concludes 'It won't be Theaetetus who figures in a judgement in me until precisely that snubness has imprinted and deposited in me a memory-trace different from those of the other snubnesses I've seen, and similarly with the other things you're composed of. Then if I meet you tomorrow that snubness will remind me and make me judge correctly about you' (209c4–9).

I think it is fairly clear that Socrates is supposing that what makes my thought a thought of Theaetetus in particular is that I have a memory-image of him that fits him and fits no one else. It is not something 'common', but is peculiar to him. One point may be made at once: what Socrates has in mind is my ability to think of Theaetetus when I am *not* perceiving him. He has apparently forgotten the perfectly correct point that he made earlier, in the discussion of the wax tablet, that it is also possible to think of something when one *is* perceiving it (e.g. as that man over there in the distance). In the latter case, what allows me to think of the thing is obviously not a memory-image, already stored on the wax tablet, but is simply my present perception. (I shall make a suggestion later as to why this apparently obvious objection is here overlooked.) But even if we too confine our attention to cases of thinking of a thing by remembering it, still what Socrates says can hardly be accepted, for the truth is that my memory-image of Theaetetus may well not be one that distinguishes him from everyone else. There may certainly be another person, perhaps 'the remotest peasant in Asia' (as McDowell translates the phrase), who looks so very like Theaetetus that my memory-image fits him just as well as it fits Theaetetus. But for all that it may still be Theaetetus that I am thinking of, and not this other lad, for example if I have met Theaetetus and have never met his double.

However it is possible that Socrates does not mean to be taken in quite this way. After all he does not exactly say that my memory of Theaetetus' snubness must distinguish it from all other snubnesses whatever, but only from all others *that I have seen*. So perhaps what he has in mind—though he does not quite say it—is that I can think of an object that I have already encountered so long as I have a memory of it that distinguishes it from all other things *that I have encountered*. But in that case, of course, he is wrong in supposing that if I can think of an object I must be able to recognize it when I meet it tomorrow. For one thing, if Theaetetus happens to be wearing a mask, or a disguise, or even a new hair-cut, then I may well fail to recognize him when I bump into him tomorrow. For another, if in fact it is his double from Asia who turns up on my doorstep, I may wrongly mistake him for Theaetetus, just because the 'distinguishing mark' that I rely on does not actually distinguish Theaetetus from everything else. Yet for all that it surely was Theaetetus whom I was thinking of yesterday when I recalled that brilliant young mathematician whom I had met one day with Theodorus in the gymnasium.

To sort out the issues involved here, let us pause to consider more directly what it is about a thought that makes it a thought of or about this particular thing rather than that one.[33] Sometimes it seems

[33] It will be obvious that what follows is heavily influenced by Russell's views on acquaintance. (See in particular his 'Knowledge by Acquaintance and Knowledge by Description' and 'On the Nature of Acquaintance', esp. pp. 167–8.) But I shall part company with Russell before the end.

fairly clear that the answer is that the thought contains a uniquely identifying description, which seems to be what Socrates means by a 'distinguishing mark'[34] and the thing in question is the one and only thing that satisfies that description. For example, suppose that I think, because I have been told, that the President of the MCR is a woman, and suppose that I know nothing else about the person in question. Then it appears that the only reason why what I think could be said to be *about* one person rather than another is that it is about that person, whoever it is, who satisfies the description 'the President of the MCR'. For I have no other link with the person in question than one which makes use of that description. But it cannot be right to say that a thought *always* attaches to the particular object that it is a thought of in this indirect way, via a description. For suppose now that I am looking at the person standing in front of me, and I have a thought which I express to myself as 'That person is a woman'. Then the only relevant description that I am using is that the thing in question is a person, and of course there are lots of things that satisfy that description.[35] But it will pay us to consider this kind of case a little more carefully.

You may reply that I do have at my command a description that that person and only that person satisfies, namely 'the one and only person now standing in front of me'. For the sake of argument, let us for the moment grant this reply. Then what has happened is that we have found a description that uniquely fits one particular object by making use of a relation in which it stands to another particular object, namely me. So we can simply renew the question: what is it that makes my thought a thought about *me* in particular, rather than anything else? Is it because I am really using a description which I and only I satisfy? Well, no doubt I could produce such a description, for example[36] 'the one and only person who is exactly

[34] Notice that a distinguishing mark is supposed to be an 'account', i.e. something that can be expressed in words, and something that fits only the thing it is an account of, such as 'the brightest of the heavenly bodies'.

[35] It may be objected that I am describing the thing not only as a person but also as *that* one. The phrase 'that person' may, of course, be applied to many different people in different situations, but it may be said that in the *present* situation it applies to just one person, namely the one I am looking at. I say more of this objection later, but for the moment I simply stipulate that a demonstrative such as 'that' is not to count as *describing* the thing demonstrated.

[36] Russell would prefer the suggestion 'the one and only person who is having *this* sense-datum'.

here', but again this is a description which uniquely fits one particular thing (me) because it specifies a relation which that thing bears to some *other* particular, in this case a particular place. So we renew the question again, and so on. Generally, in a situation where I can think of a person because I am looking at her (or perhaps him, if my thought is mistaken), it seems impossible to find a description which I will believe to fit that person uniquely except one that describes it by relating it to some other particular thing, and that merely postpones the question. And even if, after much thought, I could come up with a description which I believed to fit that person uniquely, but which did not contain within itself a reference to any further particular, still it seems obvious that my original and simple thought 'That person is a woman' did not make use of any such complicated description. So the first conclusion to draw is that it must be possible to refer to a particular thing in one's thought, not in the indirect way that relies on a description, but in some more direct fashion.

So far it is open to you to hold that there are just a few very special things—perhaps just myself and the present time—that I can refer to in this direct way, and all other things are referred to indirectly, via descriptions relating them to these special things. But actually I do not think that is a very plausible position to hold. If we go back to the original situation, it may first be observed that the description 'the person in front of me' will not in fact serve to fix who it is that I am thinking of. For example, we can easily imagine that there are actually two people in front of me, though one is somehow screened from me and I only see one. Then clearly the one I am thinking of is the one I do see, and not the one I don't see, though both satisfy the description. (Or again, the person I am looking at may not be in front of me at all, though I believe that she is, because I have not noticed that I am looking in a mirror.) You will naturally reply by changing the description, say to 'the person I am looking at'. But this too may give the wrong result, if what I am looking at is not a person at all, but—say—a waxwork. For then it will be the waxwork I am thinking of, and mistaking it for a person, but it does not satisfy the description proposed. You will presumably change the description again, say to 'the one and only thing which I am looking at and which I take to be a person', and I will concede—at least for the sake of argument[37]—that we do now have a description which fits the thing I am thinking of and nothing else. But it has now become an implausible suggestion that this description is one that I am actually using to myself, in my thought, for it employs concepts which are too sophisticated.

A very small child, or an animal, can presumably look at things without yet having the general concept of looking at something. Similarly a child, or an animal, can presumably take a thing that it is looking at to be this or that, without yet having the general concept of taking a thing to be something-or-other. And a child at any rate—though one *might* hesitate about an animal—can presumably think, of a thing that it is looking at, that it is a woman, long before it has mastered these relatively sophisticated concepts of looking at something and taking it to be something-or-other. But if the child has not mastered the concepts involved, then it *cannot* be using the suggested description in its thought, and we must presumably say that it is thinking of the person in front of it 'directly', and via no uniquely identifying description. So this must be a possible thing to do. And if it is possible for the child, then it must be possible for me too, and is—I would say—what generally happens. For although I do have the relevant concepts, there is no reason to suppose that I am actually using them. When I express my thought in language, I will use a demonstrative ('*that* person') to do so, and this represents a mental analogue of pointing to something—a kind of inner pointing, one might say. But to point at something is not to describe it—not even as 'the thing I am pointing to'.

Now if I can refer to something without describing it when I am perceiving it, it is plausible to suppose that this is because my perception of it gives me some kind of 'causal contact' with the thing. This is the main idea behind the so-called 'causal theory of perception', according to which to perceive a thing is—very roughly—to have experiences that are caused by that thing.[38] Certainly, we have to add some further conditions. In the first place, the causation must be 'of the right kind'. For example, if someone

---

[37] But what if I am suffering from a hallucination, and there is nothing at all that I am actually looking at (and taking to be a person)? Consideration of this case may lead one to suppose, with Russell, that the only things that I can directly refer to are my own sense-data. I do not think we need follow Russell so far, but it would be too much of a digression to argue that here.

[38] The recent revival of this theory is largely due to Grice's paper 'The Causal Theory of Perception' (1961).

hits me on the head with a hammer (from behind), and that causes me to have a visual experience which is just like that of seeing him, we would not wish to infer that I do see him. This is because, although it is the right kind of experience for seeing him, and is caused by him, it is not caused in the right way. Another condition is that the experience should have some suitable kind of 'fit' with the object that causes it. For example, if my eyes are open and directed at a person in front of me, and the light rays impinging on my retina somehow cause me to have an experience which is just like the experience of seeing a stormy sea, with waves breaking at the foot of the cliff, then again we shall say that this does not count as seeing the person. For there is no suitable 'fit' between the thing that causes the experience and the experience that it causes. It is no doubt very difficult to state these extra conditions in any precise way, and I shall not attempt to do so,[39] but the main idea behind the causal theory of perception does seem to be correct. The idea is, then, that I can think of the thing, not via some description which it and it alone satisfies, but because I am linked to it by a suitable causal connection: it is the causal origin of some experiences in me, and those experiences furnish the *aspect* under which I think of it, the way in which it is presented to me. That is, they provide the answer to the question of how I am thinking of the thing—not by providing some *description* through which I am thinking of it, for I have just argued that the thought is not relying on any uniquely identifying description, but by showing in what way the thing is figuring in my thought. Usually, I do not pay any attention to the kind of experience I am getting when I look at, and think about, an object. But my thought does still rely on those experiences, for it would have been a different thought if the experiences had been different (though it might still have been a thought of the same thing).

Now it would appear that we can generalize this idea of thinking of a thing, not via a description of it, but via some suitable causal contact with it. So far, we have talked only of perception, but it is easy to generalize the idea to apply to memory too. Just as the causal theory of perception seems very persuasive, so also does the causal theory of memory,[40] which claims—*very* roughly—that a genuine memory must be caused by the thing or event it is a memory

---

[39] For a discussion of some of the problems involved see e.g. Strawson's 'Causation in Perception' (1974).

[40] The standard exposition is 'Remembering' by Martin and Deutscher (1966).

of, and must again have some suitable 'fit' with that thing or event. So the suggestion will be that if I do remember something then I can thereby think of it, not because I have any description of the thing that singles it out from all other things, but because I am causally linked to it by the fact that it is the causal origin of the memory which is the aspect under which I think of it. A more daring generalization is to suggest that the causal contact we are concerned with need not be a 'direct' contact between me and the thing I am thinking of, but may be an indirect contact that goes via someone else. This idea is embodied in Kripke's 'causal theory of proper names'.[41] His main idea is that I may 'inherit' a proper name from someone else, who uses it to refer to a particular object, and then I too can use the name to refer to the same object, but without having any description that fits that object uniquely, because I have also 'inherited' the causal contact with the object that bears the name. It is true that Kripke's theory is framed as a theory that more directly concerns what it is for a name to refer, in the public language we all use, rather than what it is for a thought to refer. But one may well feel that essentially the same idea could be applied in either case. It is also true that Kripke's theory (deliberately) does not provide for anything that would count as the 'aspect' under which I am thinking of the thing—an aspect that should have some suitable 'fit' with the thing—when I am thinking of it 'by name'. But it may justly be said that this is a weakness of his theory.[42] However, it would take us too far afield to explore the Kripkean theory of names here, and it is time to return to the concerns of the *Theaetetus*.

I have been suggesting that it is a mistake on Socrates' part to suppose that if I am able to think of a thing at all then I must already have some 'distinguishing mark' for it, which discriminates it from all other things. For it may be that what enables me to think of the thing is that I have some suitable kind of causal connection with it, even though I have no description that it and it alone satisfies. In fact Socrates' own position appears to be a curious amalgamation of what we now think of as two *different* ways of being able to think of a thing. For he apparently says that in order to think of a thing I must have a description that identifies it uniquely, and yet the example

[41] See his *Naming and Necessity* (1980), esp. pp. 91–7.
[42] For *one* way of developing this point, see Evans's article 'The Causal Theory of Names' (1973).

that he uses (my remembering Theaetetus) is much more plausibly regarded as one in which it is my causal contact with the thing, and not my ability to describe it, that explains why it is that thing that I am thinking of. But it is not altogether clear that it is fair to look at Socrates' position from this modern perspective, for the modern perspective also involves a severe limitation on what may be allowed to count as a description. For example, I have excluded the demonstrative 'that', the pronoun 'I', and proper names. But it is not obvious that Socrates would be bound to agree that these expressions should be excluded from what he calls 'distinguishing marks'. He might, for example, wish to say that when I am looking at a thing directly then I do have a distinguishing mark for it, namely that it is *that* thing. Similarly, my distinguishing mark for myself may simply be that it is *me*, and so on. So all we can fairly conclude about this point is that what Socrates says *looks* like a mistake, but we cannot be sure until we have more information on what he would count as a distinguishing mark.

The next objection, however, applies to any reasonable way of understanding distinguishing marks, namely that they do not, as Socrates seems to suppose, always provide one with a way of recognizing the same thing again. For example, suppose that I am looking at, and thinking of, the red billiard ball on the table in front of me. Whether I distinguish it from others simply as *that* one, or whether I have a genuine description that applies to it and it alone— say 'the only billiard ball now on the table'—in either case it is clear that there is no reason to suppose that I will be able to recognize it if I meet it tomorrow. With such things as persons a good memory of what they look like will, in practice, give us a way of recognizing the same one again, at least in ordinary circumstances. But persons are a rather special case. I may remember perfectly well what a particular billiard ball looked like, and I may also know that the ball I have in mind is the one and only ball that satisfies the description 'the billiard ball on the table at noon yesterday', but neither of these will help me to pick out that same ball again from a clutch of exactly similar balls. In effect, the point here is simply an application of the point that we saw to lie behind Plato's problem of false belief, namely that the same thing may be presented to me under many different aspects. There is therefore no reason to suppose that my ability to think of it under one aspect (e.g. when I am looking at it, or remembering it) will also ensure that I can correctly identify it with, or distinguish it from, something presented under another aspect. Plato seemed to be at least half way to grasping this point in his discussion of the wax tablet, but—if so—he has now overlooked it once more.

There is yet a third objection to Socrates' argument on this issue. Let us grant, for the sake of argument, that if I can think of a thing at all then I must have some distinguishing mark for it, which fits that thing and nothing else. Let us also grant that the distinguishing mark will be—or include—something like a memory of that thing, which does give me a means of recognizing that same thing again, at least in ordinary circumstances. Still it does not follow that I can *state* that distinguishing mark, and very often I cannot. For example, my distinguishing mark for Theaetetus may be that I met him yesterday and he looks like *that* (pointing to a memory-image). But there is a clear sense in which I cannot *state* this mark, in that I cannot explain it to anyone else. No one else can look into my memory and see the image I am pointing to, and the probability is that I am quite incapable of either giving a verbal description of it, sufficiently detailed to allow others to pick out Theaetetus by relying on it, or reproducing the image in any other publicly accessible way (e.g. by drawing it). But surely I do not count as being able to 'give an account' of something unless I can *express* this account in some way.

You may reply that I can, in a sense, express this 'account' *to myself* simply by conjuring up the relevant image—or perhaps several images, full-face, half-face, side-face, and so on. But this seems plausible only because most of us are in fact quite good at conjuring up visual images, though even here there is plenty of room for doubt. I, at any rate, have often gone to meet someone with whom I am perfectly familiar, and whom I recognize by sight without any difficulty, and yet found that I could not conjure up a convincing image on the way. But the objection is perhaps stronger if we turn to the case of recognizing someone by his or her voice, which is a thing that most of us can do (in suitable cases), even though we are mostly rather bad at 'auditory images', and cannot express even to ourselves what a person's voice sounds like. Yet it may be the relevant part of the 'distinguishing mark' all the same (e.g. if the person is known to one only by telephone). There are in fact all sorts of clues that we use to recognize people, even though we are not aware that we are using them, and therefore cannot say what they are. This point is just a special case of the very general point that one may well have an ability to do something—in this case, an ability to recognize (in suitable circumstances)—without the ability to *say how* one does it, even to oneself.

There are, then, plenty of steps that may be inserted between the ability to think of something and the ability to *state* some mark by which the thing may be recognized. One can think of something without having a distinguishing mark for it (in a reasonable sense of what is to count as a distinguishing mark); one can have a distinguishing mark without being able to recognize the thing; and one can have the ability to recognize without being able to say how one does so. It is rather puzzling that Plato himself apparently failed to notice any of these objections. In particular, he has earlier said himself that one may think of a thing by perceiving it, and that this is different from thinking of a thing by remembering it, and yet his argument here overlooks that point. We may add that it really does seem rather obvious that a memory-image is not itself an 'account', in any reasonable sense of that word, and yet the 'distinguishing marks' that this argument is about are all supposed to be 'accounts'. We shall have to enquire later why Plato should have apparently overlooked these rather obvious criticisms. But one might perhaps feel that even though the argument is unsatisfactory, still the conclusion that Plato is seeking to draw from it is correct. For though there are, as we have said, several steps that may be inserted between thinking of a thing and stating a mark which distinguishes it from everything else, still it may seem that none of them is a very plausible candidate for what makes the difference between thinking of the thing and really *knowing* it.

If that is how we feel, it is probably because we begin with higher expectations of what genuine *knowledge* of a thing will amount to. Thus, we may have started with the idea that to know a thing is to know what it *is*, in the sense of what it is *to be* that thing. That is, it is to be able to give a suitable answer to the Socratic question 'What is X?', which must be an answer that states the 'essence' of X, however exactly that is to be understood. (Clearly, the suggestion that to know a thing is to be able to analyse it into its elementary constituents was intended as a suggestion along these lines.) Now if we begin with this attitude, then we will no doubt agree with Socrates in rejecting the suggestion that to have an 'account' is just to have some distinguishing mark or other, for we will claim that one knows a thing only when one can give a *special kind* of distinguishing mark for it, viz. one that reveals its 'essence'. Perhaps it is true that one cannot think of a thing at all without having *some kind* of distinguishing mark for it, or perhaps it is at least true that one cannot have the ability to recognize a thing, in the various settings in which it occurs, without having *some* suitable distinguishing mark. But there is no reason to suppose that *these* distinguishing marks have to give the 'essence' of the thing, and therefore no reason to suppose that they suffice for knowledge. On this view, then, Socrates has drawn the right conclusion, even if the argument that he actually offers may be faulted.

But on this view of the situation, Socrates' *next* step is quite unwarranted. He ought to have continued in some such way as this: if *any* kind of distinguishing mark will do as an 'account', then—as I have just shown—we cannot explain knowledge as true belief plus an account. So we ought now to look for some other account of 'an account', perhaps as a special kind of distinguishing mark. But that is not what he does say, for what actually happens is that he jumps straight to the conclusion that *no* account of 'an account' will do, and so infers (at 210b1–2) that knowledge *cannot* be true belief plus an account. But surely he is not entitled just to take it for granted that there is no other way of understanding an 'account' besides those that he has explicitly considered? If Plato has an answer to this last objection, it must be one or other of these: *either* he takes it that his previous objections to an 'account' as an enumeration of elements may be generalized into objections against *any* more specialized accounts of what an 'account' is; *or* he takes it that the final point that he makes in this present argument is one that can be so generalized. Let us come, then, to his final point, to which we have not yet given any attention.

Socrates in fact presents his argument in the form of a dilemma. One alternative, he says (εἰ μέν, 209d5), is to suppose that knowledge is attained by adding a *true belief* of some distinguishing mark, and that alternative he dismisses as absurd for the reasons we have been considering. The other alternative (209e6–7) is to suppose that knowledge is only attained by adding *knowledge* of a distinguishing mark, but that alternative, he objects, is evidently circular. It simply defines knowledge in terms of itself (209e7–210a9). But it is extremely tempting to suppose that Plato does not mean these as *alternative* objections, so that the second applies only if the first does not, since the second objection appears to apply *anyway*. Moreover, it appears to apply *whatever* view we take of what an 'account' should be. Apparently, to have a true belief as to what the correct account of a thing is will never be enough to ensure that one knows what the thing is, since the true belief may be arrived at by some kind of accident—e.g. as a result of an orator's persuasion (as at 201a–b), or as a result of teaching which is not yet properly understood (as at 207d–208b), or perhaps just as a result of a mere dream which one finds oneself trusting (cf. 202c). Hence, if accounts are relevant at all, then we can only say that to know what a thing is one must *know* the correct account of it, and this shows that no definition of knowledge along these lines could succeed: it will always turn out to be circular.

As a matter of fact, this objection of circularity is altogether less convincing when we recall the distinction between *connaître* and *savoir*. For we begin with the question of what it is to know a particular thing, e.g. the person Theaetetus or the word 'Theaetetus', which appears to be a case of *connaître*. It is then suggested that this is a matter of knowing a (or the) correct account of the thing, and this is clearly a case of *savoir*: it is knowing *that* Theaetetus is the man who . . ., or knowing *that* 'Theaetetus' contains the letters 'T', 'H', 'E', . . . (in that order). On the face of it, this explains one kind of knowledge in terms of *another*, and so is not circular but merely incomplete: we now have to go on to explain *savoir*. But there are two ways in which one might try to reintroduce the objection of circularity. The first goes back to the claim underlying the discussion of false belief, and to the first half of the present argument: we object that knowing Theaetetus is being explained as knowing some fact about him, but one cannot know anything about Theaetetus unless one can *first* believe it, and one cannot believe anything about Theaetetus unless one *already* knows him. That is, knowledge of facts *presupposes* knowledge of the things that those facts concern, and hence cannot be used to *explain* knowledge of things without circularity. However, if this is the way that the circularity charge is supposed to be working, then my previous criticisms of the first part of the argument appear to destroy it. We may agree that one cannot know any fact about an object unless one can in some way *think of* that object, but there are various ways in which we can distinguish thinking of an object from knowing it.

Knowledge and Belief

The second way of reintroducing the circularity charge goes back
to considerations stemming from the discussion of Socrates' dream,
and is altogether more compelling. Knowing the word 'Theaetetus'
is being explained as a matter of knowing *that* its constituent letters
are 'T', 'H', 'E', etc., and the objection is that one cannot know this
fact unless one already knows the *letters* concerned. Thus knowledge of one thing (the word) is being explained in terms which
presuppose knowledge of *other* things (the letters). So if we begin
without any understanding of what it is to know a thing (of any
kind), this explanation will not help us. Moreover, it does appear
that this objection can be generalized to apply at least to most
plausible versions of what a suitable 'account' is, for the objection is
that one cannot know that the correct account of a thing is such-and-
such unless one knows the things—whatever they are—that are
mentioned in the account.[43] And this objection now stems not from
any mistaken views on what it is to be able to think of something
but from a thesis specifically about the nature of knowledge, viz.
that if knowledge is to be based on anything, then what it is based
on must itself be knowledge. This thesis certainly does appear to
have the consequence that any attempt to explain knowledge in
terms of 'accounts' will fall to the charge of circularity, even
though we fight hard to preserve a distinction between *connaître*
and *savoir*.

It is worth remarking that many other accounts of what knowledge
is are open to a similar charge of circularity. Thus, suppose we take
the once popular idea (about knowing *that*) that one knows that *P* if
and only if

  (i) it is true that *P*;
  (ii) one believes that *P*;
  (iii) one has evidence or grounds for this belief, which justifies it,
      or entitles one to hold it, or something of the kind.

On this account, one's knowledge that *P* is based upon something
else, namely the evidence, and we shall surely wish to say that if the
evidence is merely believed, but not known, then it is not an
adequate basis for knowledge. So it seems that condition (iii) must
be rephrased as

---

[43] For example, one cannot know that Theaetetus has such-and-such a special
kind of snubness without knowing that snubness.

(iii) one *knows* certain evidence, which justifies . . .,

and the account then collapses into circularity, for knowledge of one thing (the conclusion) is being explained in terms of knowledge of something else (the evidence for it). In fact, further reflection on this kind of account of what it is to know something is likely to persuade us that yet further circularities need to be introduced. For example, if the evidence itself is known, but the inference one draws from it is in some way mistaken, then the conclusion one reaches is surely not known, even though it might happen to be true. So we shall find ourselves wishing to say that not only must the evidence be known but so also must every other belief that one relies upon in inferring the conclusion from it.[44] But we need not pursue that issue further, for the main damage has already been done.

Now an account of knowledge which is circular is not necessarily *wrong*. What it says may be perfectly correct, even though we do not accept it as an adequate analysis of the notion because it is not sufficiently informative: it could not be used to explain that notion to someone who did not already have it. But with the present example the circularity also seems to show that the account must be wrong, for it apparently leads to a vicious regress. It states that in order to know one thing (the conclusion) I must first know something else, the evidence for it. But now, how will I get to know that evidence? If we apply the same account as before then in order to know it I must have yet further evidence for it, which again is evidence that I have to know, so again I must have yet further evidence in favour of it in turn, and so on indefinitely. But this appears to be impossible. For if knowledge of one thing always rests upon knowledge of something else, it would seem that knowledge could never get started. So it is very tempting to conclude that it cannot be right to say that knowledge of a fact always requires an 'account' of that fact, in the form of further facts which justify or explain the original fact. The second part of the *Theaetetus*, as we have said, is not concerned with knowledge of facts in general, but rather with knowledge of things (or knowledge of what a thing is). But the same vicious regress apparently threatens in either case. If to know what a thing is always involves the ability to give an 'account' of that thing, and the 'account' will always mention other

---

[44] This is *one* way of meeting Gettier's celebrated argument, in his 'Is justified true belief knowledge?' (1963).

things, then apparently one cannot know what one thing is without first knowing what some other things are, and again it appears that knowledge (of what a thing is) can never get started. In either case, then, we find that the circularity which seems unavoidable when we try to explain knowledge in terms of accounts is one that gives rise to a regress that would certainly appear to be vicious. If this is so, then we can very fairly conclude that knowledge is *not* true belief with the addition of an account, just as it *is not* either perception or true belief on its own (210a9–b2). Although there may be many versions of what an 'account' is that we have not considered, they will all be open to the same objection—a circularity that gives rise to a vicious regress.

But I must end this section with a note of caution. *We* find the objections of circularity, and of a vicious regress, to be the most interesting points raised in this closing section of the *Theaetetus*, mainly because they do seem to be objections of a very general nature, and they do affect more modern approaches to the question 'What is knowledge?' But it is not obvious that Plato viewed the matter in the same way. For one thing, it is not clear that he was paying any attention to the distinction between knowing a thing and knowing a fact, a distinction which does seriously complicate the objection of circularity. For another thing, if the complication had been pointed out to him explicitly, one might well suspect that he would wish to overcome it in the wrong way. He would wish to say that one cannot explain knowing an object as a matter of knowing that it has such-and-such an account, because knowing any fact about an object presupposes knowing that object itself. But the interesting form of the circularity objection is that it presupposes a knowledge of *other* objects, viz. those mentioned in the account. But finally, and most importantly, Plato does not himself present the circularity objection as if it were a *general* objection, applying to all versions of 'an account'. On the contrary, it looks more like a mere afterthought, taking no more than twelve lines, and tacked on to the end of the main objection to an 'account' as a distinguishing mark, which runs for one and a half pages. It blocks a conceivable escape from *that* objection, but is not presented as having any wider significance at all.

It is therefore not at all clear that the moral which I have just been trying to draw from the last few lines of the dialogue is a moral that

Plato himself saw those lines as having. What moral, then, did he wish us to draw from his apparently unsuccessful attempt to explain how knowledge might be said to require an account?

4. LINES OF INTERPRETATION

I shall discuss three rather different approaches to the interpretation of this final section of the *Theaetetus*, namely those of Cornford (1935), Fine (1979*b*), and White (1976). My remarks about Cornford will be brief, but in discussing Fine and White I shall also take the opportunity to mention passages in other late dialogues which have something to tell us about Plato's later thoughts on knowledge.

(i) *Cornford's Interpretation*

Cornford of course holds that the whole of the *Theaetetus* is an indirect recommendation of the view of Plato's middle period, that only forms can be known, and he includes as part of that view that anyone who knows a form must be able to give an account of it. So in this final section of the dialogue we are intended to see that the difficulties which are raised about accounts all stem from the fact that we are trying to apply the notion to perceptible things. They would not arise if we recognized that 'the objects of which knowledge must give an account are not concrete individuals but objects of thought, and that the simpler terms in which the account must be stated are not material parts but higher concepts' (p. 154).

Now there is one section of the discussion which suits Cornford's interpretation rather well, and that is the argument about the 'distinguishing mark' at 209a–d. We noted that it is crucial to that argument that all distinguishing marks are treated as being on a par with one another, so that once you have one such mark nothing is gained by adding another. This, Cornford says, is inevitable when we are confining attention to particular things such as the sun or Theaetetus, for particular things do not *have* essence-revealing definitions, as Aristotle later argued.[45] But of course the point would not apply to forms, which do have such definitions

---

[45] *Metaphysics* Z15. (Aristotle too takes the sun as his example, and argues that it cannot be defined.)

(Cornford, pp. 161–2; cf. Gulley, 1962, pp. 103–4). This, it must be admitted, is quite a possible view of the moral to be drawn from this particular argument, but when we turn to consider the other arguments Cornford's general line of interpretation seems very implausible indeed.

First, it is not true that all the examples we are given are examples of knowing a 'concrete individual'. Admittedly, when the theory of Socrates' dream is first introduced it appears that the author has particular perceptible individuals in mind (p. 209 above), but in all the subsequent illustrations and applications of this theory it is knowledge of a general type, and not a particular individual, that is being discussed. When Plato speaks of knowing a letter, a syllable, or a word it is always knowledge of the type that is in question, and not knowledge of this or that particular concrete token. (At one point the argument clearly depends upon this: at 207e–208a it is assumed that the first syllable of 'Theaetetus' is the *same* syllable as the first syllable of 'Theodorus', and hence is correctly spelled with the *same* letters.) The same is evidently true of knowing the notes which are the elements of music (206a10–b3), and of knowing what a wagon is (207a). So there is nothing to prevent us from supposing that essence-revealing definitions may be available in these cases, and we surely are not meant to see anything absurd in the idea that one reveals the essence of a syllable by spelling it into its constituent letters.

No doubt there are some differences between analysing a syllable into its letters and analysing a form in terms of 'higher' forms (which is what Cornford regards as the right way of giving an account), but the differences do not seem to be of any importance to the argument. First, it seems clear that there will be a problem about 'highest' forms, which cannot be analysed any further; and second, where a form does have some suitable analysis, it seems clear that I may have a true belief concerning its analysis which is not yet knowledge (as with the child spelling 'Theaetetus'). But then, if we try to avoid this difficulty by saying that to know a form one must *know* its correct analysis, the account of knowledge does apparently collapse into circularity. That is, what seem to us to be the *main* problems developed about an 'account' as an enumeration of elements evidently *do* apply to 'accounts' as analyses of forms, and it is difficult to believe that Plato has not noticed this. (And incidentally it is worth noting that the dilemma as to whether a whole is or is not all its parts (which is used against Socrates' dream) might well seem to be more, rather than less, upsetting when applied to the analysis of forms. Thus, supposing that the form 'man' can be correctly analysed by the account 'Man is a rational animal', should we say that the form 'man' is or is not the same as the two forms 'animal' and 'rational'?[46])

I think, then, that we can abandon Cornford's interpretation. It suits this section of the dialogue no better than it suits the first part (pp. 101–5, 146–50). In fact, one might reply to him in exactly the same way as Socrates replies to Theaetetus' first attempt to say what knowledge is: 'But that wasn't what you were asked for, Theaetetus. You weren't asked which things knowledge is of . . . but what, exactly, knowledge itself is' (146e7–10). Cornford, it appears, has been answering the wrong question.

(ii) *Fine's Interpretation*

Whereas Cornford pays very little attention to the two problems which strike us as the important problems that this discussion of 'accounts' introduces, namely the question of how to halt a vicious regress of accounts, and the threat of circularity, other interpreters give them pride of place. I shall take Fine's interpretation to consider in detail, since she holds not only that Plato was mainly concerned with these problems but also that he here provides an answer to them.

I have already considered her account of how the dream theory is refuted (pp. 216–18 above), but more needs to be said about the moral that she sees Plato as drawing from this refutation. On the face of it, there are two possible morals: one is that knowledge does not always require an account, as there will have to be simples which do not themselves have an account, but must be knowable, since they are used in giving accounts of other things[47]; the other is that although there may be things which can be called simple still they will have accounts for all that. Fine takes the second alternative, offering two reasons. The first is (p. 380) that when Theaetetus accepts that there is no account to be given of the letters 'S' and 'O'

---

[46] In a way, this is a question that bothered Aristotle. At least, it is closely related to his question 'In what way is a definition a unity?' See his discussions at *Metaphysics* Z12 and H6.

[47] Robinson (1969, p. 55), Runciman (1962, p. 40), Crombie (1963, p. 114), White (1976, pp. 178–9).

he at the same time actually gives a (partial) account of them. He says 'In fact, Socrates, "S" is one of the unvoiced consonants, only a noise, which occurs when the tongue hisses, as it were' (203b3–4). Are we not meant to see that after all there are accounts of the letters? But of course this by itself is not yet very convincing, (*a*) because while letters and syllables are being used merely to illustrate our theory it does not matter whether letters actually are simple (p. 211 above), and (*b*) because anyway the problem seems merely to be postponed. Supposing that we can give a (partial) account of the letter 'S' as an unvoiced noise, can we then go on to give accounts of being unvoiced, and being a noise, and then further accounts of these accounts, and so on indefinitely? (Cf. McDowell, 1973, pp. 240–1.) Fine's second reason (pp. 384–5) is that when Socrates concludes his theoretical objection to the dream theory he very clearly says that elements and complexes are equally knowable, *and equally have or lack accounts* (205d7–e4). So here he undeniably retains the association between being knowable and having an account.[48] However it is not clear how significant this point is, for when he restates his conclusion at the end of his second and empirical objection the association is dropped. At that point he merely claims that letters are knowable—and indeed more clearly knowable than syllables—but he no longer claims that they have an account (206b5–11).

Now on my account of the empirical objection this is exactly the right conclusion for him to draw, since what he there counts as knowing the letters is simply the ability to recognize them, and distinguish them one from another, in all the various combinations in which they occur. And it seems clear that one could have this ability without being able to produce anything that would qualify as an 'account' of a letter. But Fine sees the passage differently, for in her view Plato is here telling us how to *give* an account of elements. She comments 'one does not understand a discipline's elements until one understands the system to which they belong; conversely, understanding any system consists in understanding how its elements are interrelated'. And a little later she sums this up as 'accounts of elements consist in locating them within a systematic framework, interconnecting and interrelating them' (p. 386).

---

[48] But I have argued, *ad hominem*, that Fine's own account of the theoretical objection would not justify this conclusion (p. 218).

Pursuing this idea, Fine interprets the argument to show that one may spell the word 'Theaetetus' correctly, but without having knowledge of it, much as I do. But she goes on to draw the rather large conclusion that 'no description of an isolated entity ever amounts to knowledge' (p. 392 n.). This conclusion she then applies to explain why the argument about the distinguishing mark did not appear to Plato to suffer from an obvious weakness: he ignores the possibility that *some* distinguishing marks may reveal essence, although others do not, because he is already convinced that no one description can reveal essence. Finally, she suggests that the circularity objection that concludes the discussion is one that Plato can already meet, by deploying his 'interrelation model of knowledge'. On her view of the matter, it is perfectly correct to say that 'knowledge of *x* is correct belief about *x* with knowledge of *x*'s difference'. Admittedly, as it stands this is circular as an answer to the question 'What is knowledge?', but we can eliminate the circularity by explaining that 'knowledge of *x*'s difference' is 'the ability to produce accounts properly relating *x* to other suitably interrelated objects in the same field' (p. 394). So in this section of the dialogue Plato has both posed some crucial problems for knowledge *and* shown how to answer them.

The attraction of this interpretation lies in its relation to other late dialogues, for much of what Plato says about his 'method of collection and division' can be seen as suggesting just such a response to the problems raised by the *Theaetetus*.[49] It is true that the bare outline of this 'method' may seem simply to ignore these problems, for it recommends us to practise collecting many different things under one genus, and then dividing that genus by successive differentiae into its various subspecies. The main illustrations of how the method may be put to work then show how it may be used to provide an 'account' of the subspecies. Thus the technique is simply illustrated at *Sophist* 219a–221c as a method of reaching an account of what angling is by starting with the point that it is a skill, and successively refining this by adding that it is a skill of acquisition, pursued by force and in concealment, i.e. a kind of

---

[49] The 'method of collection and division' is introduced in the *Phaedrus* (265d ff.), is preached and practised all through the *Sophist* and the *Statesman*, and reappears— perhaps in a slightly altered form—at *Philebus* 16b–18d.

hunting, namely a hunting of animals, that live in water, and in fact of fish, which proceeds by striking the prey, with a hook. The ostensible aim of the *Sophist* as a whole is to reach a definition of sophistry along these lines, and the *Statesman* proposes to reach a definition of statesmanship in the same way.

Now at first glance this method simply ignores the problem posed by Socrates' dream, since it allows us to reach definitions of the species of a genus, but not of the genus itself. Evidently a highest genus cannot be defined in a similar fashion, and yet it must presumably be known if the definitions of its species are to yield knowledge of them. But Plato would appear to be supposing that it is the process which he calls 'collecting' which gives knowledge of the genus, just as it is 'dividing' which gives knowledge of the species, and if we ask what the genus is to be collected from the only possible answer seems to be 'its species'. Thus it appears that species and genus are each grasped by seeing how they relate *to one another*, and Fine's 'interrelationship model of knowledge' is beginning to appear. But we can perhaps go further.

There is a curious passage in the *Sophist* which may indicate that Plato is putting yet more weight on interrelationships. By 252e we have reached the conclusion that some 'kinds' will 'combine', but others will not. (For example, motion and rest will not combine with one another, but each will combine with being.) At 253a it is noted that the same applies to letters, for some will combine to form pronounceable syllables, while others will not, and at 253b the same point is extended to musical notes, the idea being—presumably— that some combinations are harmonious and others discordant. It is inferred that, just as it needs skill (τέχνη) to say which letters or which notes will combine, so also it will require knowledge (ἐπιστήμη), and perhaps the greatest knowledge, to say which kinds will combine with which. At this point (253c6) the Eleatic Visitor exclaims that we seem to have stumbled across an account of the philosopher, for it is the philosopher who can divide things according to their kinds, and who can see both the one form embracing many others and the many embraced by it. This appears to say that it is the philosopher who can practise the method of collection and division, and this we are told precisely is 'knowing how to distinguish, according to kind, in what way things can and cannot combine' (253d9–e2). Now if this last remark is intended generally—as it seems to be[50]—it apparently implies that to practise collection and division on the letters, or the notes of music, *is* to discern the pronounceable or harmonious combinations that they can form, which is not quite what one might have expected. And even if the last remark is only intended to apply to combining forms, still we apparently have a rather remarkable implication, namely that the subsequent attempt in the *Sophist* to detail just what combinations there are among the 'five greatest kinds' that it considers is *itself* regarded as an exercise in collection and division. In either case, there appears to be rather more to 'collection and division' than one might at first have thought.

In fact the implication for letters and musical notes is confirmed by the *Philebus*, if it is fair to say that what that dialogue discusses at 16b–18d is (a version of) the method of collection and division.[51] Applying its general doctrine specifically to letters and to notes, that passage first claims that one does not count as being knowledgeable (σοφός) about them until one can see not only that the relevant sound (in speech, or in music) is in a way both one and infinitely many (or indeterminate), but also into how many distinct varieties it falls, and of what kinds (17b–c). Elaborating this for the case of music, it goes on to say that one must know how many intervals there are, and which of them are concordant, and the different lengths that notes may have, yielding different rhythms. This, it urges, is the right way to look at *any* case of a one and a many (17d). We are then offered a somewhat obscure distinction between the right procedure for someone who starts from a one, and must discern a suitable number within it, before resigning it to the indefinite, and someone who starts from the reverse position. If one is forced to begin with the indefinite, one should again discern a suitable number within it, before ending with a one (18a7–b3). This latter is then illustrated with reference to the letters again, con-strued as the elements of phonetics. Beginning with the infinite (or indeterminate) sound, one should first distinguish those that are voiced (i.e. the vowels), those that are not voiced but do have sound of a kind, and those that are neither. Then within each of these one should distinguish the various subvarieties, until one reaches the

---

[50] The previous five lines have been concerned with forms (ἰδέαι), and have consistently used the feminine. This last remark speaks of 'things' that combine using the quite general neuter plural (ἕκαστα).

[51] There are many vexing questions affecting the interpretation of this passage which I shall here ignore.

number of each, and all of them can then be called 'letters' ('elements') (18b6–c6). The final step seems to be regarded as reaching a 'one', namely the genus 'letter', which has thus been reached from its various species and subspecies. It is a bond binding all the letters into one, for 'none of us could learn even one of them by itself, apart from all the others' (18c7–d2).

The first part of this passage (on musical notes) evidently does aim to stress the importance of discerning the permitted combinations, and while this stress is not so clear in the second part (on letters) it must still be intended. Although the second part seems mainly concerned just with a phonetic classification of the letters, still Plato presumably meant us to see that the principles of classification will have implications for combination. (For example, a letter which is neither voiced nor sounded cannot be pronounced in isolation.) Besides, it is only if we do pay attention to the importance of seeing how the letters relate to one another that we can understand his apparently extreme claim that one cannot learn one letter without learning all the rest as well. Practising 'collection and division', then, does seem to be strongly connected, in Plato's mind, with discerning 'combinations'.

We may conclude that there is quite good evidence, in the *Sophist* and the *Philebus*, for the view that Plato came to adopt something like Fine's 'interrelationship' view of knowledge: knowledge is primarily directed not at isolated items but at systems of interconnected items, and one knows the system when one has grasped the interconnections. A difficulty for Fine's interpretation (which she acknowledges, p. 395 n.) is that when Plato is speaking in this vein, of the importance of grasping how things combine, he describes it as the task of 'dialectic', and the special province of the philosopher, but he does *not* clearly say that this is the way to give an 'account' of each thing.[52] On the other hand it is fair to say that he has not ceased to think of 'accounts' as important for knowledge. A particularly interesting passage here is *Statesman* 285d8–286a7.[53]

This passage tells us that some things (τὰ μὲν τῶν ὄντων) have sensible likenesses which it is easy to point to, and by means of which they may be grasped without an account. But for the most

[52] Fine's one example is the occurrence of '*logos*' at *Sophist* 253b10, but the context here is not sufficient to determine any precise meaning for the word.

[53] *Laws* x. 895d4–5, and *Letter* vii, 342b ff. (discussed below) might be cited for the same conclusion. (*Laws* xii. 967e4 appears to concede that not all things have a λόγος, but in this context λόγος appears to mean 'proof' rather than 'account'.)

important things (τὰ μέγιστα καὶ τιμιώτατα) there are no such clear images, and these incorporeal things (ἀσώματα) can be revealed only by an account. For that reason one must practise giving an account of *everything*, for even in a case in which it is not essential it is a necessary training for the important cases in which it is essential. Here it is allowed that in simple cases one may know what a thing is without being able to give an account, and an example of this might well be the knowledge of letters that we all acquire at school. (A little earlier, at 277e–278b, this has been described in terms very similar to the *Theaetetus* as the ability to recognize and distinguish each letter in all the combinations in which it occurs, and it is cited as an example of how one can make things clear by examples.) But it is also implied that if one can know what a thing is then it must be possible to give an account of it, since that is what we have to practise doing even in simple cases, and is the only possible way of acquiring knowledge in more important cases. When we put together this insistence on accounts with the other passages which talk of the importance of principles of combination, then we do reach a view that is very similar to that which Fine credits to Plato in the *Theaetetus*.

I have thought it worth while to draw out this account of what knowledge is, because it is a possible speculation that Plato himself thought of it as the answer to the *Theaetetus'* problem of how to halt the apparently vicious regress of accounts. But the most that could be maintained with any plausibility is that Plato thought out this answer to the problem *after* he had written the *Theaetetus*, for the answer is surely *not* to be found in the *Theaetetus* itself. All that is said in the *Theaetetus* is that one counts as knowing the letters when one can distinguish each by itself (206a5–8), that one counts as having learnt the notes perfectly when one can 'follow each and say which sort of string it belongs to' (which, I presume, is a way of naming the note) (206a10–b3), and that one does not count as knowing the word 'Theaetetus' if one sometimes mistakes the letter 'TH' for the letter 'T' (207e7–208a3). These passages evidently do not contain even the remotest hint of the rather sophisticated view of knowledge that we have been discussing. Fine's account, then, must certainly be rejected as an interpretation of what is said in the *Theaetetus*, and at best it is an account of how Plato later responded to the problems that he here raises.

But is even this correct? In Fine's view, the later theory was designed to meet two main problems from the *Theaetetus*. One of these is the problem posed by Socrates' dream, that it does not seem that accounts can go on for ever, and the other is the problem raised under the second sense of 'account', that apparently one could believe a correct account without this belief amounting to knowledge. It seems that this must lead us to say that what is required is knowledge of the account, and then—as the end of the dialogue points out—we are apparently defining knowledge in terms of itself. But the truth is that the 'interrelation' theory of knowledge offers no solution to the second of these problems, and Fine's attempt to argue that it does is quite inadequate. (She says 'when one can expand one's claims beyond an isolated description of one object to a description of its interconnections in a systematic framework . . . it would be unreasonable to suppose that that ability could be exercised in the absence of knowledge' (p. 397). But there is no reason to agree with this, for after all one might have the whole systematic description off by heart, and without understanding it. At any rate the author of the *Seventh Letter*, as we shall see (pp. 254–8), did not agree with it.) As for the way in which the later theory is supposed to resolve the first problem, it does this by admitting that 'accounts will circle back on themselves', for the account of one element of a system will relate it to others, and the accounts of those others will, *inter alia*, relate them to it. But although this may be what Plato intends when he speaks of the importance of knowing how things combine, he never says so at all explicitly, and we have had to put different passages together to extract this implication. So it may also be that the implication was not intended, and that the later theory was not in any way influenced by further reflection upon Socrates' dream. But anyway the important point, for our purposes, is that the later theory certainly does not tell us what Plato thought of Socrates' dream at the time when he was writing the *Theaetetus*.

(iii) *White's Interpretation*

In contrast to Fine, White sees very little importance in the problems posed by the apparent regress of accounts and the objection of circularity. On his view, the moral that emerges from the two treatments of an 'account' as an enumeration of elements is just that, when investigating the question 'What is knowledge?', there is no advantage to be gained by distinguishing between what is simple and what is complex. For it turns out that each must be equally knowable, and anyway the ability to spell out the elements of a complex is not sufficient to ensure a knowledge of it (p. 179). Similarly, he dismisses the circularity objection in a parenthesis of one line, as an evidently hopeless attempt to escape from the main argument about the distinguishing mark (p. 180). The crucial problem of the dialogue, as he sees the matter, is the one raised by this latter argument.

Plato, he implies, has never been particularly drawn to the view that a definition will analyse a complex thing into its constituents,[54] but he *has* always thought of a definition as a distinguishing mark. 'From the beginning', White says, to define an object has been 'to be able to say wherein that object differs from other objects' (p. 180). But if that is indeed the only role that a definition has, then certainly this argument about a distinguishing mark is crucial. For it apparently shows that a definition can only tell you how to do what you must be able to do already, as soon as you can think of the thing whose definition is being sought after. Either, then, you cannot think of the thing at all, or—if you can—then you already have a definition of it.

Without commenting on the validity of this argument, White regards it as posing a problem which Plato could not see how to resolve, and moreover essentially the *same* problem as the old paradox of enquiry at *Meno* 80d–e. This paradox, he says, has now 'come home to roost', with some help from what the *Cratylus* has had to say on names. When we set ourselves to answer the question 'What is virtue?', we use the name 'virtue' to pick out the object of our search. But the *Cratylus* has said that the role of a name is to pick out and distinguish one object from others,[55] which is not unreasonably interpreted as implying that he who can understand the name can himself pick out and distinguish the object named from all others.[56] It follows that if I can understand the question

---

[54] But notice that in our dialogue the definition of clay as earth plus water, and the suggested definition of knowledge as true belief plus an account, could naturally be seen as conforming to this view.

[55] e.g. 388b10–c1, 422d1–e1, 428e1–2, and elsewhere.

[56] Contrary to what White suggests, this implication is not made explicit in the *Cratylus*, though it is suggested that one who has command of a name will be able to think of the object named (434e6–7).

'What is virtue?' then I can already distinguish virtue from other things. Or, to put the same point in the language of the *Theaetetus*, if I can understand the question then I must be able to understand it as a question which is *about virtue*, and therefore I must be able to think of virtue. But, according to the argument in question, that implies that I can already distinguish virtue from other things. Either way, if I can understand the question, then I can already do what finding the answer to it was supposed to enable me to do, so apparently I must already know the answer to it. And if I do not know the answer, then that simply shows that I do not understand the question, in which case there is again nothing that I can do by way of seeking for an answer to it.

Now if Plato was caught by this puzzle it was certainly not for the reason that White gives, namely that 'from the beginning' he has always thought of the role of a definition as being *simply* to distinguish the object defined from all others. There is a clear counterexample to this claim in the early *Euthyphro* at 9e–11a, where Socrates is prepared to grant for the sake of argument that what is holy is the same as what is loved by the gods, but still complains that this is not an adequate definition of the holy: it gives only an accident (πάθος) of holiness, and not its essence (οὐσία). Rather closer in date to the *Theaetetus*, one might also cite *Phaedrus* 245c–246a, where we are first offered a definition of the soul as that which moves itself, and this is made the basis of an argument for its immortality. But having settled the question of how the soul is to be defined—glossed here as the question of what its *nature* is (φύσις)—Socrates goes on to raise what he clearly views as a different question, namely the question of what kind of a thing it is (οἷόν ἐστι, 246a4). And the long account which he then proceeds to give, though admittedly it is based upon simile and metaphor at many points, is surely an account which he takes to distinguish the soul from all other things. So if Plato has now come to think that the *only* role of a definition is to distinguish the thing defined from all other things, this is surely a change in his thinking.

But perhaps there are reasons for this change within the *Theaetetus* itself. The difficulties raised for the conception of a definition as an enumeration of elements may have seemed to Plato to be difficulties that would affect all conceptions of a definition as a special type of account that reveals essence. And certainly when meeting the first of those difficulties (posed by the dream theory) he had fallen back upon a conception of what it is to know a thing which took this simply to be a matter of being able to recognize the thing and distinguish it from other similar things. As I pointed out, it is this conception that is used in the empirical objection to the dream, and one might well suggest that it also lies behind the objection raised under the second sense of 'account'. For the idea there may well be that the child who is still learning to spell does not count as knowing the spelling of the word 'Theaetetus' because he does not *know* its first letter, in that he cannot always recognize it when he hears it, and distinguish it from others. Again, there is a similar concern with recognizing and distinguishing in the final argument, where it is (wrongly) assumed that what enables me to think of Theaetetus will also allow me to recognize him again and distinguish him from others, which is to say—on the present conception of knowledge—that I thereby know him. But now, it *is* true to say that Plato has *always* thought that a definition of a thing is needed if that thing is to be known. When we put this together with the present conception of what it is to know a thing, we can apparently infer White's claim that the only role of a definition is to distinguish the thing defined from other things. It is not that this has been how Plato has thought of definitions all along, but rather it is a position to which he is now driven by the revised conception of knowledge.

One might add at this point that the revised conception does appear to be a perfectly reasonable conception of what it is to know a thing, where the things we are concerned with are either particular concrete individuals or such things as the letters of the alphabet, or the notes of music. Moreover, it does indeed leave the role of a definition somewhat obscure, for the truth is that we can have the ability to recognize and distinguish a thing without yet being able to state any 'distinguishing mark' for it. Nevertheless Plato clearly overstates his case when he argues that definitions, so construed, *could* not be of any use, and White would seem to be right to observe that the argument that Plato does use is one that reinstates the old paradox of inquiry from the *Meno*. If, in order to think of a thing at all, I must *already* know it, then there appears to be no room for an inquiry which one could characterize as a search for knowledge of that very thing. But could Plato have been convinced—or even half-convinced—by an argument that led to a conclusion that seems so very paradoxical?

The paradox of inquiry is not the least bit convincing when

applied to particular things such as the person Theaetetus. The question 'Who is Theaetetus?' can sensibly be asked by one who has *some* way of thinking of Theaetetus, even if it is only via a description such as 'the man you have just mentioned under the name "Theaetetus" ', or via a perception of him as that man over there (perhaps wearing the name-tag 'Theaetetus'). And clearly one can be in this position without yet *knowing* Theaetetus, either in the ordinary sense of that phrase (which is—*very* roughly—a matter of being familiar with him and his ways), or in the sense proposed for this discussion, namely being able to recognize him and distinguish him from others (on the basis of one's memory). Indeed, Plato has already made that point himself, in his discussion of the wax tablet, which is precisely designed to explain how one can think of a thing by perceiving it, and *without* yet knowing it.

It would seem, then, that either Plato had not noticed these implications of his argument that White stresses, or—if he had noticed them—then he must have been aware that the argument is mistaken. On the latter view it is used to round off the dialogue in a neat way, and to set the reader thinking, but it does not—as White suggests—reveal any real perplexity within Plato himself. But I imagine that White would reply to this that although the argument is presented as an argument about knowing a particular individual, namely Theaetetus, that is not how Plato himself is thinking of it. His attention is actually focused on knowing the forms, and it was not obvious to him that there must be something wrong with the paradox of inquiry when applied to forms (as in the *Meno*). Certainly the claim made by that paradox is a claim that he would *wish* to resist, but—as White sees the situation—the *Theaetetus* ends with a grave doubt as to whether it *can* be resisted. In support of this interpretation, White goes on to draw attention to the so-called 'philosophical digression' of the *Seventh Letter* (342a–344c), where again he sees the paradox of inquiry as the key to the discussion.

The authenticity of the Platonic letters is disputed, but for the sake of argument I shall accept White's view that at least the passage which interests us was written by Plato. (If it was not by Plato, then it is very difficult to suggest who else might have wished to attribute these views to Plato, unless it was someone who had himself heard Plato saying such things. As will become clear, the views are by no means a précis of what may be found elsewhere in Plato's writings.) Now if the *Seventh Letter* was indeed written by Plato, then it was written in 353 BC, which is near to the end of his life, and well after the *Theaetetus*. But White's discussion passes over the epistemological passages of the intervening *Sophist*, *Statesman*, and *Philebus* as directed to different and irrelevant problems (p. 199). On his account the *Seventh Letter* takes up where the *Theaetetus* left off, with the paradox of inquiry as its crucial problem.

The relevant passage sets out to be an explanation of why Plato has not himself written any treatise expounding the things that most concern him, and why Dionysius (who apparently has written such a treatise) could not have learnt anything from Plato on these matters, since they had only one philosophical session together. So it is mainly concerned to stress the difficulty of imparting knowledge on the central topics of philosophy.

It tells us that in order to reach knowledge of any thing there are three things which we must use, its name, its definition (*logos*), and its images.[57] For example, we have the name 'circle', the definition 'what has boundaries everywhere equidistant from its centre', and images of circles drawn or turned on a lathe. The first two of these are found in speech, the third in bodies, and to these we must add a fourth which is found only in the soul, namely knowledge, understanding, and true belief.[58] Of these[59] the understanding in the soul is the most akin to the object we wish to know, namely the circle itself, and the others are far removed from it. Now the images are an inadequate guide, for any physical circle will be 'full of the opposite' to the real circle, in that its circumference will contain stretches that are actually straight. Again there is no reliability in the name (οὐδὲν βέβαιον), because it is clear that the word 'circle' could have been applied to straight lines, or indeed anything else. The same therefore applies to definitions too, since these are composed of names

---

[57] Contrary to *Statesman* 285e–286a (discussed above, p. 248–9) the *Letter* implies that images will *always* be available.

[58] ἐπιστήμη καὶ νοῦς ἀληθής τε δόξα (342c4–5). White suggests that the unexpected coupling of knowledge and true belief is due to the fact that the *Theaetetus* ends by being unable to distinguish them, but see n. 60 below. (The passage uses now 'knowledge' and now 'understanding' to describe the goal of the inquiry.)

[59] It is not clear whether 'of these' (342d1) means 'of knowledge, understanding, and true belief' or whether it means 'of names, definitions, images, and what is in the soul'. Contrary to Harward (1932, p. 215) and Morrow (1962, p. 239) I think the second is more likely, since our passage does not distinguish between knowledge and understanding.

and other expressions (ὀνόματα καὶ ῥήματα). Thus all of the four are defective, and yet they are all indispensable aids to knowledge of the circle itself, and we cannot do without them (342a7–e2; 343a4–b6).[60] But as well as the defectiveness of our four instruments there is also—and more importantly—the problem that, because of the weakness of language,[61] they do not adequately distinguish between what a thing [essentially] is (τὸ τί, τὸ ὄν ἑκάστου) and what it is like (τὸ ποῖόν τι). What we seek to know is the former, but each of the four can bring the latter to the soul instead, and this is something easily refuted by perceptions,[62] which confuses everyone. Although we can ordinarily hold our own well enough in debates upon matters where we are not accustomed to seek the truth, but are satisfied with an available image, it is different when the questions concern the real thing itself. There any exposition in words can be made to appear ignorant, not necessarily because the speaker himself is ignorant, but because the 'four' that he employs are defective (342e2–343a1, 343b7–e1).

There are many surprising features of this passage, but one thing that emerges very clearly is that the endeavour to know a thing does not terminate with the formulation of a definition or account of it. On the contrary, the passage seems to suppose we *begin* the inquiry with a definition already available, but that this cannot be relied upon any more than the name can, 'because of the weakness of language' (διὰ τὸ τῶν λόγων ἀσθενές, 343a1). However, the reason given for this 'weakness' seems very unconvincing, being simply the observation that any word *might* have meant something other than what it does mean. Although that is no doubt a perfectly correct observation, it does not seem enough by itself to license the very sceptical position on language that the passage seems to adopt, namely that no words ever do have a clear meaning. Nor is it obvious why this supposed fact should lead us to confuse what a thing is with what it is like, or should render even one who does know what he is speaking of open to apparent refutation.

---

[60] The text seems to imply that knowledge (sc. of the circle?) is an indispensable but defective aid towards knowledge of the circle. Perhaps what is meant is that knowledge of its name, definition, and images is essential to knowledge of the thing itself. (But 342a7–b3 is rather against this.) Alternatively the suggestion may be that true belief of the circle is an essential aid towards knowledge of it.

[61] It is not clear why the defectiveness of images should be set down as a weakness of *language*.

[62] I have no explanation to offer of why an account which says what a thing is like should be easily refuted *by perceptions*.

Some of these difficulties, however, are lightened if we consider the context of our 'digression', which makes it perfectly clear that what is mainly in Plato's mind is the *teaching* situation. He is concerned with how knowledge of the most important topics in philosophy can be imparted by one man to another (341b–e, 344c–345b), and he wishes to say that this cannot be done by setting down the truth in a written treatise for others to read, or by expounding it in a lecture, or by engaging in a single session of debate. Now there is nothing surprising in the suggestion that the *teacher* starts with definitions already worked out, and we can easily conjecture why 'the weakness of language' nevertheless obstructs him. For when we are dealing with the most important topics in philosophy—and not, e.g., the simple question of what a circle is—it is plausible to suppose that matters can be accurately stated only with the help of a technical vocabulary. But the technical vocabulary is likely to be misunderstood by the audience. (Plato must have been familiar with this problem. We are told that he gave a 'Lecture on the Good' which appeared to his audience to be mainly about numbers rather than about goodness, and which evidently puzzled them a great deal.) And it is tempting to add a further conjecture here, namely that the technical vocabulary will naturally use ordinary words in senses that *resemble* their ordinary senses. If so, this could well lead us to say that an audience who understood those words in their ordinary senses would at best understand what the thing was *like*, but not what it *is*. Moreover, a disputant who relied upon the ordinary senses of those words could well make it seem that the speaker did not know what he was talking about. Much of the passage, then, makes rather good sense if we suppose that what Plato really had in mind when he talked of 'the weakness of language' was the problems that arise from a technical vocabulary which uses familiar words in specialized and unfamiliar senses.

This, however, cannot be the way that White understands things, for on this way of taking the passage the correct conclusion to draw is not the strong conclusion that the knowledge we are concerned with cannot be set down in words at all, but only the weak conclusion that it cannot be set down in words which any ordinary person will easily understand. At one point the *Letter* appears to concede this. As in the similar (but less detailed) attack on writing at *Phaedrus* 274b–278b, it allows that a man who does understand the truth may write out a reminder for himself—but, it adds, there is no point in so doing: there is no danger of forgetting what can be set down so shortly (344d9–e2). But interpreters have often been tempted to see the *Letter* as drawing the strong conclusion, because of what it says about the way that knowledge *is* eventually obtained (or imparted).

Earlier, at 341c5–d2, we have been told that these matters are not statable (ῥητόν), as are other things that one learns (ἄλλα μαθήματα), but after much joint discussion and a life lived together, suddenly light is kindled as by a leaping flame, and thereafter nourishes itself in the soul. Then, when we come back to this point again in the longer account at 343e1–344c1, we are told that one must spend a long time with 'the four', going always from one to the other, and then with difficulty knowledge will come to one who is naturally fitted for it. (That is, one who is quick to learn, of good memory, and with a virtuous character akin to the virtues he is wishing to know.) After a long period spent in rubbing together names, definitions, and perceptions, and in friendly refutations of question and answer,[63] with the greatest effort of which man is capable, understanding will at last shine forth. Both passages use the metaphor of light, apparently conceived in the first passage as 'leaping' from teacher to pupil, and perhaps to be understood in the same way in the second. Knowledge is apparently thought of as a kind of illumination, a revelation of what was hitherto shrouded in darkness, and—if we stress the first passage—altogether inexpressible in language. On this account, then, the reason why Plato never has written any treatise on what most deeply concerns him, and never will, is simply that it cannot be put into words at all.

It is by stressing the lack of connection between what we can know and what we can say that White obtains his interpretation of the doctrine of the *Seventh Letter*, as a last and somewhat despairing attempt at resolving the old paradox of inquiry. That paradox is essentially a paradox about *recognition*: it asks how one can ever be in a position to recognize a thing that one discovers *as* the thing that one was looking for. As it appeared in the *Meno*, it was the problem of how one could be so placed that, while not yet being able to formulate the definition of a form oneself, one could nevertheless recognize a proposed definition as the correct one. To this problem

---

[63] The perceptions evidently correspond to the 'images' which are the third of 'the four'. Do the friendly refutations perhaps correspond to the fourth, namely what is in the soul?

the theory of recollection was supposed to provide an answer, namely that once upon a time we did know the correct definition of the form, so if we now stumble across it, or hear it from another, then it will fall into place with the familiar 'click' of memory, and that will reveal to us that it is correct. But this never was a very satisfactory solution to the problem (since it ignores the possibility of a delusive 'click' of memory), and anyway there is no reason to suppose that Plato retained the theory of recollection to the end of his life (p. 22). So, on White's account, it is not surprising that the problem is posed once more in the final argument of the *Theaetetus*, but this time without a solution. The *Seventh Letter* then tries again with a different 'solution', but it is now very much more radical. For the *Meno* had presumed that it *is* possible to recognize a definition as correct, and had tried to explain how, but the *Seventh Letter* simply denies that this is possible. Definitions cannot be any more 'correct' as accounts of forms than names can be 'correct' as names of them. This is not just because (as I suggested earlier) it all depends upon how the definition is understood, but because there simply is no genuine connection between what words can say and what it is to know a form.

The result is that one never does have any adequate conception of the form that one is searching for before one finds it, for the names, definitions, and images that one has to begin with simply do not specify what it is that one is searching for. For that reason, there is nothing that counts as *recognizing* the form that one eventually does see *as* the one that one was searching for. As White puts it, when the light dawns, it is 'simply a matter of enjoying the spectacle, as it were—like gazing at an unidentified landscape, as opposed to seeing and recognizing places which one has sought . . . You are apprehending something that you were not apprehending before, as though a light had illuminated the darkness. But it must not be thought that you *recognize* the particular things which you see, or that you know them to be something which you have sought' (p. 207). The result is that Plato has surrendered to the paradox, accepted that it has no solution, and drawn the consequence that indeed there is no such thing as inquiring into a form, as he had originally conceived it.

A point that White does not stress as he should is that, on this interpretation, the doctrine of the *Seventh Letter* is simply fantastic. If we stick to Plato's own illustration, the situation White envisages would appear to be this. You and I have spent many long hours rubbing together the name 'circle', the definition of a circle, and images of the circle. We have been asking and answering questions about circles, and perhaps about other related concepts, e.g. those occurring in the definition of a circle. Eventually, illumination comes, and there, revealed to our gaze, are some new and unexpected objects. But we do not in any way *recognize* them as the objects we have been searching for, and there is no reason to suppose that these objects in any way *are* what we have been searching for. Perhaps what we see are indeed the forms of the circle, the straight, the equal distance, and so on, but if so we have no means of telling which is which. Perhaps, indeed, they are quite different forms, say the forms of earth, air, and water, or the forms of justice, virtue, and equality. There is no way in which we can tell what forms these newly revealed objects are, since there is nothing that counts as recognizing a form, and no reason to suppose that what we now see is in any way related to those earnest discussions of a circle that somehow sparked the vision. For indeed on White's account there just is no relation between the forms that we see and the names, definitions, and images that we employ as a means of coming to see them. But this is manifestly absurd. If it is indeed what the writer of the *Seventh Letter* intended, then he was a fool and an idiot, and we need pay him no further attention.

If the *Seventh Letter* is to be taken at all seriously, then we can surely draw from it the opposite conclusion to the one that White draws: the author is *not* in any way concerned with the paradox of inquiry. He must be taking it for granted that we do in some way *recognize* which form is which, but since he does not say anything very much about how we do so, this is not a problem that was exercising him. In fact it seems to me that White himself has very largely manufactured this problem, by taking altogether too literally the idea that knowledge is here conceived of as a kind of *vision*. Once upon a time, in the *Phaedo*, Plato did subscribe to a theory that leads straight to this conclusion (chapter I, section 2(ii)). But that was many years ago, and there is really no good reason to say that the *Seventh Letter* returns to the same naïve viewpoint. The *only* relevant evidence is that it twice makes use of the metaphor of light: when understanding is finally attained, it is as if a light had been kindled. But we do not have to suppose that Plato means this metaphor to be taken in any more literal way than the many other

perceptual metaphors that we and he constantly use about understanding. We too say 'the light has dawned', just as we speak of
'seeing the point', 'viewing things in perspective', and so on. But we
do not mean to suggest that understanding is in any serious way like
gazing in a good light, and there is not much reason to suppose that
Plato wishes to suggest this either.

What the *Seventh Letter* is mainly concerned to say is that genuine
understanding of philosophically difficult concepts cannot be
gained either by reading a written treatise, or by listening to a
lecture, or in a single tutorial. Anyone who teaches philosophy must
be familiar with this thought, and must agree that there is a great
deal of truth in it. One simple reason is that words may always be
misunderstood, and we could easily add various other ways in which
understanding may fail. (Though we would not offer this as an
excuse for not trying to write, or to lecture.) Pressed with the
questions 'What then *is* understanding, and how *is* it to be
imparted?', we will be tempted to reply to the second as Plato does,
that it requires time, effort, and plenty of opportunity for question
and answer. But in reply to the first we may well not be able to say
much more than he can, using metaphors ('it nourishes itself') that
we do not know how to spell out in any literal way.

I conclude that the *Seventh Letter* gives no support to White's view
that the paradox of inquiry remained in Plato's mind as a serious
problem. The *Letter* (if it is genuine) can certainly be cited to show
that, at a date much later than the *Theaetetus*, Plato did still suppose
that the 'account' of a thing was an indispensable aid to knowledge
of it, but that he also recognized that 'accounts' by themselves are
not enough: they do not guarantee understanding. However, the
Seventh Letter simply ignores the old paradox of inquiry, and I think
it extremely probable that the *Theaetetus* is equally unperturbed by
it. In fact, I see no good reason to suppose that that paradox played
any important role in Plato's thought after the *Meno*, and one may
doubt whether it really had much importance even then. Certainly it
is used there as the occasion for introducing the theory of recollection, but the importance of that theory—so far as the *Meno* is
concerned—is that it seems to provide some explanation of how
a priori knowledge is possible, and we do not need the paradox in
order to see that a priori knowledge does call for some explanation.
Anyway, whatever is the case with the *Meno* itself, there is nowhere

else in Plato's writings where he shows signs of taking that paradox seriously, and no reason to say that it continued to bother him.[64] But of course White is right to claim that the last argument of the *Theaetetus* does apparently commit Plato to that paradox. Could Plato have both noticed this and continued to believe that the argument was valid?

Well, yes, I think he could have done. But to explain how one needs to pay more attention than White does to the earlier arguments about accounts. To continue with the line of thought that I introduced on pp. 252–3, we may say that this part of the *Theaetetus* in effect poses a dilemma. If on the one hand we suppose that knowing a thing involves the ability to give an account of it in the usual Platonic sense of that phrase, according to which a given thing has just one proper account and no more, then we run into an important objection. We may take the analysis of a thing into its elementary parts as typical of accounts of this kind, and when we think about this it becomes clear that accounts of this kind must eventually run out. We may also add that it will be possible to have a true belief of the account that does not yet amount to knowledge, which shows that knowledge anyway cannot be *defined* as the possession of an account, but the more important objection is the first one. If what we are considering are special essence-revealing accounts, then there must be some things which can be known (because they figure in the accounts of other things) but which do not themselves have such accounts. So we now turn to the other horn of the dilemma and allow that *any* 'distinguishing mark' will do as an account. But on this alternative Plato thinks (mistakenly) that if one can distinguish an object then one must already have a 'distinguishing mark' for it, so in effect we have identified knowing a thing with the ability to recognize it and distinguish it from others. And this is, anyway, not an unreasonable view in itself. But Plato also thinks (mistakenly) that I cannot even think of a thing without, in *this* sense, knowing it. So on this view accounts have nothing to do with it, since there is nothing to which an account can be added in order to produce knowledge.

Now it was correct to conclude that, on this conception of what it is to know a thing, accounts are unimportant. But it was a mistake to suppose that we cannot distinguish this kind of knowledge from the

[64] The similar paradoxes at *Euthydemus* 276d–277c are clearly there treated as *silly* puzzles, of no importance.

mere ability to think of a thing, and a mistake that Plato should not have made. For his example here is knowing, or thinking of, a perceptible thing, and he has *already* explained, in his discussion of the wax tablet, that I can think of what I perceive, whether or not I also know it. But I am sympathetic to White's view that what is really in Plato's mind is the case of knowing or thinking of a form (by which I just mean, in the present context, an item that Plato would take to be grasped by the mind, independently of perception). And we have noted that he did *not* see how to generalize the distinctions of the wax tablet to apply to forms. Perhaps, indeed, it is not unreasonable to suggest that there is no distinction to be drawn between being able to think of a form and knowing it, where this just means being able to recognize it and distinguish it from others?

Now *in a way* this commits Plato to the paradox of inquiry. One cannot first pick out some form (e.g. by name) and then set about the search for knowledge of that form, in *this* sense of 'knowledge'. But one can, of course, seek for knowledge of it in *other* senses of that word. One can, presumably, engage in a search for an account of the thing that reveals its essence. So, in another way, this argument does not commit Plato to the paradox, for when its conclusion is rightly understood it is not paradoxical. The only difficulty that might seem to emerge is that the first horn of the dilemma has shown that there will be some forms—perhaps being, sameness, and difference would be examples?—which do not have essence-revealing accounts. Perhaps in their case we have to accept that the only sense in which they can be known is just that they can be thought. But it is not obvious that that is a wholly unacceptable conclusion.

This line of interpretation has something in common with White's: like his, it does assign an important role to the argument about the distinguishing mark. But, unlike his, it stresses the contrast between accounts as genuine analyses and accounts as mere distinguishing marks, and for that reason it credits Plato with a line of thought that he may well have believed to be correct. To give it a name, I shall call it my interpretation.

Perhaps the most obvious objection to it is this. As I construe the situation, Plato is *mainly* interested in what it is to know a form throughout this last section of the dialogue, for it is with forms in mind that he has so often said in the past that to know a thing one must be able to give an account of it. Now most of the discussion takes letters and syllables as its example, and it is not at all difficult to see these as illustrating forms. (They are certainly used in this way at *Sophist* 253a.) But in the final argument, where in fact we *have* to see the argument as concerned with forms if it is not to be refuted by something that Plato has already said, he in fact switches his example to the perceptible individual, Theaetetus. How is this to be accounted for? Well, I think the explanation probably lies in the fact that this final argument also returns to the image of the wax tablet. Socrates says (mistakenly) that it is what is imprinted on his wax that enables him to think of Theaetetus, and hence to recognize him (and therefore, on the present account, to know him). But he has *also* told us that there is something imprinted on his wax that gives him his grasp of the forms. He would rather not talk explicitly about that, because he now does not know quite what to say about how those impressions got there in the first place, and he has been preserving a discreet silence on that topic. That is why he actually takes as his example the more straightforward case of an ordinary perceptible object. But he thinks (rashly) that it will not affect his argument, because in each case his argument concerns what one can do as a result of having a suitable impression on the tablet of one's mind.

As for the argument itself, it is certainly strange that Plato should have accepted the view that an image on one's wax tablet would itself qualify as an account. But from the present viewpoint this is no longer a serious mistake on his part, for it can be seen simply as a concession made for the sake of argument. That is, I conceive of Plato's actual train of thought as moving in the opposite direction to the way in which his argument is explicitly set out. As it is set out, the argument begins with the idea that an account may be merely a distinguishing mark, and infers that it will enable one to recognize the thing that it is an account of. But I imagine Plato himself as beginning with the idea that to know a thing (in particular, a form) is to be able to recognize the thing (e.g. as it occurs in discourse), and to distinguish it from other similar things (other forms). He believes that (in the case of forms) we can do this only because we have a suitable image on the wax. So *if* accounts are relevant to this kind of knowledge, then we must allow that these images may be called accounts. The straightforward way of continuing the argument from this point would be to protest that images are not accounts. But

Plato prefers to proceed more circuitously. Suppose that we allow them as accounts, of a kind. It *still* will not do to say that knowledge (of this sort) arises by the addition of an account to some other and independent ability, that we could possess without having any such 'account'. For there is no way of even thinking the form that does not rely upon this image. Thus, even if images are permitted as accounts, still the proposed definition of knowledge will not be satisfied.

(iv) *Summary*

Against Cornford, I agree with both Fine and White (and, I think, nearly all other interpreters) that the problems which Plato here develops for accounts do apply, and were intended to apply, to knowledge of forms just as much as to knowledge of other things. In fact I think that it is mainly knowledge of forms that Plato is interested in, for that would explain why he failed to notice that the earlier wax tablet contains a conclusive objection to his final argument about accounts as distinguishing marks.

I agree with Fine in supposing that Plato recognized that the theory of Socrates' dream poses a crucial problem about accounts, and that he was well enough aware that this problem does not depend upon taking an account to be just a listing of elementary parts. On more or less any view of what a definition or an analysis is, it *looks* as though we are going to have to admit that definitions must end with indefinables. On my interpretation Plato does admit this, or at any rate he deliberately explores the consequence of admitting it, namely that it must be possible to know some things without any account of this kind. On Fine's interpretation, he does not admit it, and he continues to maintain that suitable accounts are always required, which he does by allowing that accounts may go round in circles. Now I certainly have to admit that *later* dialogues support Fine's view. At any rate the *Statesman* claims that there always are suitable accounts (and so does the *Seventh Letter*), and if Plato really has appreciated the problem posed by Socrates' dream then he must presumably have in mind some such solution as Fine suggests. There are things in what he says about 'collection and division' that do lend this conjecture some indirect support. But, against Fine, there is no hint of this view in the *Theaetetus* itself, whereas there are quite strong indications that Plato is falling back upon a less exacting conception of knowledge. So it seems to me that my interpretation fits the *Theaetetus* better than Fine's does. We are all agreed that the second objection raised to accounts as enumerations of elements, namely that one may believe such an account without having knowledge, is in itself a perfectly good point. It recurs in the *Seventh Letter*, but one would hesitate to say that that *Letter* provides any solution to the problem raised, since it has nothing but metaphor to offer when trying to say what genuine understanding is. What is not clear is whether Plato connects this point in the *Theaetetus* with the circularity objection that ends the dialogue. There *is* a natural connection, and *if* Plato saw the circularity objection as an important one, then no doubt he drew it. Moreover it is tempting to suppose, with Fine, that Plato did see the importance of the circularity objection, for this would explain why he feels entitled to conclude that there is *no* way of understanding an 'account' which will permit us to define knowledge as true belief plus an account. (But we should not suppose, as Fine does, that Plato found a way of meeting this objection, either now or later.) But I am more inclined to agree with White that Plato has not really grasped the importance of the circularity objection, for he does not even state it as a complete objection on its own, as he certainly should do on Fine's interpretation, and he evidently does not *say* that it applies to all versions of an 'account'. In fact what he does say gives so little prominence to this objection that it seems to me more plausible to suppose that it was not playing any prominent role in his thought either.

It may perhaps be objected that to place an argument right at the end of the book *is* to give it prominence. And this objection may be reinforced by the observation that the *Theaetetus* not only ends with a problem of circularity; it also begins with one. At 147a–b Socrates complains that one who does not yet undertand what knowledge is equally cannot understand any supposed examples of it (such as geometry or shoemaking), and an account in terms of examples is therefore circular. If the whole discussion is framed, at the beginning and at the end, by objections of circularity, should we not infer that Plato did see this as a crucial problem? However, I do not find this convincing. It is perfectly clear that Plato's *main* objection to an account in terms of examples is not that it is circular but that it does not tell us what we want to know: we want to know what the examples all have in common, and the list of examples simply does not tell us this. This is the objection that he puts first (146e), and it is surely the one that matters to him. If he does go on to add a further objection of circularity, that is no doubt because he had once upon a time believed that his main objection could be strengthened in this way (*Meno* 79b–c), and he has not thought about the matter further. But he should have done, for in fact the circularity objection at the beginning of the book is a bad one (pp. 32–4 above). By contrast, the circularity objection at the end is *potentially* a very good objection indeed, but the qualification 'potentially' cannot be omitted. As the objection is actually presented, it is merely one half of a dilemma, and I agree with White in supposing that it was the *other* half that Plato was mainly concerned with.

The question that was exercising him, in this last argument of the dialogue, was this. We have been driven to admit that indefinables must be knowable, since otherwise no definition could yield knowledge at all. But apparently the only kind of knowledge that could apply to indefinables is the ability to recognize them, and distinguish them from other similar things. And we do have to admit that this ability *is* a kind of *knowledge*, in order to resolve that first problem. But can we say that *this* kind of knowledge involves *any* sort of 'account'? The correct answer is that it does not, and this is in effect the answer that Plato gives, though he presents it more circuitously. His claim is rather that, even if you so understand the notion of an 'account' that the ability to recognize does involve an account, still it cannot be represented as arising by the *addition* of that account to some independently existing ability. For—at least in the case of a form—one cannot think of the thing at all without having the ability to recognize it and discriminate it from its fellows. Either way, then, we cannot say that knowledge always involves the addition of an account, for *this* kind of knowledge is a counter-example. The suggested definition of knowledge must therefore be rejected.

To put this conclusion in the somewhat peculiar terms in which this discussion is officially conducted, it is this: knowledge cannot be defined as true belief plus an account, because *some* knowledge is simply true belief and nothing more. But why does Plato use such evidently inappropriate terminology?

VII

EVALUATION

1. THE COHERENCE OF THE *THEAETETUS*

When the *Theaetetus* raises the question 'What is knowledge?' it does not suggest that there are different kinds or varieties of knowledge to be distinguished. On the contrary, it apparently presumes that there is just one single and unitary concept of knowledge that we are to inquire into. Is that how Plato himself saw the problem? Did he suppose that the various suggestions that he puts forward, discusses, and rejects should all be understood as suggested analyses of this one concept? If so, he was certainly confused, and it must be admitted that first appearances do quite strongly suggest this.

The major confusion is, of course, the apparent confusion between knowing things and knowing that. The first part of the dialogue ends by claiming that knowledge is unlike perception, since it always reaches truth and perception never does. This, of course, is quite acceptable as a claim about knowing that (if, as seems to be the case, perceiving that is not allowed to count as perception). Accordingly, the second part begins by proposing to look for knowledge in the region of belief, and specifically true belief, and so far everything is in order. We thus expect the two suggestions discussed in the second part to be, first that knowing that *P* is no different from truly believing that *P*, and second that it differs only by the addition of an 'account', which we expect to be an account of why it is the case that *P*—e.g. a 'working out of the reason ' (αἰτίας λογισμός, p. 16)—or something of that kind. But this is not at all what happens. In fact the suggestion that is actually discussed in the last section of the dialogue is that to know a thing is to be able to give an account of that thing, in addition to merely being able to think of it. So there has been a complete change of subject. But there is no indication that Plato has *noticed* this. To think of a thing is not the same as to have any belief, or make any judgement—for we think of a thing when we are merely wondering about it—and it cannot be done either truly or falsely. That is, to think *of* is not the same as to think *that*, and only the latter can be true. But Plato continues to say that it is *true* thought (or belief, or judgement), with an account, that he is discussing, even when it is quite clear that he is not. (There are clear examples at 208e3 and 209a1–2, where he is introducing his final argument.)

If we look now at the way that the topic of knowing a thing, rather than knowing that, first enters the discussion, again first appearances suggest that important distinctions are not being drawn. As soon as the second part has started, Plato begins to use the verb 'to know' with a direct object, for it is used in this way in his opening puzzle about false belief. The idea here is that one must know the things that one's belief is a belief about, and yet at the same time this idea apparently leads to paradoxical conclusions. So when it is concluded, at the end of this discussion, that we should not have tried to unravel these paradoxes until we had first decided what knowledge is, one might naturally expect the subsequent investigation to be directed to this point. That is, its problem should be: what exactly is this relation which a thinker must have, to the things that his thought is about, if he is to be able to have that thought at all? But again it would not appear to be *this* topic that is next pursued. In the passage immediately following we revert to thinking of knowledge as knowing that, in order to refute the view that it is the same as truly believing that, and we then move on to consider the view that knowing a thing involves being able to give an account of it. But it is surely very implausible to suppose that in order to have a thought at all I must first be able to give an account of the things that my thought is about. Thus the suggestion that is actually explored in the last section of the dialogue appears to be totally irrelevant *both* to the idea that introduces the second part (which concerns knowing that) *and* to the idea that gives rise to the problem of false belief (which concerns knowing things, but a quite different kind of knowing things).

Another point that one might note is this. The verb δοξάζειν standardly means to think that (or believe, or judge), but early in the discussion of false belief Plato begins to use it with a direct object construction, as he is also using the verb 'to know', so that it has to be translated 'to think of' (or 'to believe about', or 'to have in one's judgements', or something similar). But he then proceeds, at

190a, to explain how he is understanding this verb, and his explanation is evidently an explanation of thinking *that* (for he explains it as a matter of reaching a *verdict*). But the verb continues to be used to mean 'think of' (as well as 'think that'), even in the passage where it is defined as meaning 'think that'. A nice example here is 190c5–7, where the definition is recalled and the verb is used in different senses in successive lines. A fairly close translation of the Greek would be 'If to say to oneself is to think, then no one who says and thinks both the things concerned . . . will say and think that the one is the other'.[1] Here 'say' and 'think' mean 'say that' and 'think that' in their first and third occurrences, but they mean 'speak of' and 'think of' in their second occurrence. Plato apparently regards both uses of the verb as covered by his account of thinking as saying things to oneself, whereas in fact only one of them is. Again the natural inference seems to be that he simply has not noticed that two distinct uses are involved.

On this view the *Theaetetus* as a whole is simply a muddle. Broadly speaking, its first half is about knowing that, and its second half is about knowing things, but since Plato thinks that it is the same topic that he is addressing in both parts, one can only say that the discussion as a whole is just incoherent. Now this *may* be the right account of the matter, but it does involve certain difficulties. For example, why, on this interpretation, does Plato never even consider the view that the right kind of 'account', that should be added to true belief to turn it into knowledge, is 'a working out of the reason'? If he is aware that what he is talking about at this stage of the dialogue is knowledge of things, rather than knowledge of truths in general, then this omission is, of course, entirely to be expected. But if he is not aware of this, then it is really very surprising. Again, why is Plato not prepared to admit that some things, namely (in his view) our experiences, are known by being perceived? They are things perceived, and they are also things that are, and on this interpretation Plato can hardly be relying on the point that we do not perceive *that* they are. It would plainly be unreasonable to credit him with a distinction between perceiving things and perceiving that, while at the same time denying him any grasp of the distinction between knowing things and knowing that.

On the other hand these points are entirely intelligible if we

---

[1] εἰ τὸ λέγειν πρὸς ἑαυτὸν δοξάζειν ἐστίν, οὐδεὶς ἀμφότερά γε λέγων καὶ δοξάζων . . . εἴποι ἂν καὶ δοξάσειεν ὡς τὸ ἕτερον ἕτερόν ἐστιν.

suppose that Plato is aware that the subject has been changed from one part of the dialogue to the other. In fact, *given* this change of subject, it can reasonably be said that the proposals made, and the arguments used, are in each part perfectly appropriate to their topic, and it is only the terminology of the second part that is strange. The terminology certainly is strange. It is distinctly unusual Greek to use the verb δοξάζειν, with a direct object, to mean something like 'think of', and it is quite inappropriate to qualify this use of the verb by 'truly' or 'correctly', as the text often does. But at the same time one must observe that the double usage of the verb δοξάζειν is in fact perfectly clear, and there is very seldom any doubt as to which way the verb should be taken.[2] More importantly, the inappropriate uses of 'truly', 'correctly', and so on, *never* affect the argument. So one might suggest that this strange terminology is acting as a kind of smoke-screen: it seems to be designed to conceal the fact that we have changed the subject, but the discussion that goes on underneath it is a perfectly good discussion of the new subject[3] and not a bungled attempt to continue the old one.

But why might Plato have wished to put up such a smoke-screen? One obvious point is that it allowed him to leave the discussion of knowing that and believing that in a very unfinished state, without having to admit this explicitly. All that we are told about this kind of knowledge is that it is sensible to look for it in the region of belief, but that it is more than just true belief. That is no doubt perfectly all right as far as it goes, but it does not seem to go very far. (Of course Plato may have realized that the difficulties which he raises for an account as an enumeration of elements *could* be adapted to apply also to an account as a working out of the reason, i.e. a proof or explanation. But that is only a conjecture.) But I think a more important consideration is this. If Plato had told us clearly that he was changing the subject, then he would also have to admit that the concept of knowledge is not, after all, the simple and unitary concept it apparently pretends to be. But in that case the correct procedure would be to begin with a 'division' of knowledge into its various types and kinds.[4] But it would not be at all surprising if Plato

---

[2] There is just one point at which I disagree with McDowell's translation on this question (p. 165 n. 9).

[3] I shall shortly elaborate this claim, which denies the criticism made on p. 269.

[4] It seems to me probable (but not certain) that Plato had by this time written at least the first part of the *Phaedrus*, which contains his first fairly explicit essay in such a division, namely the division of madness.

did not feel competent to undertake such a task. (Even in the later *Philebus*, where he seems to promise such a division, it does not really materialize.) The 'smoke-screen', then, enables him to avoid it, and to allow the outward structure of his discussion to conform to the initial suggestion that there is just one concept of knowledge that is discussed all through. But, I suggest, he indicates clearly enough that he is not as confused as this seems to suggest. The second part of the dialogue at once introduces the verb 'to know' with a direct object, and in case the reader fails to notice the point— for it is, after all, quite an ordinary use of the word—it very soon starts to use the verb 'to believe' in the same way. But that is noticeable, and we should be properly alerted.

One's first impression of the *Theaetetus*, then, is that it is simply muddled. Sometimes it is concerned with knowledge of truths, and sometimes with knowledge of things, but it has not noticed the difference. But on second thoughts this seems to me to be improbable. Setting aside the short and unimportant passage which argues that to know a truth is not the same as to believe it (200e–201d), and looking beneath the strange terminology of the second part, one can say that the first part concerns knowledge of truths and the second concerns knowledge of things. Moreover, it seems that Plato *is* aware of this distinction, for otherwise one would expect his discussion to be considerably more chaotic than it is. So apparently he has deliberately changed the subject. I now wish to introduce a third thought: there is not actually any change of subject, for the problem which the second part of the dialogue is concerned with is precisely the problem of whether the conclusion of the first part can be maintained. The plot of the *Theaetetus* as a whole is, I suggest, this.

The first part assumes that knowledge is always knowledge of truths, and it argues on this basis that knowledge is quite unlike perception. Perception is directed to simple objects, while knowledge, like belief, is directed to something complex. The point here is that judgements are complex, and made up out of several terms. But the second part begins by raising a question about the judger's relationship to the terms of his judgement. He must, presumably, grasp these terms in some way, and it is at first natural to say that he must know them. This admittedly seems to give rise to a problem about how false belief is possible, and that problem is then pursued, but left unresolved. But so far as the main plot is concerned, the important point is this: if the judger does have to *know* the terms of his judgement, then after all knowledge can be directed at simple items, and so cannot be distinguished from perception in the way suggested. So the question is: do we have to say that the terms of the judgement *are known*?

Now the discussion of false belief has pointed out that where the terms in question are perceptible objects we need not say this. For we can distinguish between knowing and merely thinking of a perceptible thing, and it may therefore be possible to reserve the notion of knowing a perceptible thing for something that does 'reach truth', in that it consists in knowledge of some fact or facts about the thing. This would no doubt be embodied in a suitable 'account' of the thing. But can we also say the same for imperceptible objects (forms)? Certainly Plato always used to hold this view about what it was to know a form, but now it appears that the point that lies behind the theory of Socrates' dream is an insuperable objection. Apparently the kind of 'accounts' that are suitable for forms must eventually run out, and we shall have to admit that there is a way of knowing something which does not involve an account. This will be, presumably, the ability to recognize the thing and distinguish it from others, for we do in our ordinary way of speaking count that as knowledge. But—at least in the case of a form—this just *is* the ability to think of the thing, i.e. it is exactly what is needed if one is to make judgements in which that thing occurs. We therefore *do* have to admit that there is a kind of knowledge which does not 'reach truth', for it involves no 'account' which would express that truth. This kind of knowledge must, then, be directed to its simple objects (especially forms), in much the same way as perception is also directed to its (simple) objects. And the result is that the conclusion of the first part cannot be maintained, for there is one kind of knowledge which is very like perception.

There is, then, this perfectly coherent line of argument that holds the *Theaetetus* together, though certainly it is not lying clear upon the surface. If anything at all like this was in Plato's mind as he composed the second part of the dialogue, then we must say that he was writing enigmatically (as he is also in the contemporary *Parmenides*). One has to think quite hard about the issues involved, and their relationship to one another, before anything like the plot I have outlined begins to emerge. This, I imagine, is quite deliberate on Plato's part. He wants us to have to think about these issues, and he is not, as in the dialogues of the middle period, trying to make clear to us the truths that he is confident that he has discovered. This, I believe, is because he is not at all confident himself. He too is still thinking about these issues, and I do not imagine that he is *satisfied* with the line of argument that he here presents. He does not *wish* to admit that there is anything that can properly be called knowledge but yet does not involve 'an account', and so cannot be said to 'reach truth'. In later dialogues, as we have noted, he has rethought his position and he does not admit it. So, as I see his position, when he here presents a line of argument which seems to show that this must be admitted, he is offering us what he sees as a problem, and not a solution. But he has seen very much more deeply into the problem now than he ever had before.

2. RESOLUTION OF PLATO'S PROBLEM

I end this discussion with a word on Plato's problem, as that has now emerged. It arises through a misconception on his part, but one that stems from long-standing views about the forms, and leads to too crude a view about what it is to understand a judgement. One can see without much difficulty that there must be *something* wrong with the problem I have just outlined. One can perceive an object without recognizing it for what it is, and the first part of the dialogue relied upon this point in its final argument. For to recognize is to make a judgement. But if there is any sense in which one can be said to 'know' the terms of one's judgement without recognizing them, this must be irrelevant. For knowledge without recognition—if there is such a thing—evidently cannot explain how one 'grasps' the terms of the judgement sufficiently to understand the judgement itself. But let us look into this a little more closely.

Let us grant, for the sake of argument,[5] that a judgement is always complex, and so can be regarded as made up from several terms. Let us also, for simplicity, limit our attention to nice simple subject–predicate judgements, such as the textbook example 'Socrates is wise'. Now one begins on the wrong foot if one supposes that to grasp such a judgement one must first grasp the term *being*, expressed by the word 'is', which here links the two terms expressed by 'Socrates' and by 'wise'. For the expression '. . . is wise' is better

---

[5] Cf. p. 194 n. 34.

regarded as one that is grasped as a whole, as is the single verb 'talks' in 'Socrates talks'. Of course one can later admit that there is a significant complexity within '. . . is wise', just as there is also a significant complexity (between verb-stem and verb-ending) within the one word 'talks'. But it is sensible not to make things too complicated at the beginning. We will do better to suppose that our simplest statements contain one subject-expression (ὄνομα) and one predicate-expression (ῥῆμα), as Plato himself later does.

The reason why I say that it is misleading to start in the way that Plato seems to in the *Theaetetus*, breaking the statement up into three components, is that it too readily encourages us to start thinking in terms of abstract objects. We very naturally think that we grasp what is expressed by 'Socrates' because we are acquainted with the thing it stands for, namely the man Socrates. Then it is not too unnatural to suppose that we grasp what is expressed by 'wise' because we are equally acquainted[6] with the thing that it stands for, namely wisdom. The idea that a word such as 'wise' stands for some object is not particularly repelling. But having come this far we will evidently be tempted to go on to the last step, and say similarly that we grasp what is expressed by 'is' because we are acquainted with what it stands for, namely being. Admittedly, one *can* be led to essentially the same position even if one starts by considering the predicate '. . . is wise' as a whole. I think it is less natural to suppose that '. . . is wise' stands for some object, and more plausible to say—as Plato does say later in the *Sophist*—that the role of a name is to stand for an object, while the role of a predicate is something different. But nevertheless one could suppose that '. . . is wise', taken as a whole, does stand for something, say being wise. At any rate, Russell at one stage adopted just such a view.[7] On this account, a simple judgement such as we are considering will contain a subject-expression and a predicate-expression, and to understand it one needs to be acquainted with the two objects they stand for. The subject-expression will stand for an ordinary kind of object, which one will often be acquainted with by perception, while the predicate-expression will stand for something which Russell calls a universal, which one is acquainted with in a different way. This

---

[6] Nothing will hang on the word 'acquaintance', which I use simply because it was Russell's word. The point is that we understand an expression by being in some suitable relation to the object that the expression stands for.

[7] See his 'Knowledge by Acquaintance and Knowledge by Description'.

differs from Plato's theory in the *Theaetetus* only in unimportant ways (mainly concerning what acquaintance with a universal is[8]).

But Russell later came to see, for very good reasons, that this theory was a mistake. First he realized that an acquaintance with the various items that occurred in one's judgements was not *sufficient* to explain how one understood the judgement. This is basically because a mere acquaintance with some item that a predicate stands for is not enough to explain what is meant by applying that predicate to a subject. The simplest way of making this point is by considering a slightly more complex kind of statement, e.g. one in which a relation (a dyadic predicate) is applied to two subjects, as in 'John hit James'. Knowing what 'John' stands for, and what 'James' stands for, and what 'hit' stands for (namely past hitting, I suppose), cannot tell one the difference between 'John hit James' and 'James hit John'. One who cannot tell the difference between these two evidently does not know what either of them means. The same point also applies, though it is perhaps less easy to see in this case, to the simple statement 'Socrates is wise'. To know which item the expression '. . . is wise' stands for is not yet to know what is meant by fitting the expression 'Socrates' into its gap. For it will not tell you the difference between 'Socrates is wise', which *says* something, and 'Socrates, wisdom' or 'Socrates, being wise', which do not.[9] Plainly, what we need to understand is what it is that '. . . is wise' *says* about the subject it is applied to, and not what item (if any) it *stands for*.[10]

Further reflection on this point led Russell in the end to admit that one might understand the statement 'Socrates is wise' without being acquainted with any item that '. . . is wise' stands for. He began by conceding that such an acquaintance was not *sufficient* for understanding the statement, and eventually came to see that it was not *necessary* either.[11] In this, he was surely right. We do not have

---

[8] Russell thought that acquaintance with universals arose through perception. Plato evidently denies this, but tells us nothing positive about how it does arise. (He speaks mainly of 'thinking' or 'knowing' the universal, but also of 'considering it' (ἐπισκοπεῖν, 185e7), of 'reaching out for it' (ἐπορέγεσθαι, 186a4), and of 'grasping it' (ἐφάπτεσθαι, 190c6, d9). He also compares it to having an impression on one's wax tablet, and to having a bird in one's aviary.)

[9] The same applies to Plato's version 'Socrates, being, wisdom'.

[10] This is what Russell means when he says that in order to understand a predicate one must 'bring in the form of a proposition' ('Lectures on Logical Atomism', p. 205).

[11] See his *The Analysis of Mind* (1921), p. 228.

to suppose that the expression '. . . is wise' stands for any such object as a universal is supposed to be, in order to explain how we understand it. Nor do we have to suppose that the two words which it contains each stand for an object, one for the Platonic form of being, and the other for the Platonic form of wisdom. To understand the expression '. . . is wise' is indeed to know what it means, but what it means is not an object, or a combination of two objects (being and wisdom). What it means, that is to say, is not something that we can name, but rather something that we can *state*. There is, of course, some controversy over precisely the right way to state the meaning of such an expression. A popular view nowadays would be that we state the meaning of '. . . is wise' when we say: the expression '. . . is wise' is true of a thing if and only if that thing is wise.[12] This conforms to the idea that meaning is essentially a matter of truth-conditions. But there are many other views about meaning now available, and I do not intend to discuss which of them should be adopted.

We are now in a position to return to Plato's problem. In order to understand the statement 'Socrates is wise' I do indeed have to know what '. . . is wise' means. But this is not a matter of knowing the object that it means, or of standing in any other relation to the object that it means, for what it means is not an object. Rather, to know what '. . . is wise' means is to know *that* something-or-other (e.g. that it is true of all and only those who are wise). So this is a kind of knowledge that *does* 'reach truth', even though it need not issue in any very informative 'account'. That is, one can know what '. . . is wise' means without being able to provide any useful *analysis* of the concept of wisdom. But, for all that, the relevant knowledge is a case of knowing that, and not of knowing an object.

Now it has been simpler to make this point by talking explicitly of what an *expression* means, and you may object that the topic is supposed to be judgements and not sentences. Despite what the *Theaetetus* says at 190a, it is not obvious that one needs to know what any *expression* means before one can judge that Socrates is wise. For the sake of argument I grant this, but the point that I am after may be made without explicitly bringing in expressions and their meanings. It may be said that in order to be able to judge that

---

[12] This is not, as it may appear to be, a tautology. One who *misunderstands* the expression '. . . is wise' may suppose that it is true of a thing if and only if that thing is foolish.

Socrates is wise one must know what being wise is (or what wisdom is). But still this is a matter of knowing *that*, and not a matter of knowing any *object*. It evidently cannot be said that to know what being wise is is to know being wise (or that to know what wisdom is is to know wisdom). Whether or not there are such objects as being wise, or wisdom, it is still quite wrong to suppose that one has to know *those objects* if one is to grasp the judgement that Socrates is wise. Knowledge of *objects* has nothing to do with it.

Incidentally we may add here that a similar point holds about the subject-term 'Socrates'. To understand the statement 'Socrates is wise' one must, in a suitable sense, know what 'Socrates' means; and to judge that Socrates is wise one must be able to think of Socrates. But in either case this requirement can apparently be satisfied if I merely know of Socrates via some such description as 'the man whom you mentioned just now, using the name "Socrates"'. If this is all the information that I have about Socrates, then it may be said (somewhat misleadingly) that I do in a way know who Socrates is (namely, the man you have just mentioned), but it certainly cannot be inferred that I know Socrates. Equally, if what enables my thought to be a thought about Socrates is that I stand in some appropriate causal relationship to him—e.g. I can perceive him—then again it cannot be inferred that I know him, in any ordinary sense of that word. So the truth is that knowing objects is not in any way a precondition of being able to make judgements: neither one's understanding of the subject nor one's understanding of the predicate need involve knowledge of this kind.

Thus Plato's problem collapses: we do not need to invoke any kind of knowledge that does not 'reach truth' in order to explain how we understand judgements,[13] even though it is admitted that judgements are complex, put together from several terms, and that we understand the judgement only because we understand the terms that it contains. One can see very well why Plato thought there was a problem here. Beginning from the position that predicate-terms do stand for objects, i.e. forms, he was inevitably led to think that to understand them we must in some sense know those forms. I have only resolved his problem by denying the premiss from which he started—or, at least, by arguing for its irrelevance. Alternatively, we may put the situation thus. If one

[13] I am not claiming that *all* kinds of knowledge do 'reach truth'. But that is a large topic, which there is no need to pursue here.

does wish to hold on to the view that understanding a predicate is a matter of knowing a form, then a detailed investigation shows that this is a case of knowing that, rather than of knowing an object. But it is not at all surprising that Plato should have thought otherwise.

LIST OF WORKS CITED

A. On Plato

ACKRILL, J. L., 'Plato on False Belief: *Theaetetus* 187–200', *Monist* 50 (1966), 383–402.

ALLEN, R. E. (ed.), *Studies in Plato's Metaphysics*, London, 1965.

BOSTOCK, D., 'Plato on "Is Not" ', *Oxford Studies in Ancient Philosophy* 2 (1984), 89–119.

——*Plato's Phaedo*, Oxford, 1986.

BURNYEAT, M. F., 'The Material and Sources of Plato's Dream', *Phronesis* 15 (1970), 101–22.

——'Protagoras and self-refutation in Plato's *Theaetetus*', *Philosophical Review* 85 (1976*a*), 172–95.

——'Plato and the Grammar of Perceiving', *Classical Quarterly* 26 (1976*b*), 29–51.

CHERNISS, H. F., 'The Relation of the *Timaeus* to Plato's Later Dialogues', *American Journal of Philology* 78 (1957), 225–66. (Reprinted in Allen.)

COOPER, J. M., 'Plato on Sense-Perception and Knowledge (*Theaetetus* 184–6)', *Phronesis* 15 (1970), 123–46.

CORNFORD, F. M., *Plato's Theory of Knowledge*, London, 1935.

CROMBIE, I. M., *An Examination of Plato's Doctrines*, vol. 2, London, 1963.

FINE, G. J., 'False Belief in the *Theaetetus*', *Phronesis* 24 (1979*a*), 70–80.

——'Knowledge and *Logos* in the *Theaetetus*', *Philosophical Review* 88 (1979*b*), 366–97.

GOSLING, J. C. B., *Plato*, London, 1973.

GULLEY, N., *Plato's Theory of Knowledge*, London, 1962.

HARWARD, J., *The Platonic Epistles*, Cambridge, 1932.

HICKEN, W. F., 'The Character and Provenance of Socrates' "Dream" in the *Theaetetus*', *Phronesis* 3 (1958), 126–45.

HOLLAND, A. J., 'An Argument in Plato's *Theaetetus* 184–6', *Philosophical Quarterly* 23 (1973), 97–116.

JACKSON, H., 'Plato's Later Theory of Ideas: the *Theaetetus*', *Journal of Philology* 13 (1885), 242–72.

LEWIS, F. A., 'Two Paradoxes in the *Theaetetus*', in *Patterns in Plato's Thought*, ed. J. M. E. Moravesik, Dordrecht, 1973, 123–49.

LUTOSLAWSKI, W., *The Origin and Growth of Plato's Logic*, London, 1905.
LYONS, J., *Structural Semantics: An Analysis of Part of the Vocabulary of Plato*, Oxford, 1963.
MCDOWELL, J., *Plato: Theaetetus*, Oxford, 1973.
MEYERHOFF, H., 'Socrates' "Dream" in the *Theaetetus*', *Classical Quarterly* 8 (1958), 131–8.
MORROW, G. R., 'Aristotle's comments on Plato's *Laws*', in I. Düring and G. E. L. Owen (edd.), *Aristotle and Plato in the Mid-Fourth Century*, Göteborg, 1960, 145–62.
——*Plato's Epistles*, Indianapolis, 1962.
——'Plato and the Mathematicians', *Philosophical Review* 79 (1970), 309–33.
NAKHNIKIAN, G., 'Plato's Theory of Sensation', *Review of Metaphysics* 9 (1955), 129–48, 306–27.
OWEN, G. E. L., 'The Place of the *Timaeus* in Plato's Dialogues', *Classical Quarterly* 3 (1953), 79–95. (Reprinted in Allen, and cited from there.)
ROBINSON, R., 'Forms and Error in Plato's *Theaetetus*', *Philosophical Review* 59 (1950), 3–30. (Reprinted in his *Essays in Greek Philosophy*, Oxford, 1969, and cited from there.)
ROSS, W. D., *Plato's Theory of Ideas*, Oxford, 1953.
ROWE, C. J., M. WELBOURNE, and C. J. F. WILLIAMS, 'Knowledge, Perception, and Memory—*Theaetetus* 166b', *Classical Quarterly* 32 (1982), 304–6.
RUNCIMAN, W. G., *Plato's Later Epistemology*, Cambridge, 1962.
RYLE, G., 'Plato's *Parmenides*', *Mind* 48 (1939), 129–51, 302–25. (Reprinted in Allen, and cited from there.)
——*Plato's Progress*, Cambridge, 1966.
SAYRE, K. M., *Plato's Analytic Method*, Chicago, 1969.
——*Plato's Late Ontology*, Princeton, 1983.
TAYLOR, A. E., *Plato: the Man and his Work*, London, 1926.
WATERFIELD, R. A. H., 'The Place of the *Philebus* in Plato's Dialogues', *Phronesis* 25 (1980), 270–305.
WHITE, N. P., *Plato on Knowledge and Reality*, Indianapolis, 1976.
WILLIAMS, C. J. F., 'Referential Opacity and False Belief in the *Theaetetus*', *Philosophical Quarterly* 22 (1972), 289–302.

B. Others

ARMSTRONG, D. M., *A Materialist Theory of the Mind*, London, 1968.
BERKELEY, G., *A New Theory of Vision, Principles of Human Knowledge*, and *Three Dialogues* (many editions).
EVANS, G., 'The Causal Theory of Names', *Aristotelian Society Supplementary Volume* 47 (1973), 187–208.

FREGE, G., 'On Sense and Reference', in his *Philosophical Writings*, ed. P. T. Geach and M. Black, Oxford, 1952, 56–78.

GETTIER, E. L., 'Is Justified True Belief Knowledge?', *Analysis* 23 (1963), 121–3.

GRICE, H. P., 'The Causal Theory of Perception', *Aristotelian Society Supplementary Volume* 35 (1961), 121–68.

HUME, D., *Treatise of Human Nature* (many editions).

KANT, I., *Critique of Pure Reason* (many editions).

KRIPKE, S. A., *Naming and Necessity* (revised edn.), Oxford, 1980.

——'A Puzzle about Belief', in *Meaning and Use*, ed. A. Margalit, Dordrecht, 1976, 239–83.

LOCKE, J., *Essay Concerning Human Understanding* (many editions).

MARTIN, C. B., and M. DEUTSCHER, 'Remembering', *Philosophical Review* 75 (1966), 161–96.

PUTNAM, H., 'The Meaning of "Meaning" ', in his *Philosophical Papers*, vol. 2, Cambridge, 1975, 215–71.

QUINE, W. V., *Word and Object*, Cambridge, Mass., 1960.

RUSSELL, B., 'On Denoting', in his *Logic and Knowledge*, ed. R. C. Marsh, London, 1956, 41–56.

——'Knowledge by Acquaintance and Knowledge by Description', in his *Mysticism and Logic*, reprinted Harmondsworth, 1953, 197–218.

——*Problems of Philosophy*, London, 1912.

——*Our Knowledge of the External World*, London, 1914.

——'On the Nature of Acquaintance', in his *Logic and Knowledge* (supra), 125–74.

——'Lectures on Logical Atomism', ibid., 177–281.

——*The Analysis of Mind*, London, 1921.

STRAWSON, P. F., 'Causation in Perception', in his *Freedom and Resentment and Other Essays*, London, 1974.

INDEX

Ackrill, J. L., 163n., 170–3, 178–9, 181, 189, 280
Allen, R. E., 280–1
analysis *see* definition
Antisthenes, 202n.
Aristotle, 9n., 22–3, 29, 46n., 105, 110, 131, 202n., 216n., 241n., 243n.
Armstrong, D. M., 144n., 281
aviary, 185–93, 196, 276n.

being v. becoming, 24–6, 30, 51, 106n., 147–9
being = essence, 36, 78, 138–42, 235–6, 241–2, 256
being = existence, 53, 76–8, 129–30, 165–9, 193–5
being (predicative), 76–8, 129–32
belief, identified with perception, 26–7, 30–1, 146, 149
belief of (opp. belief that), 164, 176, 268–72
belief v. judgement, 124, 156–7
Berkeley, 114, 118, 136, 151, 154, 281
Bostock, D., 15n., 197n., 280
Burnet, J., vi
Burnyeat, M. F., 90–1, 111n., 112n., 119n., 128–32, 137, 140, 202n., 204n., 280

changes (events), fast and slow, 54–8, 60–70, 75, 81, 107, 152–3
Cherniss, H. F., 9, 280
chronology, 1–14, 148–50
circularity, 32–4, 236–40, 245, 250–1, 266–7
collection and division, 245–9, 271–2
collections (of perceptions), 66–70, 75, 78–9, 81–2, 116, 134, 153–5
'common things', 110–12, 118–28, 133–7, 140
complexes *see* simples
connaître/savoir, 27–30, 37, 41, 129, 132, 137–8, 147n., 164, 199–200, 237–8, 268–74

Cooper, J. M., 119–25, 132–7, 139, 141, 280
Cornford, F. M., 10n., 11n., 31, 62n., 101–5, 119n., 128–9, 146, 151, 163n., 171, 172n., 186n., 189n., 198n., 216n., 223n., 241–3, 265, 280
Cratylus, 23, 110
Crombie, I. M., 62n., 64, 106n., 109n., 134–7, 151n., 152n., 162n., 204n., 243n., 280

de dicto/de re, 173–5, 183–5
definition (analysis), 35–6, 203, 206–11, 241–3, 251–3, 255–7, 265
Deutscher, M., 231n., 282
distinguishing marks, 225–36, 241, 245, 251

Evans, G., 232n., 281
events *see* changes
experts (wisdom), 32n., 85, 89, 92–7, 133, 146
explicit/tacit knowledge, 33–4, 37n.

falsehood, 11–12, 161–97
Fine, G. J., 162n., 171n., 198, 208n., 216–18, 220n., 221n., 223n., 243–50, 265–6, 280
flux doctrine *see* Heraclitus
forms, 15, 17–31, 98–9, 101–5, 146–50, 191, 241–3, 246–7, 254–60, 263–5
Frege, G., 163n., 175n., 184n., 281

Gettier, E. L., 239n., 282
Gosling, J. C. B., 106n., 198, 280
Grice, H. P., 230n., 282
Gulley, N., 62n., 119n., 242, 280

Harward, J., 255n., 280
Heraclitus (flux doctrine), 23–4, 44–83 *passim*, 89n., 99–110, 112, 116, 147–8
Hicken, W. F., 202n., 280
Holland, A. J., 114n., 280
Hume, 54n., 82, 96, 136, 154, 282